The Worth of the University

The Worth of the University

RICHARD C. LEVIN

Yale UNIVERSITY PRESS   NEW HAVEN & LONDON

Yale University Press books may be purchased in quantity for
educational, business, or promotional use. For information, please
e-mail sales.press@yale.edu (U.S. office) or
sales@yaleup.co.uk (U.K. office).

Designed by John Gambell and Rebecca Gibb.
Set in Yale Design type by Integrated Publishing Solutions,
Grand Rapids, Michigan.
Printed in the United States of America.

Library of Congress Control Number: 2013930709
ISBN 978-0-300-19725-9 (hardcover: alk. paper)

A catalogue record for this book is available from the Library of
Congress and the British Library.

This paper meets the requirements of ANSI/NISO Z39.48-1992
(Permanence of Paper).

10 9 8 7 6 5 4 3 2 1

Contents

Color plates follow page 132.

Introduction

I AM pleased to offer a selection of speeches and essays from my second decade as president of Yale. This collection is a sequel to *The Work of the University*, which contains the principal writings of my first decade.

Many of the speeches in this volume focus on themes I enunciated in my inaugural address in 1993: forging a strong partnership with the city of New Haven, rebuilding Yale's physical plant, strengthening science and engineering, and internationalizing the University. But I hope that this book captures also the essence of what is both the work and the worth of the University: the joy of scholarship, the beauty of students awakening to the life of the mind and pursuing their passions, the lively interaction of students and teachers in quest of truth.

I have spent 43 years at Yale — as student, teacher, scholar, and president. It has been the most extraordinary privilege to learn and to serve in the company of scholars who are international leaders in their fields and students of incomparable promise, energy, enthusiasm, and achievement. The job of president has its challenging moments, but for me it has been abundantly fulfilling, and a great joy.

I have been immensely fortunate in having exceptional teachers and colleagues. The first section of this book reflects on some of these sources of inspiration, briefly on two institutions that have shaped me and then on four individuals who have inspired and taught me.

The second section contains addresses to incoming freshmen. It is daunting, but ultimately very satisfying, to find a new way, every year, to convey the same basic message: make the most of the amazing resources of Yale College; open your minds and take on the new and the unfamiliar; then discover what you love and pursue it with passion.

My job has given me extraordinary opportunities. Among them is to speak on behalf of higher education as a whole to enunciate its broad mission and social purpose. The speeches in the third section of this book develop these ideas for audiences in Athens and London as well as Washington, New York, and Cleveland.

One of the great pleasures of my work has been the privilege of presiding over Yale's annual Commencement Exercises. Each year, I am deeply moved by the view from the platform: nearly 20,000 joyous and amazingly diverse friends and relatives of our graduates, bursting with pride. In the fourth section I send off our seniors to the challenges, opportunities, and responsibilities that lie before them.

I believe that, in this era of growing global interdependence, universities such as Yale must teach and exemplify good citizenship not only for their local communities and their nations, but also for the entire planet. Global citizenship is a theme articulated in some of my speeches to freshmen and seniors, but it is also the focus of the writings in section five.

Expanding Yale's involvement overseas has been a special passion of mine, and the selections in the sixth section reflect some of the exceptional opportunities I have been given to become involved with the development of higher education throughout Asia.

In the final section I return to my roots as an economist. The piece on patents in India and the United States may seem arcane to some readers, but it reflects an area of my scholarly expertise that I was able to put to practical use by contributing to an eleven-year effort to reform U.S. patent law. The final chapter expresses my observations about the causes of and the policy response to the economic crisis of 2008.

To lead an institution of the size and complexity of Yale requires motivating and mobilizing a great many people. No president can do this alone. I have had the good fortune of working with a group of academic leaders that I believe to be unmatched in higher education, and perhaps in any organization. My gratitude for their efforts is boundless. Each of the four provosts I appointed has gone on to lead one of the world's great universities: Alison Richard to Cambridge, Susan Hockfield to MIT, Andy Hamilton to Oxford, and now Peter Salovey will follow me at Yale. And, among many other extraordinary officers, deans, directors, department chairs, and college masters too numerous to mention, there are those few committed leaders who have been with me from the beginning, or very nearly so, and they deserve special thanks: Linda Lorimer and Dorothy Robinson, Bruce Alexander and David Swensen, Tom Beckett and Robert Blocker. I have been blessed as well with an astonishingly devoted supporting cast in the President's office and the President's house, led by Regina Starolis, Nina Glickson, Penny Laurans, and Pat Chase. I am also indebted to Ted Wittenstein for his help in selecting and organizing the pieces in this volume, and to Ted, Nina Glickson, Penny Laurans, and Linda Lorimer for their close reading and editorial suggestions.

Finally, if I have failed to say this clearly enough in the papers collected here, let me say it now. To be truly effective, a leader must have two attributes: a willingness to put the institution first, over and above any personal needs or desires, and a moral anchor, a firm commitment, in the toughest of situations as well as every day, to do what is fair, just, and right. I was blessed to have parents who believed in these values and inculcated them in me, and I have been doubly blessed to have a life partner, Jane, who never loses sight of these principles, and who helps to keep me faithful to them.

SOURCES OF INSPIRATION

Stanford and Yale

WHEN I arrived at Stanford's Wilbur Hall in the fall of 1964, little did I imagine that the day would provide material for a welcoming address to Yale College freshmen thirty-one years later. In this, as in so many ways, Stanford formed me for the life Jane and I have lived. We never left school; we just moved to a different one.

I have been privileged to test Stanford from many perspectives – as an alumnus, as a professional colleague of fellow economists, as a parent of two going on three students, as a parent of a young member of the faculty, and as the president of a rival institution. Stanford passes each test with banners waving overhead.

Yale and Stanford are so very different. Yale is a stronger community. Students live in the same residential college for four years, where responsible adults look after them and care about them. The average Yale undergraduate has a wider circle of acquaintances than her Stanford counterpart and joins more organizations. Alumni are more strongly

Written as a Classbook entry for the Class of 1968, on the occasion of my thirty-fifth Stanford University reunion in 2003.

invested in the place. Intellectual life is more intense, and the commitment to public and community service runs deeper.

But Stanford has its own virtues, just as distinctive and important. After 111 years, it clings to all that is best about the American West. The restless spirit of the frontier survives; the winds of freedom blow. Independence, innovation, and entrepreneurship are prized. Students are irreverent, open, and curious. For the student with a strong anchor, Stanford is an invitation to self-discovery. It was for me. It gave me a running start, and I have never looked back.

Eliot of Harvard

SEVERAL YEARS ago, I was asked to deliver a midsummer lecture to a group of university presidents on the subject of leadership. Initially, I planned to draw lessons from the work of the greatest of my Yale predecessors, as well as several presidents with distinguished careers at other institutions. The more I read, the more convinced I became that one leader stands above all others in the history of American higher education. He, alas, was not a Yale man.

Charles Eliot served as the president of Harvard University for forty years, from 1869 until 1909.[1] He was, almost certainly, the most influential university president of his time. I believe that it is fair to say that, cumulatively, the changes he wrought at Harvard had as significant and as enduring an impact on higher education in the United States as the accomplishments of any university president before or since. He became

Published in *The Yale Review,* vol. 99 (4) (Oct. 2011), pp. 1–15.

1 Where specific citations are omitted, I have drawn primarily on two excellent biographies of Eliot: Henry James, *Charles W. Eliot* (1930), and Hugh Hawkins, *Between Harvard and America: The Educational Leadership of Charles W. Eliot* (1972).

a national figure during the second half of his tenure as a spokesman for liberal individualism and an advocate of school reform. In retirement, he championed continuing adult education through his role in conceiving and editing the *Harvard Classics,* a multivolume series of the great works of Western civilization.

In the contemporary discussion of leadership — in general management and public life as well as in education — much is made of the importance of vision. We expect good leaders to have a vision, to state it clearly and frequently, and to take actions that advance toward its realization. In these respects, Eliot was truly extraordinary. From the very beginning, he articulated a clear and ambitious vision for transforming Harvard. His vision had three major components. First, he envisioned an undergraduate curriculum with more freedom to choose among a wider variety of elective courses. Second, he wanted to provide greater opportunity for future teachers and scholars to pursue advanced subjects beyond the bachelor's degree, and, third, he wanted to elevate to a higher standard Harvard's professional schools of law, medicine, and theology, and open them only to those who had already completed an undergraduate degree. His ultimate goals were ambitious, but he managed expectations so that gradual progress toward them was regarded as success. He restructured the presidency so that he could spend more time on his highest long-term priorities. He took risks, persevered in the face of initial failure, and understood when it was most advantageous to act on his own and when he needed to build support within the faculty. He selected strong leaders for supporting roles, and he aligned their incentives so that their personal triumphs were institutional triumphs. I will comment on each of these attributes of Eliot's leadership as I tell his story.

Among Eliot's accomplishments at Harvard, the best known was his transformation of the undergraduate curriculum from one that was largely a prescribed set of required courses to a completely unconstrained set of elective courses. In fairness, Eliot was neither the first champion of the elective system, nor was he the first to introduce elective courses at Harvard. But he took the idea to its logical and, indeed, ideological conclusion. In Eliot's view, the well-prepared student should be entirely free to shape his (Harvard educated only men in these years) own education. He railed against the defects of coercion, and supported instead the use of incentives to bring coherence to a potentially unstructured course of study. He seized upon the clever idea of awarding "honors" only to those graduating seniors who took a sufficient number of courses within a single discipline and earned sufficiently high marks. Thus, Harvard under Eliot was the first U.S. university to conceive of the undergraduate "concentration" (as it is still called today at Harvard) or "major" (as it is called elsewhere in the United States), although it did not actually require students to select a major subject.

When I claimed that Eliot took the elective system to its ideological conclusion, I meant this quite literally. He began with the assertion in his inaugural address that "the young man of nineteen or twenty ought to know what he likes best and is most fit for."[2] We might think of this as an opinion rooted in developmental psychology, rather than political ideology. But later in his career, he began to see the elective system as yet another step in the gradual emancipation of man from tradition and tyranny. Grandiosely, he claimed the system of elective courses was "an outcome of the Protestant Reformation . . . an outcome of the spirit of political liberty."[3] He believed it was a natural extension of the freedoms that America granted its citizens in religion, political life, and economic

2 Charles William Eliot, "Inaugural Address as President of Harvard, 1869," reprinted in Richard Hofstadter and Wilson Smith, eds., *American Higher Education: A Documentary History* (1961), p. 608.
3 Eliot, "Experience with a College Elective System," unpublished address, 1895, cited in Hawkins, *supra* note 1, p. 94.

activity. Few educators today would carry Eliot's logic quite so far. Most U.S. universities now offer an abundance of elective courses, but choice among them is typically constrained by requirements that students display some degree of breadth across different fields of study, as well as some degree of concentration on a major field.

Although Eliot's reforms of the undergraduate curriculum were regarded at the time as his primary contribution, I would like to emphasize instead a more enduring contribution, his leadership in transforming Harvard into a modern university. Although this took decades to accomplish in full, what is remarkable is that a vision of what was needed was clear to him upon assuming the presidency at age 35, and the most critical steps in the transformation were all taken in his first decade of service.

To understand what Eliot accomplished and how he accomplished it, one has to begin with a sketch of Harvard in 1869. Though a university in name, Harvard was then a small undergraduate college, enrolling about 150 students in each class, surrounded by a relatively young "scientific school" and three loosely affiliated professional schools of law, divinity, and medicine. The president had focused historically on the college, where he typically taught classes and preached sermons in the chapel. The Lawrence Scientific School commanded some presidential attention, since it had been founded only two decades earlier and frequently came into conflict over laboratory space and equipment with the older, more established, and wealthier college. But presidents before Eliot had paid little or no attention to the professional schools, which had very small, self-governing faculties and were mired in complacency. For example, the language describing the Law School's entry requirements and course of study had not been altered by one word in twenty years, and the School's annual reports, submitted to the president by its three faculty members, had contained the following sentence for ten consecutive years: "There have been no new arrangements in relation to the organization of the School or the course of study."[4] Harvard's faculty was the most distinguished in the nation, but Yale had a better claim to being a national institution. Only 30 percent of Harvard's students came from outside New England, compared to more than 60 percent of Yale's.[5]

To this parochial, college-centered institution, Eliot brought a transformative vision. Like others in his time, such as Daniel Coit Gilman, the first president of Johns Hopkins, Eliot took inspiration from the superior training in research offered by German universities. But unlike Gilman, he did not seek to replicate the German model. Just months before he was offered the Harvard presidency, he wrote in the *Atlantic Monthly* magazine:

> [A] university, in any worthy sense of the term, must grow from seed. It cannot be transplanted from England or Germany in full leaf and bearing. . . . When the American university appears, it will not be a copy of foreign institutions, or a hot-bed plant, but the slow and natural outgrowth of American social and political habits. . . . The American college is an institution without a parallel; the American university will be equally original.[6]

Eliot was correct to say that the evolving American university would be original, but he erred in characterizing it as "a slow and natural outgrowth of American social and political habits." He made it happen faster than he himself imagined possible.

Eliot's vision of an American university involved three central elements: an undergraduate college devoted to general education without

4 James, *supra* note 1, p. 267.
5 Edward D. Page, "Two Decades of Yale and Harvard: A Retrospect," *The Nation* (Feb. 18, 1886), pp. 3–4.
6 Eliot, "The New Education," *Atlantic Monthly,* vol. 23 (Feb./Mar. 1869), pp. 202–20, 365–66, reprinted in Hofstadter and Smith, *supra* note 2, pp. 636–37.

premature specialization, opportunity for those with an undergraduate education to pursue advanced study and research in the arts and sciences, and a set of professional schools such as law, medicine, and divinity for those who had already experienced the rigors of a broad and general undergraduate education. To get from the Harvard of 1869 to this ideal model of an American university required moving the institution in two different directions: toward the European model of graduate education in the arts and sciences, and away from the European model of early concentration on professional education.

Modern university presidents would recognize instantly what Eliot perceived as one of the greatest obstacles to the realization of his vision: the demands and expectations that, as president, he spend much of his time engaged in activities that contribute only minimally to the advancement of the institution. He tackled this problem courageously; he immediately freed himself from the president's traditional pedagogical and disciplinary obligations by creating the position of Dean of Harvard College. This gave him the time to preside, not simply at meetings of the College faculty, but at meetings of the faculties of all the schools. And meet they did. Eliot's biographer, Henry James (a nephew of the famous novelist), indicates that in his first year the faculty of the College met forty-five times, while the scientific school and the professional school faculties met forty-four times. Eliot often extended these meetings until eleven in the evening, encouraging free discussion and asking questions designed to explore the minds of his colleagues about changes that he was contemplating.[7] Thus, he prepared the ground for reform, knowing that the faculty's support would be necessary for much that he hoped to accomplish.

Eliot also moved quickly to prepare the way for both an expansion

7 James, *supra* note 1, pp. 243–44.

and a greater integration of the schools into a single university. Employing a judicious mix of top-down authority and bottom-up persuasive talent, he acquired a significant quantity of adjacent land (a top-down initiative), and he persuaded the faculties to put all schools on a common academic calendar and, soon thereafter, to open all courses to any student in the university.

Graduate Education

Let us now consider how Eliot managed the evolution of Harvard toward graduate education. He first articulated a very clear vision of what he hoped to accomplish. I hesitate to say this so bluntly, but what he wished to do was imitate Yale! He noted that the Lawrence Scientific School founded at Harvard in 1846 had been intended to permit advanced study beyond the bachelor's degree, but in fact the overwhelming majority of its students were simply pursuing bachelor's degrees in scientific subjects as an alternative to attending Harvard College. For the few graduates pursuing further study, there was no organized program or formal course of study. Yale, by contrast, had formalized postgraduate study by creating the Department of Philosophy and the Arts in 1847 to offer advanced instruction in philology, philosophy, and natural science. In 1869, Eliot wrote: "The history of the development of the Department of Philosophy and the Arts in Yale College is so full of instruction as to justify . . . dwelling upon it at some length; it is at once an epitome of the past history of scientific instruction in this country, and a prophecy of its future."[8]

In 1860, Yale became the first university in America to offer the Ph.D. degree — which was earned after two years of study by evidence of high

8 Eliot, "The New Education," reprinted in Hofstadter and Smith, *supra* note 2, p. 628.

attainment in two branches of learning. Only candidates with the bachelor's degree, or those who passed an equivalency examination, were eligible to undertake doctoral studies. By 1869, Yale had awarded thirteen students the Ph.D., causing Eliot to opine: "This legitimate success at Yale, on a really high level, if also on a modest scale, points the way to improvements which ought soon to be made at all the more important American 'universities,' which will then better deserve their ambitious title."[9] I have yet to discover in the writings of any other Harvard president such generous praise of Yale.

There is a lesson in this, for Eliot's willingness to learn from the experience of others is another mark of his greatness. An outstanding leader should recognize and acknowledge the deficiencies of his institution and be willing to borrow and adapt superior practices employed by others.

Determined to create an organized course of advanced study, worthy of those who had already graduated from Harvard College, Eliot displayed in his first years two other attributes of a great leader: a willingness to experiment and perseverance in the face of failure. His predecessor, Thomas Hill, had instituted what were called University Lectures. These were short courses taught by scholars from both Harvard College and outside, and they chiefly provided an opportunity to expose graduates and undergraduates alike to advanced ideas, mostly in the sciences. Eliot decided to adapt this institution to his purposes. He invited the most distinguished intellectuals in Boston and New Haven to give two series of lectures — one philosophical and one literary. Ralph Waldo Emerson, Charles Sanders Peirce, James Russell Lowell, and William Dean Howells were among the distinguished lecturers, who were compen-

9 *Ibid.*, p. 629.

sated by charging those who enrolled $150 for each series, an amount equivalent to the prevailing annual tuition of Harvard College.

Eliot declared the lectures intended for advanced students, but open to the public, including women. This was a bold and risky experiment, but because the University Lectures were already in place and were not considered part of the curriculum of the college, or any of the other schools, Eliot was able to introduce his new scheme from the top down, without faculty approval.

There is another lesson in this; it is easier for a president to initiate new programs and even new schools than to modify existing ones, which would typically require faculty approval. Today, at least in America, only the most courageous president would attempt to reform an existing curriculum from the top down; curriculum reform is almost always the work of a faculty committee, which can be encouraged from the top but rarely directed. Thus, when I initiated a comprehensive review of the undergraduate curriculum at Yale in 2001, I put the task in the hands of a forty-two-member committee of faculty and students. I met with the committee several times and pointed them in what I considered the right direction, but they reached their own conclusions. By contrast, in areas previously uncharted by Yale — such as advanced education for mid-career professionals — I have been able to create entirely new programs strictly from the top down. The Yale World Fellows Program, which brings together emerging leaders from around the world for an intense period studying global issues, is a case in point.

To return to Eliot, and to speak frankly, his first attempt at graduate education was a dismal failure. One hundred and fifty-five people enrolled in one or more of the two courses, making the lectures economically viable, but only four recent graduates of the College enrolled in the philosophical course, while six enrolled in the literary course. These young men were the only attendees who sat for examinations on the lecture material. The remainder of the audience was adult gentlemen and women seeking intellectual enrichment, not the aspiring professors and teachers whom Eliot hoped to attract.

Undaunted, Eliot varied the experiment the next year, offering a large number of short courses, available for ten dollars or less per course. But again the results disappointed. In his annual report, Eliot wrote that the University Lectures "have not induced Bachelors of Arts of this University to remain in Cambridge for purposes of independent study, and they have not attracted to the University advanced students from other places."[10] Showing where he was headed next, Eliot went on to say, "Advanced students want profound, continuous and systematic teaching." He suggested that "fresh utterances of distinguished scholars who were not professional teachers" had failed the mark. What was needed were resident teachers who were professional instructors.

And so, learning from failure and but still focused on his original goal, Eliot came to the two-pronged approach that gave him the outcome he desired. First, he had to organize the resident faculties to provide the needed advanced instruction. He did this by creating, in effect, a "graduate department," governed by the "Academic Council," a recreation of a dormant institution consisting of the professors and assistant professors in all the schools. With Eliot presiding, the Council formally inaugurated the degrees of Master of Arts, Doctor of Science (S.D.), and Doctor of Philosophy (Ph.D.). In 1873, twelve years behind its New Haven rival, Harvard awarded its first doctorates.

Second, he had to expand the size of the faculty, to bring in those who had not invested a career in the still largely prescribed curriculum of the college. Here two of Eliot's principal objectives dovetailed perfectly. He wanted advanced courses suitable for graduate students, and he wanted to increase the number and variety of elective courses in the undergradu-

10 Eliot, "Annual Report, 1871–72," cited in James, *supra* note 1, p. 251.

ate college. Thus, Eliot embarked on a hiring spree, and here, unlike presidents today, he had free rein. Curricular changes required faculty approval, as they do today, but the appointment of faculty was entirely in the president's hands, subject only to the approval of the Corporation, Harvard's governing board. And here Eliot made an indelible mark— altering more than the organization of the institution, going to the heart of its substance. Though he failed to entice the pair of distinguished Yale professors who were his very first targets, within four years, Eliot hired more than two dozen new members of the faculty, including Henry Adams (perhaps America's greatest historian), Oliver Wendell Holmes, Jr. (a constitutional scholar who later became a Justice of the Supreme Court), William James (a philosopher who explored the foundations of psychology), C. C. Langdell (a distinguished legal scholar who invented the "case method" of teaching law), and Charles Eliot Norton (a distin- guished art historian and founder of *The Nation,* a well-known magazine of political and cultural commentary).

Eliot's recruitment of such extraordinary individuals reminds us that nothing we do is more important than selecting the best people. Al- though few of us have the authority to appoint faculty directly, most of us appoint administrative officers, deans, and department chairs. These administrators inspire the faculty to maintain high standards and seek continuous improvement throughout the institution. We should all ask ourselves whether we are giving the selection and recruitment of out- standing talent the attention it deserves.

The new faculty hired by Eliot gave Harvard the capacity to educate graduate students more effectively and to expand the elective system in Harvard College. During Eliot's first decade, the number of required undergraduate courses diminished from 40 to 22, and the number of electives permitted rose from 20 to 34, chosen from a substantially larger menu. By 1884, all courses for sophomores, juniors, and seniors were elective, and, for the first time, the elective system was extended to freshmen, who were allowed to choose more than half their courses.

Similarly, Eliot's vision of a rigorous program of graduate education required some time to come into being. Even after the doctoral degrees were introduced, very few courses were offered exclusively for graduate students. Instead, Ph.D. students simply had the opportunity to choose from the growing menu of elective courses those they had missed as undergraduates. It was not until 1890, spurred by the success of Johns Hopkins in graduate education, that Harvard turned its "Graduate Department" into a full-fledged Graduate School, and began to create a serious course of graduate study in the several disciplines.

Professional Education

Of all Eliot's reforms, the most distinctly personal and original was his transformation of professional education. Nearly twenty years before Eliot took office, Francis Wayland, the president of Brown University, had advocated the elective system for undergraduates, and Harvard had begun to introduce elective courses before Eliot greatly expanded their number. Both Yale and Johns Hopkins established doctoral programs before Eliot, through trial and error, moved Harvard toward the form of graduate education that became the American standard. But Eliot's views on professional education, and the reforms he initiated, had no significant precursors.

Eliot was appalled by the condition of professional education as he found it in 1869. In his *Atlantic Monthly* article, he observed: "The term 'learned profession' is getting to have a sarcastic flavor. Only a very small proportion of lawyers, doctors, and ministers, the country over, are Bachelors of Arts. The degrees of LL.B. and M.D. stand, on the average, for decidedly less culture than the degree of A.B., and it is found quite possible to prepare young men of scanty education to be successful pulpit exhorters in a year or eighteen months."[11] Eliot went on, using the example of the University of Michigan, to note that both the standard of admission and the duration of the course of study were insufficient to produce truly learned professionals. Only 12 percent of Michigan's law students and 5 percent of its medical students had bachelor's degrees on admission, and the formal course of study in law was only one year.

Eliot found matters no better at Harvard upon assuming the presidency. The vast majority of students enrolled in the Schools of Law, Medicine, and Divinity were admitted directly from high school. And the standards for graduation were minimal: three years in residence without examination in the Divinity School, eighteen months without examination at the Law School, and a year of study (plus three to six months' work with a practitioner) at the Medical School. There was no concept of progression within the curriculum; courses might be taken in any order.

In his efforts to transform the situation he confronted, Eliot displayed many of the characteristics of an effective academic leader. He had a clear and well-articulated vision. He set ambitious goals. He patiently devoted the time required to win over complacent members of the faculty. He took significant risk. He used the authority of his office to initiate some changes from the top down, and he employed his persuasive powers to win support for changes from the bottom up.

In his earliest annual reports, Eliot made clear what he hoped to accomplish—to raise the standards for admission and graduation, and to bring greater coherence to the curriculum of each professional school. Within two years, each of the major schools made dramatic progress.

The Divinity School was the most easily reformed, for the conditions

---

11 Eliot, "The New Education," reprinted in Hofstadter and Smith, *supra* note 2, p. 635.

Eliot sought had once been the norm. At his urging, the faculty quickly restored an earlier requirement that candidates for admission demonstrate mastery of Greek and Latin, and the School established a requirement that graduates must pass an examination.

The Law School presented a greater challenge, since the faculty was complacent, training was haphazard, and the curriculum had no logical progression from elementary to advanced courses. Fortunately for Eliot, one of the School's three senior faculty members resigned, insulted by the new president's stated desire for reform. This gave Eliot the opportunity he needed. He promptly appointed C. C. Langdell, a legal scholar of the first rank, and persuaded the remaining two senior faculty members to elect him as dean. Langdell made Eliot's agenda his own, extending the period of study from one to two years and requiring satisfactory performance on examinations for graduation. He divided the curriculum into first- and second-year courses, and he went well beyond Eliot's own aspirations for improving legal education. He pioneered the teaching of law through the study of decided "cases" rather than treatises. Under Langdell's leadership, with Eliot's unwavering support, the Law School flourished, enrolling an ever-increasing percentage of students who held bachelor's degrees. Within a decade, a college education, or an examination demonstrating equivalent preparation, became a requirement for admission, as Eliot had hoped.

The Medical School presented the greatest challenge of all, for the leader of the faculty, Dr. Henry Bigelow, was inalterably opposed to change. Faced with intransigence, Eliot wisely employed a mix of top-down and bottom-up strategies. From above, he assumed control of the finances of *all* the professional schools, dampening the objections of the relatively prosperous Medical School. Then, coolly and patiently, Eliot presided over thirty-one faculty meetings in two years, enough to persuade the faculty to support the reforms he desired over Bigelow's continued opposition. In a colorful account, Oliver Wendell Holmes, Sr., a distinguished member of the medical faculty, described the young president's clarity of purpose and strength of character:

> He [Eliot] comes to the meeting of every Faculty, ours among the rest, and keeps us up to eleven and twelve o'clock at night discussing new arrangements. He shows an extraordinary knowledge of all that relates to every department of the University, and presides with an *aplomb*, a quiet, imperturbable, serious good-humor, that it is impossible not to admire. . . . I cannot help being amused at some of the scenes we have in our Medical Faculty, – this cool, grave young man proposing in the calmest way to turn everything topsy-turvy. . . .
>
> "How is it? I should like to ask," said one of our number the other evening, "that this Faculty has gone on for eighty years, managing its own affairs and doing it well, – . . . and now within *three or four months* it is proposed to change all our modes of carrying on the school – it seems very extraordinary, and I should like to know how it happens."
>
> "I can answer Dr. [Bigelow's] question very easily," said the bland, grave young man: "there is a new President."[12]

In the end, the faculty completely overhauled the curriculum, bringing a logic and coherency to the course of study, extending the program from eighteen months to three years, requiring the satisfactory completion of annual examinations to progress to the next year of study, and, finally, requiring satisfactory performance on final examinations in all nine of the principal areas of medicine, rather than merely five of nine, as had been previously required.

In raising the standard of medical education so radically, Eliot took considerable risk. Since the imposition of more rigorous standards was

12 James, *supra* note 1, pp. 283–85.

bound to reduce the number of students, the School's financial stability was placed in jeopardy. But Eliot believed that Harvard's higher calling was to raise the standard of the professions throughout the United States, especially the standard of medical practice. If this required additional funds, he argued, new endowment would be sought. But standards should not be compromised.

As it turned out, the size of the class declined by 35 to 40 percent, but students now enrolled for three years instead of eighteen months. Three years after the reforms were introduced, the Medical School earned a substantial surplus.

Guidelines for Leadership Recapitulated

Having told the story of Eliot's early years, let me summarize what it teaches us about leadership:

1. *Develop a vision and communicate it.* Eliot did this brilliantly in his 1869 *Atlantic Monthly* articles and his inaugural address. From the beginning it was clear that he had three major priorities: expanding the elective system for undergraduates, developing a serious program of graduate study in the arts and sciences, and raising the standards of the professional schools. He returned to these themes regularly in his annual reports.

2. *Set goals that are ambitious but achievable.* Expanding the elective system, creating a serious graduate program, and transforming the professional schools into schools for college graduates — these were all ambitious goals. Eliot knew that none could be achieved in short order; he spoke of a "slow and natural evolution." By not raising expectations counterproductively, he had the freedom to move gradually, yet he

seized the opportunity to make very rapid progress in the first
decade of his presidency.

3. *Free up enough time to concentrate on major initiatives.* Eliot
   recognized this from the beginning. He immediately appointed a Dean of Harvard College to relieve himself of
   numerous duties, so that he might have time to attend the
   meetings of the professional school faculties, where he sought
   major changes.

4. *Take risks.* The University Lectures were a worthy attempt to
   jump-start the transition to graduate education, and Eliot did
   not shy away from confronting the powerful leaders of the
   Medical School where an important issue of principle was at
   stake.

5. *Don't be deterred by initial failures. Some good ideas deserve a
   second try.* Having failed to stimulate interest in graduate
   education with the University Lectures, Eliot moved directly
   to the introduction of doctoral degrees.

6. *Know where top-down and bottom-up work best.* Land purchases, administrative reorganization, and, in his day, faculty
   appointments were all domains of action reserved to the
   president. Eliot devoted extensive time to winning faculty
   support in areas where he needed to persuade, such as
   curriculum reform in the college and admissions requirements in the professional schools.

7. *Select strong leaders for supporting roles, and give them sufficient
   freedom to take initiative on their own.* The appointment of
   C. C. Langdell as Dean of the Law School is an excellent
   example. He not only followed through on Eliot's intentions
   to strengthen admissions standards; he independently
   developed a new pedagogy – the case method – that became
   the dominant paradigm for teaching law.

8. *Align incentives.* To encourage specialization where most courses were elective, Eliot supported the award of honors only to students with a sufficient number of courses in one discipline, as well as high marks.

Conclusion

On the twenty-fifth anniversary of Eliot's election to the Harvard presidency, one hundred and ten years ago, the faculty offered this tribute: "It is the period of the present administration that will be remembered hereafter as the epoch in which the University was first fairly able to take its place among the great seats of learning of the world."[13] The assessment rings true; to this day no other American university president has matched the legacy of Charles Eliot.

13 Cited in Hawkins, *supra* note 1, pp. 78–79.

The Astonishing Joseph Stiglitz

NOW THAT Joe Stiglitz is 60, he appears to us as one of a small number of the most distinguished members of our profession. But when I entered graduate school at Yale in 1970, Joe was entirely, completely, and absolutely in a class by himself. At 27, he had already published more than twenty articles in major journals, edited Paul Samuelson's papers, and earned the rank of full professor. The adjective *prodigious* barely does justice.

Among the graduate students in economics it was believed that Joe was the youngest full professor in Yale's history. Now that I am in a position to know, I can tell you that it isn't true. In 1802, Yale's president, Timothy Dwight, intent on introducing science to the college curriculum, tapped a brilliant twenty-three-year-old student of law and classics, Benjamin Silliman, made him a professor, and sent him off to Philadelphia and then Europe to learn some science. Dwight made a good bet; Silliman became one of the most influential scientists in America during the first half of the nineteenth century. Joe had a tougher route

Remarks on the 60th birthday of Joseph Stiglitz, former Yale professor of economics, public servant, and Nobel Laureate, October 24, 2003.

to the top. He couldn't rely on the largesse of Yale's president; he had to earn the votes of tenured members of the Economics Department.

Joe's early productivity was legendary. It seemed to us that if he had an idea one day, he had a paper the next. That's a slight exaggeration, but there is little doubt that he slept fewer hours in a week than there are hours in a day. We suspected that he slept in his office, but no one ever stayed at work late enough to prove the proposition. His rumpled shirts were all the evidence we had. He was never tired. Because he was doing what he loved, there was always a smile on his face and a sparkle in his eyes.

Joe's apparent disorganization seemed hard to square with his productivity. There was the occasional line, delivered with an innocent smile, "Oh, did I say I'd get your paper back today?" or "Oh, did we have an appointment this morning? Sorry I missed it." In his office every surface was filled with stacks and stacks of reprints and working papers, more papers than we graduate students believed we would have time to read in our entire careers. In retrospect, we now know that Joe probably hadn't read most of them. But from time to time he would astonish us by digging into the middle of a pile and extracting just the one that was needed to point us in the right direction.

Joe's disorganization reached into the classroom. In the required theory courses, Joe would often need to be reminded where he had left off last time. It didn't matter. He had the whole script in his head. Once launched, he blitzed through the material with ease, perhaps with a little too much speed. Some were left behind, but those of us who struggled and stayed with him were amply rewarded.

A highlight of my four years in graduate school came in the fall of 1972, when Joe offered a course labeled something like "Advanced Topics in Economic Theory." To give you an idea of how immensely productive Joe was in this period of his career, the two-hour lectures he delivered each week were not fourteen of Joe's greatest hits. They were fourteen of Joe's current hits. Each lecture was based on a paper Joe had not yet published. And they spanned most of the major fields of economic inquiry.

And this, of course, is what is most astonishing about Joe's early years, and, indeed, his whole career: he has written important papers in almost every area of economics. By the time he left Yale in 1974, at the age of 31, Joe had published seminal papers in no less than nine major fields: growth theory, information economics, macroeconomics, finance, public economics, international trade, development, technological change, and labor economics. And important work in industrial organization was in the pipeline. From the definition of risk to corporate financial policy; from portfolio theory to the effects of taxes on efficiency and risk-taking; from the short-run behavior of output, employment, and wages to the theory of exhaustible resources; from factor price equalization to the economics of sharecropping to the effects of discrimination in labor markets — one could go on and on and on. To characterize the influence of, let's say, the top twenty of Joe's first fifty papers would take, I suspect, the rest of the evening and most of tomorrow.

So what is it that drives this powerful engine of creativity? I think it is a dual passion. First, as anyone who was ever his student or collaborator knows, Joe loves the game itself, the sheer fun of building and manipulating a model to see where it leads. And second, he is relentlessly curious about what economics can tell us about the world it purports to represent, and especially curious about how we can understand the effects of the anomalies and imperfections that make the actual world different from the textbook world of general equilibrium.

These two passions and the relationship between them, I think, explain a lot about Joe. In particular, they help us to understand the evolution of his career from one deeply engaged in advancing the frontier of economic theory to one equally deeply engaged in the world of policy. When I was working on my dissertation, I would sometimes, in our one-on-one sessions, confront Joe with an empirical anomaly. He loved these challenges, and he would immediately begin thinking about how to construct a model that would explain it. We see this in Joe's published work. He only rarely seeks, as most theorists do, to solve a puzzle that arises strictly within the literature of theory; most of the time, he tackles an empirical anomaly straight on.

The path from this kind of theory to policy is a natural one. Over time, the balance shifts from creating a new theory that explains the world to using the theories we have to improve the world. And for Joe in particular the path was pretty direct, because his instincts, sentiments, and politics have always been on the side of social justice.

I want to close by remarking on one more dimension of Joe, for I suspect it is a reason that so many of us are here tonight. And that is his generosity and warmth. Over the years, I have shared reminiscences with some of Joe's other graduate students and junior collaborators. We all had the same, remarkable experience of a mentor who, busy and accomplished as he was, always had time to talk. We were always welcomed with a smile and, more often than not, we were treated to the immense pleasure of watching Joe, in the midst of conversation, bound out of his chair to the blackboard, sputtering with excitement, to develop a new idea.

Joe, speaking for your legions of students, thank you for inspiring us. And speaking for everyone here tonight, with respect and admiration, we salute you for all you have accomplished and for all you have given us.

Repairing a Bicycle

I HAVE learned two things from Bill Brainard — how to repair a bicycle and how to run a university. Actually, I have learned a lot more from Bill, although I must admit I never really understood most of the stuff Bill taught us in first-year macroeconomics. But let me focus on the two examples I mentioned because they reveal so much about a truly extraordinary teacher and friend.

About a dozen years ago, when my two sons were teenagers, we planned a bicycle trip to France. Since we were going on our own, and might conceivably experience a breakdown at some distance from a repair shop, it occurred to me that it might be useful to know a few simple things beyond being able to say to the repair man: "Le vélo ne marche pas."

You have to understand. I was a complete mechanical incompetent. I grew up in one of those families where the answer to "How many people does it take to change a light bulb?" was two: one person to call the electrician and the electrician. So I enrolled in a short course in bicycle repair at Bill's home on Everit Street.

Remarks in honor of William C. Brainard, Arthur Okun Professor of Economics at Yale University, June 2006.

Now I didn't know the difference between an Allen wrench and those little flat things that you use to pry the tires off the wheel. But in the course of an afternoon, I learned how to patch a tire tube and adjust the brakes, spokes, and gears. Of course, nothing was explained in the typical manner of a how-to manual, such as "place wrench here, turn counterclockwise three revolutions." Instead, every single step was derived from the first principles of elementary physics. Never a simple derivation, mind you, but one which noted along the way every imaginable anomaly that might modify the most straightforward explanation. Terms like "torque" were frequently invoked.

As with all great teachers, it wasn't the specific content that Bill conveyed, it was the method that mattered. The lesson was simply this: when you want to fix something, start from first principles and figure out how.

That one tutorial on bicycle repair changed my life. Without the benefit of another formal lesson, I have, on occasion, to Jane's utter astonishment, figured out how to repair locks, toilets, the oil burner, and the clothes dryer.

But of course in a room full of folks who are used to keeping up with Bill Brainard, you have already guessed by now that repairing a bicycle is just a metaphor for running a university. Some of the happiest and most satisfying years of my personal and professional life were spent after Bill moved back to Everit Street from the Provost's House, and back to the Economics Department from the Hall of Graduate Studies. To my delight Bill agreed to be Director of Graduate Studies when I became Chair of the Economics Department, and we embarked on a five-year tutorial that I hope has served Yale well.

The lessons were conveyed in countless conversations in Bill's office at 28 Hillhouse Avenue, on the phone at night for hours, and, most memorably, on the sidewalk on Everit Street in the dark after work. We would talk and talk while Ellie and Jane peeked out of their respective windows trying to decide whether it would ever be time for dinner.

And the lesson of course was the same as the lesson on bicycle repair: go back to first principles and you can figure it out. Bill approached every decision confronting the Director of Graduate Studies, the Chair, the Provost, and the President just the same way he approached math puzzles, a seminar presentation, and auto repair, only here the first principles weren't the theorems of abstract math or Newtonian mechanics. They were simple human principles. Listen carefully. Make sure you hear what the other person is saying. Then try to understand why he or she is saying it: is it a matter of rational self-interest, or emotional need, or some combination of both? Confront the rational arguments with reason, the emotional needs with compassion and empathy. Be patient. The emotional issues sometimes pass, and then reason alone can prevail. Be prepared to look at the issue from all sides, again and again as circumstances change. Think it through and you can figure it out.

There is one secret to Bill's lesson: compassion and empathy are not merely instrumental. They have to be real, from the heart. Bill Brainard's heart is as big as his intellect is tenacious. We all know that. That's why we're here. That's why we love and celebrate this exceptional man who is our teacher, in economics and in life.

The Ornament of Our World

MARÍA CARED about words — whether they were found in medieval poetry, rock lyrics, or recipes. Thus it was not by accident that she chose as the title of her best-known book words used by a tenth-century author to describe Córdoba. María made the words her own, painting a vivid picture of the flourishing culture of Al-Andalus — the ornament, the adornment, that which adds beauty and brilliance to the world. To use words very precisely, María was the ornament of our world.

She added beauty and brilliance to the world in so many different ways. I leave it to others to characterize her dazzling, imaginative scholarship — so deeply learned, so highly original, so beautifully written. Her leadership of the Whitney Humanities Center was equally dazzling and imaginative. She was at once a radiant hostess and a productive academic entrepreneur — and she loved both of those roles equally. She widened the Whitney orbit to embrace hundreds of Yale faculty, postdocs, and graduate students — reaching across disciplines and divisions

Remarks delivered at a memorial service in Battell Chapel for María Rosa Menocal, Sterling Professor of the Humanities at Yale, December 1, 2012.

with an unerring taste for both quality and eccentricity. María's introductions of speakers and conferences were works of art (ornaments, actually), brimming over with insight and graciousness.

Jane and I were privileged to have many intimate hours with María. She shared our love of the kitchen — so the three of us would hang out in hers or ours, in lively conversation as María and I consumed a very good bottle of white wine before moving on to a very good bottle of red over the dinner we all had a hand in preparing. Once a year, the dinner would be a "sleepover" on Everit Street, where the after-dinner entertainment was a rock-and-roll movie — Pennebacker, Scorsese, or Haynes on Dylan, a Stones concert, or a classic Beatles film.

María would invariably bring lentils of the highest quality to these occasions, calling herself "the lentil fairy." She finally revealed her source, telling us about Kalustyan's, her favorite purveyor of spices, grains, and legumes. One day, having just a few minutes between meetings in lower Manhattan, I went quickly to Kalustyan's and emailed proudly to María that I had purchased twenty-two pounds of red, yellow, green, and black lentils in a five-minute visit. She was appalled, and excoriated me. For Maria, a visit to Kalustyan's had to be a sacred pilgrimage, not a drive-by.

We did make a sacred pilgrimage every spring — with María and Geo — to the Beacon Theater to see the Allman Brothers Band. The music was always sublime. I suspect that most of you know the connection. One of María's most brilliant essays is about the Persian romance *Layla and Majnun* — rediscovered and sanctified in our lifetime by Eric Clapton. The highlight of the canonical performance is an astonishing guitar riff by the late Duane Allman. At our last pilgrimage to the Beacon, Clapton himself came to perform with The Band, and the inevitable finale brought down the house. A performance of *Layla* by the Jamie McLean Band will close our service today.

María's passions were boundless, and she shared them generously. There are hundreds of you here who could relate your own intimate moments with María that were just as full of enthusiasm and passion and love of life as those I have described. She brought so many of us into her life, and she added beauty and brilliance to our lives – an adornment, the ornament of our world.

VARIETY AND FREEDOM:
WORDS FOR NEW STUDENTS

Encountering New Perspectives

THIS SPRING, as you were coming to the end of your high school years, I got my first inspiration for what I might say to you when you arrived here. I was sitting in the auditorium of the Whitney Humanities Center, listening to a splendid lecture by Garry Wills, a Yale alumnus who has written brilliantly on topics as diverse as Abraham Lincoln, Richard Nixon, and Catholic theology. As the topic of the annual Tanner Lectures on Human Values, Professor Wills had chosen Henry Adams, the great-grandson of John Adams whose autobiography, *The Education of Henry Adams,* was recently voted the best nonfiction work of the twentieth century.

To everyone's surprise, Professor Wills took as his text not the famous autobiography but an anonymously published, best-selling, and little-remembered political novel entitled *Democracy.* In describing the novel, Professor Wills made repeated reference to Adams' treatment of related subjects in his magisterial, nine-volume *History of the United States during the Administrations of Thomas Jefferson and James Madison.* This intrigued me, because reading and talking about history, especially the

Freshman Address, October 11, 2003.

early history of the United States, is one of my passions. And so, sitting and listening to Garry Wills last March, I decided that I would tackle Henry Adams' monumental historical work and somehow find in it material to provide a framework for this morning's welcoming address.

Months later, with summer's end approaching, I found myself in a situation I am sure each of you will confront more than once in your time at Yale. I had an assignment due, and I hadn't finished the reading. The end of August was near, and I had read only 200 of the 1,200 pages Adams devotes to the Jefferson years.

I fell back on the sound advice that Viper offered to Maverick in the classic action film *Top Gun:* "A good pilot must constantly re-assess." I re-assessed, and reached a conclusion that I now pass on to you as advice: "Don't be tempted to write papers on books you haven't read." And so I went to Plan B.

I remembered that earlier in the summer I had read two provocative new books on international affairs. One of these books, *The Future of Freedom,* was written by Yale College graduate and *Newsweek International* editor Fareed Zakaria.[1] The other, *World on Fire,* is the work of Amy Chua, a professor in the Yale Law School.[2]

Both books examine the consequences of the spread of democracy around the globe. Zakaria notes that in the year 1900 not a single country in the world established its government by an election in which every adult citizen held the franchise. Today, 119 do, nearly two-thirds of all the countries in the world. To citizens of the United States, who have enjoyed a long, continuous tradition of free elections, this would seem to be unambiguous good news. But Zakaria and Chua think otherwise,

1 Fareed Zakaria, *The Future of Freedom: Illiberal Democracy at Home and Abroad* (2003).
2 Amy Chua, *World on Fire: How Exporting Free Market Democracy Breeds Ethnic Hatred and Global Instability* (2003).

and they advance powerful arguments and abundant historical detail to support their views.

I cite these books because they exemplify an important feature of the experience you are about to have during the next four years. Both books challenge conventional wisdom and require us to reconsider what we believe to be true. And just as these books challenge us all to think for ourselves, so will your Yale College experience – from the books you read to the professors and classmates you encounter – challenge each of you to re-examine your beliefs and re-define yourself as a person.

Encouraging the spread of democracy around the globe is as old as the American republic itself. Twenty years before he sent Meriwether Lewis on his journey to the Pacific, Thomas Jefferson imagined the United States spanning the North American continent. He desired this not so much to increase the power of the young nation, but to disseminate its values and provide inspiration for the whole world. Near the end of his life, he wrote: "[T]he flames kindled on the 4th of July 1776 have spread over too much of the globe to be extinguished by the feeble engines of despotism."[3] A century later, "Making the world safe for democracy" was more than a slogan to Woodrow Wilson; it was a creed.

Today, Zakaria argues, we have come to identify democracy not with a complex of constitutional arrangements that protect individual liberty and guarantee a rule of law, but rather with one simple defining characteristic – free elections. We have made free elections a central objective of American foreign policy. Yet, as Zakaria points out, in countries without a strong constitution, an independent judiciary, a free press, and the other trappings of *liberal* democracies, elected leaders can, and often do, become tyrants. Zakaria provides many examples, such as Serbia and

---

3 Jefferson to Adams, September 12, 1821, in Lester J. Cappon, ed., *The Adams-Jefferson Letters: The Complete Correspondence Between Thomas Jefferson and Abigail and John Adams* (1959).

Ghana, to illustrate how, too often, democratically elected governments suppress liberty. In juxtaposition, he cites Singapore and Jordan, where in the absence of free elections, citizens have considerably more freedom than those in many countries with elected governments.

Zakaria not only expresses concern about democracies abroad that lack constitutional safeguards to protect individuals; he also attacks direct democracy at home. He objects to the reliance of politicians on opinion polls, the use of primaries to select presidential candidates, and the increased openness of decision processes in Congress and federal agencies — which he argues makes those bodies more, rather than less, susceptible to the influence of lobbyists. Perhaps less surprising in light of recent developments is his concern about the use of plebiscites, which California has developed to a high art. Those government agencies that function best, he argues, are those with ultimate accountability but considerable insulation from day-to-day political pressures, such as the judiciary, the Federal Reserve System, and the Securities and Exchange Commission.

Robert Kagan, another Yale College alumnus who has himself written a challenging and controversial book this year,[4] has denounced Zakaria as an "elitist" for holding views that seem to cut so against the grain of most popular thinking. Is it a problem, Kagan asks, that politicians are more sensitive to public opinion? That the discipline enforced through the "backroom politics" of parties has waned? That government decision processes are more open? Herein lies the value of encountering ideas that challenge conventional thinking. By forcing us to confront our natural bias in favor of democracy and democratization, Zakaria makes us think. And when he reminds us that virtually all his central ideas find

4 Robert Kagan, *Of Paradise and Power: America and Europe in the New World Order* (2003).

support in the *Federalist Papers,* and most especially in those written by James Madison, we are inclined to think even harder.

My role today, and that of Yale's faculty for the next four years, is not to tell you what to think about such matters as these. Rather, drawing on our experience as students and scholars, we can help you identify the sources that will best inform you. We can help to illuminate both sides of the argument, perhaps favoring one view over another and citing our reasons why. But above all our role will be to encourage you to think for yourself. So I won't tell you whether I think Zakaria is right or wrong about the relative importance of liberty and democracy abroad or about the alleged excesses of democracy at home. Just let me suggest that you read the book, and perhaps the *Federalist Papers* as well. And then, for the other side of the argument, you might start with *How Democratic Is the American Constitution,*[5] the most recent book of Robert Dahl, Yale's most distinguished political scientist of the past half century.

Amy Chua shares Zakaria's discomfort with spreading democracy around the world when in practice democracy means majority rule without the constitutional protection of the individual supported by a rule of law. But her argument extends further. She observes that the United States and international agencies like the World Bank and the World Trade Organization are not only exporting a simple-minded notion of democracy; they are also encouraging free market economics of the most rudimentary form, without the regulatory structures used in advanced economies to limit corruption, protect consumers and laborers, and moderate tendencies toward widening the gap between rich and poor. And to this potentially volatile mix of unconstrained free market democracy, she adds a new element that is frequently overlooked — the presence, in a great many developing countries, of a minority group that

5 Robert A. Dahl, *How Democratic Is the American Constitution* (2002).

controls a disproportionate share of the nation's wealth. Examples include the Chinese in Indonesia, Burma, and the Philippines; whites in South Africa; Lebanese in West Africa; the Ibo in Nigeria; and Croatians in the former Yugoslavia.

The presence of what Chua calls "market-dominant minorities" exacerbates the strains caused by global pressures to open protected markets and to democratize political systems. She cites examples of "backlash" against globalization that take three characteristic forms. One, as in Zimbabwe, is expropriation of the wealth of market-dominant minorities by democratically elected representatives of the majority ethnic group. We might think of this as democracy triumphing over market forces. The second is the formation of a ruling coalition in which the market-dominant minority exercises substantial influence, usually through ties with a corrupt government led by representatives of the majority. Marcos' alliance with Chinese in the Philippines is one such example of the market triumphing over democracy. Finally, the backlash against the dominant minority may take the form of systematic violence, or even genocide, as in the ethnic cleansing of the Croatians and the slaughter of the Tutsi in Rwanda. Chua argues that external pressures for free market democracy in the presence of a market-dominant minority will typically lead to one of these three unsatisfactory outcomes.

Professor Chua's provocative ideas won't be the only ones you will encounter in Yale College. Here you have the opportunity to interact with professors who are at the frontier of discovery, enlarging the range of what we know or providing novel interpretations of what we thought we knew. They will confront you with new perspectives, new ways of looking at the familiar, and these new perspectives will challenge you to re-examine your values, attitudes, and beliefs.

This is no less true of the classmates you will meet here and the new friends you will make. You come from all fifty states and fifty countries around the world. One of you is a tenth-generation Yalie and another, who comes from a town in the Midwest with a population of 268, is the first in his family to attend college. From the diverse experiences you will encounter, you cannot fail to learn.

The new perspectives you will confront here may unsettle you, but they will cause you to think more deeply — about yourself, your immediate community, and the wider world that surrounds you. Here you will expand your horizons, develop your critical capacities, and grow as a person in every dimension. The opportunities are boundless. I know you will make the most of them.

Back to School

WHILE YOU were making last-minute preparations to come to New Haven for pre-season practice, or one of our many orientation programs, Dean Salovey and I, along with about fifty administrative and faculty colleagues and an even larger number of indefatigable supporting staff, were embarking on a new adventure of our own. Just two weeks ago, the presidents and vice presidents of twelve of China's leading universities arrived in New Haven for an intensive ten-day course on the American university, and Yale in particular.

I was greatly pleased but not entirely surprised when, at the end of the program, our Chinese colleagues reported that they found the course very stimulating, and that they were returning home full of ideas for modifying and reforming their policies and practices. What did surprise me was how valuable the experience was for those of us at Yale who participated in teaching the course.

At the request of China's State Council and Ministry of Education, we explained the essential features of how universities work: how students are admitted, how faculty are recruited and evaluated, how research is

Freshman Address, August 28, 2004.

funded, how student participation in the classroom and in extracurricular activities is encouraged, how digital technologies are used in teaching and research, how medical schools relate to the larger university, how alumni involvement is encouraged, how funds are raised to support the university, how the endowment is invested, how long-run planning is done, how campus master plans are created and modified, and how responsibilities are divided among administrators and the faculty.

Any good teacher knows that one cannot hide one's ignorance from an inquisitive student. And we knew in advance that our Chinese students would be very inquisitive. It would not be enough for them to learn *how* Yale works; they would want to know *why*. This was no small challenge for us. Anticipating, correctly, the curiosity of our visitors, we prepared our lectures by re-thinking the answers to some very fundamental questions about why the University is organized the way it is, and about why we do things the way we do.

Among the questions we had to ask ourselves, and among those asked by our visitors, are some that pertain directly to you. Three in particular come to mind. Why is the undergraduate curriculum, at Yale as at other leading American universities, structured as it is—with two years of broad, general education followed by two years focused largely on one subject? Why is it valuable to have advanced research and undergraduate education co-located in the same institution? Why do we select students by considering many dimensions of accomplishment and potential rather than academic performance alone?

Since the experience of being a Yale undergraduate is about to be yours, I thought these questions might be of some interest. So, with the answers fresh in my mind, having been recently tested on this material, I submit them to you.

During your first two years here, you will have the opportunity to explore a broad range of subjects, choosing among literally hundreds of courses throughout the humanities, social sciences, and natural sciences that have no or few prerequisites. Indeed, you will be required to distribute your courses such that you cannot specialize prematurely. Only when you choose a major field of study, at the end of your second year, will you be required to concentrate a significant portion of your courses in one area, and only then will you be required to take certain specific courses, rather than choose among electives.

This distinctively American approach to undergraduate education is not the prevailing pattern in most other countries with strong universities. In most of Europe, India, and China, students choose their major field of study when they apply for admission. Once admitted, they do not have the freedom that you have to test your interest in a wide variety of subjects; they specialize immediately. Similarly, in much of the world, students choose a profession in their final year of secondary school; they begin the study of law and medicine as first-year undergraduates.

The freedom to explore in the first two years has not always been a feature of undergraduate education in America. Until the middle of the nineteenth century, there were very few elective courses at Yale and other leading American colleges. Everyone in Yale College took a common set of courses focused on classical Greek and Latin, science, mathematics, and philosophy, and the vast majority of students in law and medical schools entered directly from secondary schools. The expansion of the number of elective courses, the requirement that students choose a major after two years of general study, and the definition of professional schools as postgraduate institutions evolved gradually during the fifty years following the Civil War.

The most eloquent justification for a broad, unspecialized, non-vocational, and, indeed, thoroughly impractical undergraduate curriculum is found in a report written by Yale's President Jeremiah Day in 1828 that was intended, ironically, to justify retention of the prescribed classical curriculum. At the core of Day's argument was the belief, which we at Yale share today, that your education should equip you to think independently and critically, and to respond flexibly to new information, altering your view of the world as appropriate. Although Day believed that the set classical curriculum was ideal to develop this "discipline of the mind," today we encourage you to experiment broadly over a wide range of subjects, to master different ways of thinking that will prove valuable as you continue to learn and develop over a lifetime. We believe that you will be better doctors, lawyers, business leaders, teachers, scholars, ministers, artists, musicians, writers, or public servants after you have explored many subjects, and most especially after you have learned to submit all ideas to critical scrutiny and to think for yourself.

A second question we confronted in attempting to explain Yale to our Chinese visitors was why, in the same institution, do we combine research at the most advanced levels with undergraduate instruction? Again, this is not the prevailing pattern throughout the world. In many European countries, as well as Russia and China, the most distinguished scientists and scholars work in specialized government laboratories or research institutes, where they train advanced graduate students but do not teach undergraduates. That is not the practice here. Yale's most distinguished scientists and scholars teach undergraduate courses. This arrangement advantages both you and our faculty.

The advantage to you is clear. There are few experiences comparable to that of learning a subject from someone who has actively shaped the field she teaches. Such scholars understand more deeply than anyone else that our knowledge is constantly being augmented and reinterpreted. There are simply no better teachers than those who at once possess complete mastery of a field and a commitment to learning as an active, lifelong project.

The advantage to faculty is less obvious, but equally important. I have just explained to you how being asked to teach the Chinese material with which we were intimately familiar caused us to reconsider and justify things we normally take for granted. Well, so it is for scholars, enmeshed in their disciplines, who confront students as bright and curious as you. You ask the best and most challenging questions, precisely because you have yet to internalize fully the assumptions and methods that govern each particular discipline. What we teachers learn from thinking about the questions you ask in the classroom makes us better scholars, and better teachers.

A third question our Chinese visitors asked was: why do we have such a mysterious and complicated set of criteria for admitting students? In China, as in Korea and Japan and many other countries around the world, admission to the top universities is strictly determined by performance on standardized national examinations. Why are we so different?

The question has a simple answer, even if we acknowledge that our admission process *is* mysterious and complicated. We know what we are trying to accomplish, even if the decisions are hard to make.

Now you are by no means slackers when it comes to taking tests. But it was not your test scores that got you here. It was your potential to make a contribution to society, your potential to become leaders in your professions and chosen fields, your potential to become involved in public and civic life, your potential to become creative and imaginative scholars, teachers, artists, musicians, or writers. To make a judgment about your potential we used all the evidence available, not simply test scores and grades. We considered what your teachers said about you, what you said about yourselves, and what you did outside the classroom.

I am not revealing our high opinion of you to impose a burden of obligation. I mean instead to convey a sense of our confidence in you, even as you are experiencing the understandable and entirely natural anxiety of starting something new. History has proven us right in our admissions decisions; Yale graduates make an astonishingly rich array of contributions to society. But it does not happen automatically. Our job is to put extraordinary resources at your disposal; your job is to make the most of them.

In the weeks ahead, each of you will find yourself in a situation not unlike mine two weeks ago as I encountered our Chinese visitors for the first time. Just as I had to explain Yale to those unfamiliar with it, you will have to explain yourself to strangers. You will be asked to describe who you are, what you like and dislike, what you believe and do not believe. In probing conversations way past midnight, you will be challenged to explain why you have come to be the person you are. Do not shy away from these conversations; they are the beginning of your Yale education. You have so much to learn from the other people in this room. You are all alike in possessing talent and potential, and you will come to share a great enthusiasm for this place, but you have very different backgrounds, tastes, and beliefs. Just as it does in the classroom, encountering difference among your classmates will broaden your horizon and cause you to appreciate new possibilities. It will challenge you to think about yourself, to understand the person you are, and to define the person you hope to become. Welcome to four years of self-discovery. Welcome to Yale.

Friendship and Individuality

EARLIER THIS month, as I was thinking about what I might say to you on this occasion, my wife Jane and I visited the recently renovated Museum of Modern Art in New York. There it was our good fortune to see a brilliantly conceived special exhibition of the works of two French impressionist painters, Camille Pissarro and Paul Cézanne. The exhibition covers the period from 1865 to 1885, when the two artists were in very frequent contact, often spending weeks together painting side-by-side.[1]

Pissarro was thirty-five when their close friendship developed, and Cézanne was twenty-six. So they were not exactly your age. But I was struck by the many parallels between their experience and the experience that you are about to have here at Yale. And so by telling you a little about them, I hope to give you a partial introduction to your next four years.

Pissarro and Cézanne met in Paris, at the time the unquestioned capital of the world of art, and a great center of intellectual life. Unlike many

Freshman Address, August 27, 2005.

1 The historical material that follows is drawn from the excellent exhibition catalogue written by Joachim Pissarro, the artist's great-grandson: *Pioneering Modern Painting: Cezanne and Pissarro, 1865–1885* (2005).

artists, they had no connection to the upper strata of French society. Their origins were culturally diverse and middle class. Pissarro had been born in the Caribbean, on the island of St. Thomas, where his father had come from France to take over a troubled family business. Cézanne was a native of Provence, in the south of France. His father sold hats, and later founded a small bank. Both painters had mothers described as "Creole," a term which at the time referred to individuals whose ancestors included either natives or long-time European settlers of the Americas.

You, too, come to a great center of learning, to one of the world's great universities, where you will have daily contact with a faculty whose research, writing, and teaching is constantly reshaping the way we think about literature, the arts, history, nature, the economy, and society. Some of you come from great wealth, some from great hardship, but most of you, like Cézanne and Pissarro, are somewhere in the middle and come from afar. You represent fifty states and forty-two foreign nations. And you have very diverse interests: academic, artistic, and athletic, ranging from debate to drama, from science to surfing to Irish step dancing.

Cézanne and Pissarro became acquainted at a time of great unrest in the world of art. The recognized masters of the day were superb technicians who created rich, lustrous paintings, but their subject matter was highly formalized and allegorical—full of allusion to classical texts, ancient history, and mythology. These "academicians" controlled access to national recognition for younger artists, judging whose work would be shown at the great annual national exhibition—the Salon.

By the time Cézanne first arrived in Paris, Pissarro had already established himself as one of the leaders of a group of young artists in rebellion against the aesthetics of the Academy. Although they respected the technical proficiency of the academicians, the younger artists, like the romantic poets who preceded them by a half century, aimed at a radical simplicity. Instead of elaborate allegorical compositions, they preferred to respond to nature directly—expressing their individuality through painting from still life or the simplest outdoor scenes. Their intention, articulated in some of the earliest correspondence exchanged by Pissarro and Cézanne, was to give a truthful representation of one's own "sensations," one's individual experience of the physical world.

The two painters quickly developed a mutual admiration. As outsiders, they shared a common bond. Both were deeply passionate about art and committed to a revolutionary aesthetic. Both worked fanatically hard. Beyond this, Cézanne was impressed by the older artist's ability to conceptualize their work and to serve as a leader and model for the young artists who would eventually constitute the impressionist school. Pissarro admired Cézanne's audacity, his raw talent, and his extraordinary sense of color. He did everything he could to advance the younger painter's career. Indeed, throughout their lives, even when they grew distant after 1885, they took pleasure in each other's excellence.

You, too, will develop admiration for one another and come to take pleasure in each other's excellence. In these early days at Yale, as you discover in conversation after conversation the astonishing accomplishments of your classmates, you may be wondering: how can I possibly excel here? But believe me, one of the glories of this place is that there is room for everyone to excel. You will be pleased to learn that you do not need to compete with the person sitting to your right or to your left. You will find yourself rejoicing in the success of your classmates, just as they rejoice in yours. There is so much room for individual achievement here—in many different fields of study and many different activities, including music, theater, journalism, community service, athletics, and so much more.

Cézanne and Pissarro repeatedly found inspiration in each other's work. They experimented with a wide variety of techniques—borrowing them from each other, sometimes rejecting them, sometimes returning to them years later. During one period in the late 1870s, Pissarro experimented with Cézanne's much more vivid palette of greens and reds only to return to his more subtle greys. A few years later, Cézanne began to emulate Pissarro's work of the late 1860s, which resembled his own mature style more than Pissarro's work of the impressionist period.

Like Cézanne and Pissarro, you, too, will be drawn to each other, attracted sometimes by a common interest and sometimes by interesting differences. You will learn from one another. Sometimes, you will seek to be like one another. You will experiment, separately and together, trying out new ideas, exploring new subjects, and pursuing new activities. I encourage you to experiment. Yale will not serve you best if you do nothing but deepen the interests you already have, and make friends only with those most like you. You will learn the most by trying out new ideas and new activities, and by getting to know people whose experiences and values are least like your own.

As much as Cézanne and Pissarro learned from one another, each developed a distinctive individuality. Let me illustrate by reference to two pairs of paintings. The first (plates 1 and 2) depicts two representations of the same scene in Louveciennes. The first was painted by Pissarro in 1871, and borrowed a year later by Cézanne so that he might study it and make a "copy." The scene is recognizably the same, and, at this early stage of their relationship, the paintings are more alike than different. Yet there is no doubt that our two artists are experiencing something different in the same scene. For Pissarro, the world is full of browns and greys, where Cézanne sees green, red, orange, and yellow. Look at the Pissarro's finely painted details in the leaves of the trees and the pattern of stones in the wall. Cézanne sees bolder patches of color where Pissarro sees delicate detail. The overall impression is that Pissarro's image of the scene is finer, and Cézanne's is bolder.

Now consider the second pair of paintings (plates 3 and 4). These were created as the artists stood at their easels side by side, six years later. The differences are no longer so subtle. Pissarro's trees are slender, vertical, and elegant. The leaf structure is less precise than in his earlier work, but still gives the impression of lightness and laciness. His palette is more varied, but still dominated by subtle variations of grey. What cannot be seen in the reproduction is that the surface is built up by thousands of tiny brush strokes, to create a dense, lustrous image.

Cézanne's trees, by contrast, are thicker and heavier. Detail of branch and leaf structure has given way to abstract patches of paint oriented largely on the diagonal, giving this painting a geometry and a sense of motion that is radically different from Pissarro's. Cézanne's colors remain richer and more vivid; he is once again bolder and more dramatic than Pissarro. And, in contrast to the richly textured surface built up by the elder artist, Cézanne applies his patches of color with a palette knife, creating a much flatter, more uniform surface – a technique that both artists had explored together but abandoned years earlier.

I think you can see what I am trying to say. Like Cézanne and Pissarro you've come as strangers to a new place. Like them, you will become passionate about what you do here. You will work hard. I hope that, like Cézanne and Pissarro, you will aspire to change the world.

You will form close friendships here. You will find classmates and teachers you admire and wish to emulate. You will learn from them and they will learn from you. You will experiment, exploring new subjects and new activities. And all the while, in the classroom and outside, you will expand your capacity to think independently and creatively.

In the end, you will become the person you choose to become. Like Cézanne and Pissarro, you will each develop your own distinctive character. To help you do this, Yale offers you resources that are beyond imagining – teachers, classmates, libraries, and museums with few equals in all the world. The University Art Gallery has excellent examples of the work of Cézanne and Pissarro. At the reception following this ceremony, you will find a wonderful Pissarro portrait hanging over the fireplace to your left as enter the President's House. Go to it! Yale is yours. Make the most of it.

Preparing for Global Citizenship

THERE IS so much in store for you. Nearly two thousand courses, a library with endless treasures, fabulous museum collections, one of the world's most distinguished faculties, abundant athletic opportunities, and over 250 student organizations that encourage your participation in music, theater, journalism, debate, politics, and community service. There are caring masters, deans, faculty, and freshman counselors to help and advise you. And a campus architecture that is as inspiring as any in America. When it comes to deciding how to exercise your mind, your body, or your voice, the choices are entirely your own. And you will get back what you put in; the benefits from the activities and pursuits you choose will be proportionate to the effort, commitment, and passion that you devote to them.

Why, you might ask, do we shower you with such an abundance of learning and living opportunities? Why do we invest in you?

The answer is simple: because you are the future. You are immensely talented, and you have the capacity to make the world a better place. Most of you will think I am talking not about you but about your amaz-

Freshman Address, September 2, 2006.

53

ing suitemate who seems to have accomplished so much, or the person in the next entryway who seems so much better prepared and so much more self-confident. But no, I am talking about each and every one of you. Every one of you has the potential to make a difference.

And we need you. There is so much to be done. Global security is threatened by a new war in the Middle East and a persistent terrorism that strikes almost randomly at civilized peoples around the world. Global prosperity is threatened. Just six weeks ago, the global free trade regime that has brought hundreds of millions out of poverty in the past quarter century was placed in jeopardy by the parochialism of nations unable to see the common good. And our global environment is threatened. Unless we resolve to cooperate and do something about it, the biodiversity of the planet will continue to diminish at an alarming rate and global warming will transform the conditions of life and livelihood around the world.

Thanks to a revolution in communications, our world is more interconnected and interdependent than ever before in human history. Clearly, we need to understand each other better. Can Hezbollah and Israel coexist in peace? Why does Al Qaeda continue to attract young men willing to kill themselves and blow up trains, planes, and buildings? Why are the Europeans refusing to open their agricultural markets, thus impeding the continued liberalization of trade that has contributed so much to the progress of developing and developed countries alike? And why is America not leading the world's efforts to reduce greenhouse gas emissions instead of dragging its feet?

How can your Yale College experience prepare you to address questions like these? How can you use your time at Yale to prepare for global citizenship? Dean Salovey has already given part of the answer. He offered evidence that people with different cultural backgrounds and different languages see the world differently. And he suggested that bringing together classmates of diverse national origins or cultural backgrounds enriches the learning experience for everyone, improving our understanding of common subjects of inquiry. But this is not the only virtue of creating an internationally diverse student body. It also helps us to understand one another.

For Americans, understanding the thinking and beliefs of people living in China, India, the Middle East, and Africa is crucial if we are to secure peace, promote prosperity, and protect the environment throughout the twenty-first century. Understanding Americans is no less important to Chinese, Indians, Arabs, and Africans. As Yale students, your opportunity to get to know students from other countries is far greater today than it was even very recently. When I greeted my first freshman class as president of Yale thirteen years ago, only one student in fifty came from a foreign country other than Canada. Today, the number is one in twelve.

The increased representation of students from around the world has a major implication for those of you who are Americans or Canadians. It means that each of you can, without much effort, become close friends with at least one classmate from a country quite different from your own. This can be a very important start in broadening your perspective on the world. You each have a chance to begin your exploration of the world – its peoples and their diverse values – right here in New Haven. And for those of you who come from abroad, you have an extraordinary opportunity to get to know America and some very talented and promising Americans. We will do all we can to make you welcome here.

But forming friendships is only the beginning of the work that each of you needs to do to become an informed global citizen capable of bringing the world closer together. You also need to educate yourself about the world. Fortunately, you will find that over six hundred of the courses available to you deal with the language, literature, art, music, history, religion, culture, politics, economics, and sociology of other nations. I hope you will explore these subjects for the pure joy of learning about them, but I also hope that you will take time to reflect on how learning about other cultures informs your thinking about the issues that we as global citizens must confront. I recommend, most of all, that those of you who are native English-speakers master at least one foreign language to the point of true fluency. Your understanding of a foreign culture will be so much deeper if you know the language.

Finally, let me urge you to spend time abroad. With the adoption of the Report of the Committee on Yale College Education in 2003, it became an expectation that all Yale College graduates will spend a year, a semester, or at least a summer engaged in study programs or work experiences overseas. To make this expectation feasible for all, we announced in 2005 that additional funding would be provided during summers to make it possible for students on financial aid to work or study abroad. This past academic year and summer over 900 undergraduates participated in Yale-sponsored work internships, study programs, or independent research projects overseas, and by the time you finish your sophomore year, we expect that there will be a Yale-sponsored overseas opportunity for every member of your class.

There is simply no substitute for spending time in another country, immersed in another culture. Very few experiences in life provide greater insight into the strengths and limitations of one's own culture and values; very few experiences teach more about how to understand others. My wife and I spent two and a half of our undergraduate and graduate student years abroad. Our experience in Italy inspired a lifelong interest in the aesthetics of the visual arts and architecture, and our time in England exposed us to a degree of commitment to the life of the mind barely imaginable to pragmatic Americans. And yet our experience abroad also helped us to savor all the more the optimism, toleration, and democratic impulses of Americans unencumbered by the historical legacy of social class and status. We learned to appreciate not only Botticelli and the Oxford don, but Whitman, too.

If you take the time to get to know one another and the diverse points of view and values that you represent, if you inform yourselves about the world through your studies and your daily reading, if you learn a language, and if you study or work abroad—preferably for more than a single summer—you will be a more fully educated person. And you will be far better prepared for the global careers that will be possible, indeed inevitable, for your generation.

But I am suggesting more, because a Yale education is not just for your own personal benefit. Given the enormous investment that we, and your families, are making in you, you will leave here not only with abundant opportunities but also *responsibilities,* responsibilities akin to those borne by generations of Yale graduates before you, but different. Your predecessors were the stewards, first of the Connecticut Colony, then of the young Republic occupying part of the east coast of North America, and then of the vast nation spanning a continent and seeking to spread its message of freedom around the globe. Your responsibility will be different. You will be the stewards of a small planet, an interconnected world with a diverse array of peoples, cultures, and beliefs coexisting interdependently. The challenge before you is immense and without precedent. But it is a challenge worthy of your talent and promise. Seize every moment of these next four years. Take advantage of all that Yale offers. Pursue your passions, and prepare yourselves for global citizenship.

The Questions That Matter

THREE WEEKS ago, as you were beginning to prepare yourselves for your journey to New Haven, I spent a very pleasant weekend reading a new book by one of our distinguished Sterling Professors, the former Dean of the Yale Law School, Anthony Kronman, who now teaches humanities courses in Yale College. I had one of those experiences that I hope you have time and again during your four years here. I was disappointed to finish reading the book. It was beautifully written, closely reasoned, and utterly transparent in its exposition and its logic. I was disappointed because I wanted the pleasure of my reading to go on and on, through the lovely summer afternoon and well into the evening.

Professor Kronman's book, *Education's End*,[1] is at once an affirmation of the essential value of the humanities in undergraduate education and a critique of the humanities curriculum as it has evolved over the past forty years. Professor Kronman begins with a presumption that a college education should be about more than acquainting yourself with a body

Freshman Address, September 1, 2007.

1 Anthony T. Kronman, *Education's End: Why Our Colleges and Universities Have Given Up on the Meaning of Life* (2007).

of knowledge and preparing yourself for a vocation. This presumption is widely shared. Many who have thought deeply about higher education — including legions of university presidents starting most eloquently with Yale's Jeremiah Day in 1828 — go on to argue that a university education should develop in you what President Day called the "discipline of the mind" — the capacity to think clearly and independently, and thus equip you for any and all of life's challenges.[2]

Professor Kronman takes a step beyond this classical formulation of the rationale for liberal education. He argues that undergraduate education should also encourage you to wrestle with the deepest questions concerning lived experience: What constitutes a good life? What values do you hope to live by? What kind of community or society do you want to live in? How should you reconcile the claims of family and community with your individual desires? In short, Professor Kronman asserts that an important component of your undergraduate experience should be seeking answers to the questions that matter: questions about what has meaning in life.

Professor Kronman then divides the history of American higher education into three periods, and he argues that the quest for meaning in life was central to the university curriculum during the first two, but no longer. In the first period, running from the founding of Harvard in 1636 to the Civil War, the curriculum was almost entirely prescribed. At its core were the great literary, philosophical, and historical works of classical Greece and Rome, as well as classics of the Christian tradition — from the Bible to the churchmen of late Antiquity and the Middle Ages to Protestant theologians of the Reformation and beyond. In the minds of those who established Harvard and Yale and the succession of American colleges that were founded by their graduates, the classics were the ideal instruments, not only for developing the "discipline of the mind,"

2 *Reports on the Course of Instruction in Yale College* (1828), p. 7.

but also for educating gentlemen of discernment and piety. In this era, Kronman argues, the proposition that education was about how to live a virtuous life was never in doubt. Through their mastery of the great texts, the faculty, each of whom typically taught every subject in the curriculum, were believed to possess authoritative wisdom about how to live, and they believed it their duty to convey this wisdom to their students.

After the Civil War the landscape of American higher education changed dramatically, as new institutions like Johns Hopkins, Cornell, and the University of California took German universities as their model. For the first time, the advancement of knowledge through research, rather than the intergenerational transmission of knowledge through teaching, was seen to be the primary mission of higher education. As faculty began to conceive of themselves as scholars first and teachers second, specialization ensued. No longer did everyone on the faculty teach every part of a prescribed curriculum; instead the faculty divided into departments and concentrated their teaching within their scholarly disciplines.

Amidst this transformation, explicit discussion of the question of how one should live was more or less abandoned by the natural and social sciences and left to the humanities. Humanists, like scientists, became specialists in their scholarship, but they recognized that the domain of their expertise, the great works of literature, philosophy, and history—modern as well as classical—raised, argued, and re-argued the central questions about life's meaning. And they continued to see their role as custodians of a tradition that encouraged young people to grapple with these questions as a central part of their college experience. But humanities professors no longer had the moral certainty of their predecessors. They saw the great works of the past not as guidebooks to becoming a steadfast and righteous Christian, but rather as part of a "great conversation" about human values, offering alternative models of how one should live, rather than prescribing one true path. Engagement with the "great conversation" remained an important component of college education in the century between the Civil and Vietnam Wars, a period which Kronman labels the era of "secular humanism."

Kronman goes on to argue that since the 1960s, the tradition of secular humanism has been eroded – he would even say defeated – by two forces. The first of these forces is a growing professionalization, discouraging humanists from offering authoritative guidance on the questions of value at the center of the "great conversation." The second is politicization, challenging the view that the voices and topics engaged in the "great conversation" of Western civilization have any special claim to our attention and arguing for increased focus on the voices and topics, Western and non-Western, that have been excluded from the Western canon.

Kronman's argument about the contemporary state of the humanities will be welcomed by some and met with fierce resistance from many others. But the inevitable controversy about the current state of the humanities should not obscure for us this most important point: that the question of how you should live should be at the center of the undergraduate experience, and at the center of your Yale College experience.

The four years ahead of you offer a once-in-a-lifetime opportunity to pursue your intellectual interests wherever they may lead, and, wherever they do lead, you will find something to reflect upon that is pertinent to your quest for meaning in life. It is true that your professors are unlikely to give you the answers to questions about what you should value and how you should live. We leave the answers up to you. But I want to make very clear that we encourage you to ask the questions, and, in seeking the answers, to use the extraordinary resources of this place – a brilliant and learned faculty, library and museum resources that are the equal of any campus anywhere, and curious and diverse classmates who will accompany you in your quest.

Because of their subject matter, the humanities disciplines have a special role in inspiring you to consider how you should live. But I also want to suggest to each of you that questions that bear on the shaping of your life will arise in whatever subjects you choose to study. You will find that virtually every discipline will provide you with a different perspective on questions of value and lead you to fresh insights that will illuminate your personal quest.

Your philosophy professors, for example, are unlikely to teach you the meaning of life, but they will train you to reason more rigorously and to discern more readily what constitutes a logically consistent argument and what does not. And they will lead you through texts that wrestle directly with the deepest questions of how to live, from Plato and Aristotle to Kant and Nietzsche and beyond.

Your professors of literature, music, and art history will not tell you how to live, but they will teach you to read, listen, and see closely, with a keener appreciation for the artistry that makes literature, music, and visual art sublime representations of human emotions, values, and ideas. And they will lead you through great works that present many different models of how, and how not, to lead a good life.

Neither will your professors of history instruct you on the values that you should hold most close, but, by giving you an appreciation of the craft of reconstructing the past, they will lead you to understand how meaning is extracted from experience, which may help you to gain perspective on your own experience. And history, too, provides models of how one should, and should not, live.

In your effort to think through how you wish to live and what values matter most to you, you will find that challenging questions arise not only in the humanities. Long ago, I taught introductory economics in Yale College. I always began by telling the students that the course would change their lives. I still believe this. Why? Because economics will open you to an entirely new and different way of understanding how the world works. Economics will not prescribe for you how society should be organized, or the extent to which individual freedom should be subordinated to collective ends, or how the fruits of human labor should be distributed – at home and around the world. But understanding the logic of markets will give you a new way to think about these questions, and, because life is lived within society and not in abstraction from it, economics will help you to think about what constitutes a good life.

Dean Salovey has already given you some insights gleaned from his study as a professor of psychology. His discipline probes many fundamental questions. What is the relationship between your brain and your conscious thoughts? To what extent is your personality – in both its cognitive and emotional dimensions – shaped by your genetic makeup, your past experiences, and your own conscious decisions? The answers to these questions have an obvious bearing on the enterprise of locating meaning in life.

Your biology and chemistry professors will not tell you how to live, but the discoveries made in these fields over the last century have already extended human life by twenty-five years in the United States. As the secrets of the human genome are unlocked and the mechanisms of disease uncovered, life expectancy may well increase by another decade or two. You may want to ponder how a longer life span might alter your thinking about how to live, how to balance family and career, and how society should best be organized to realize the full potential of greater human longevity.

Finally, it is at the core of the physical sciences that one finds some of the deepest and most fundamental questions relating to the meaning of human experience. How was the physical universe created? How long will it endure? And what is the place of humanity in the order of the universe?

For the next four years, each of you has the freedom to shape your life and prepare for shaping the world around you. You will learn much about yourself and your capacity to contribute to the world not only from your courses, but also from the many friends you make and the rich array of extracurricular activities available to you. Your courses will give you the tools to ask and answer the questions that matter most, and your friendships and activities will give you the opportunity to test and refine your values through experience.

Let me warn you that daily life in Yale College is so intense that it may sometimes seem that you have little time to stop and think. But, in truth, you have four years — free from the pressures of career and family obligations that you will encounter later — to reflect deeply on the life you wish to lead and the values you wish to live by. Take the time for this pursuit. It may prove to be the most important and enduring accomplishment of your Yale education.

Variety and Freedom

IN A lead article last month, the editors of *The Economist*, that most pro-American of foreign publications, proclaimed, "The United States, normally the world's most self-confident place, is glum." The editors went on to note that home prices are falling faster than during the Great Depression, credit is scarce, gasoline is more expensive than in the 1970s, and the dollar is at a post–Cold War low. Popular support for free trade and open markets, the lifeblood of growing world prosperity, is lower in the United States than anywhere in the world. Our universities remain strong, but our system of K-12 education is underperforming. We lead the world in biomedical innovation, yet a large fraction of our population is medically uninsured or underinsured. Support for U.S. foreign policy has eroded around the world. And many Americans view China's emergence as a global power, so dramatically punctuated by the Beijing Olympics, as a threat rather than an opportunity. According to a recent poll, eight out of ten Americans believe that the country is headed in the wrong direction.

Amidst this midsummer gloom, as I thought about what to say on

Freshman Address, August 30, 2008.

this occasion, I turned for comfort and inspiration to one of my favorite authors, the greatest of American voices, Walt Whitman. Like Alexis de Tocqueville before him, but with greater artistry and eloquence, Whitman grasped and characterized America's historical distinctiveness and anticipated its destiny. If you want to understand in full the power and potential of this nation, take some time, lots of time, with Whitman's poetic magnum opus, *Leaves of Grass.*

But let me confine myself here to Whitman's brilliant prose essay, *Democratic Vistas,* written in 1870. Like the 1855 preface to *Leaves of Grass,* but more ordered and more rigorous, *Democratic Vistas* is, on the surface, an argument about the need for a distinctive American literature. In Whitman's view, America's historical uniqueness comes, first, from its unprecedented foundation on the rights of the individual, embodied in the Declaration of Independence, the Constitution, and its political institutions, and, second, from its unprecedented actual and potential material prosperity. But for Whitman, the achievements of America, like the deeds of the heroes of ancient Greece, would be incomplete were they not memorialized in song. He asserts that, to realize its full potential as a nation and a culture, America needs a poet, and a literature, to teach its lessons, to capture the essence of its achievements and make them permanent, and to create models of democratic heroes that inspire. From our perspective, it is clear that Whitman himself is the very poet he yearns for.

For now, I am less interested in Whitman's argument about the role of literature, and more interested in what the American song is about and what bearing this has on your next four years, whether you come from Delhi or Detroit. Whitman begins *Democratic Vistas* by observing that the greatest lessons of nature are variety and freedom, and that these are also the greatest lessons of politics and progress in the New World. What does he mean?

Let me oversimplify. Whitman's democratic vision is that in America, like nowhere else in history, every man and woman has the opportunity to be a hero. Like Tocqueville, Whitman understood that the absence of a feudal legacy not only makes individuals equal before the law, but also allows for the possibility that the contribution of a person could be measured without reference to aristocratic standards and ideals. Hence, a "democratic vista" in which excellence in all walks of life can be celebrated, and creativity of the most radical kind can flourish. In his poetry, Whitman extols, among many others, the factory worker, the farmer, and the common soldier no less than Abraham Lincoln, their great leader. In *Democratic Vistas*, he sketches the lives of four women — a housekeeper, a mechanic, a housewife, and an elderly woman who played the role of community peacemaker — each with her unique dignity and excellence, each a contributor to the well-being of others. None of these heroic women bears the slightest resemblance to the aristocratic ideal of feminine virtue. Variety (or, to use today's word for it, diversity) and freedom are the lessons of the New World.

From the native peoples and the waves of immigrants that gave America its astonishing diversity, and from the political institutions that gave individuals unprecedented freedom, came the basis of unprecedented material prosperity. Like Tocqueville before him, Whitman foresaw that, unshackled by constraints of class or authoritarian government, America's democratic creativity would inevitably result in new institutions and technologies that would secure that prosperity.

If America is now at the end of the era of sole global leadership that Whitman envisioned, it is in part because of its success, because some or all of the institutions it created — free and open markets, easy access to capital, an educational system and culture that support innovation and creativity, and a democratic polity — are being emulated elsewhere. As Fareed Zakaria, a Yale College alumnus and a trustee of the University, argues so persuasively in his new book, *The Post-American World*, the rise of the rest of the world should be seen as a great accomplishment, not a threat. The world economy is a positive-sum game. Twenty percent of the world's population has been lifted out of poverty in the past thirty years, largely in China and India. This is obviously a good in itself, one that creates opportunity for the entire world.

Let me now connect the *Economist*'s lament and Whitman's lessons to the opportunities before you these next four years. It is true that your generation will face major challenges, but it is also true that you will find the spirit of Whitman's America — the twin engines of variety and freedom — very much alive here at Yale. You will take strength from the rich diversity of your classmates, and you will find in all of them the latent capacity to take their place among Whitman's democratic heroes. Every one of you has the potential not only to make your own lives personally and professionally fulfilling but also to make a contribution to the well-being of others, on scales both large and small. The freedom you have here will give you the opportunity to discover your intellectual passions, establish your personal goals, and define the standards you will live by.

Dean Salovey has encouraged you to be adventurous in making use of Yale's resources, to take risks, and not fear failure. I would also encourage each of you to be a leader. Yale College is a virtual laboratory for leadership. We have thirty-five varsity sports, thirty-five club sports, and more than one hundred intramural teams, as well as two hundred and fifty student organizations embracing almost every imaginable sphere of activity — student government, music, film, theater, politics, journalism, and community service. So join in, learn how to work well with others, and learn how to lead.

It is important to remember that leadership takes many forms. In high school, many of you worked hard to get elected as a student government president, or a literary magazine editor, or a team captain. But from now on, leadership is not measured by a title and a line on your résumé. True leadership means drawing the best out of others and inspiring them toward a worthy goal. You do not have to be a team captain or a club president to be a leader. But you do have to participate, make a contribution, and be ready to lead when the opportunity arises. You may find an opportunity to lead by inspiring third graders in a school tutorial program, or simply by taking initiative within an organization to inspire and motivate others to accomplish more than anyone else imagined was possible.

I summon you to lead because you come to us with proven talent, keen intellect, and a demonstrated capacity for hard work. You have the ability to do more in life than just go along for the ride. If America is to revive from its current malaise and bring its extraordinary assets to bear on a post-American world, if the wider world is to awaken to the challenges that confront us all — global warming, poverty, and disease — rather than fall prey to the ideologies and interests that divide us, you must step up and be leaders.

During the next four years, Yale will provide you with an unimaginably rich array of resources that will allow you to develop yourselves as individuals and as leaders. If you choose to engage, by the time you leave here you will be prepared to contribute meaningfully to the improvement of the world around you. These four years are your time of opportunity; your parents, your teachers, and I look forward to watching you make the most of them.

Passion and Perseverance

A FEW weeks ago I was browsing in a bookstore when I noticed a new biography of Grace Murray Hopper.[1] In a flash, I knew that I would buy the book, read it, and tell you about her — one of the most extraordinary women ever to attend Yale — when you arrived here. What a perfect topic for this season, the fortieth anniversary of the first enrollment of women in Yale College.

I imagine that only a small number of you have ever heard of Grace Hopper. She was the first woman to receive a Yale Ph.D. in mathematics, the first woman in the nation to reach the rank of Admiral in the U.S. Navy, and the first graduate of our mathematics department to be awarded the Graduate School's Wilbur Cross Medal for distinguished contributions to scholarship and public service. She made her mark on the nation and the world as a pioneer in computer programming, lead-

Freshman Address, August 29, 2009.

1 Kurt W. Beyer, *Grace Hopper and the Invention of the Information Age* (2009). In the preparation of this talk I drew freely from this book as well as an earlier biography by Kathleen Broome Williams, *Grace Hopper: Admiral of the Cyber Sea* (2004).

ing some of the most important advances in the field as it developed in the 1940s, '50s, and '60s. Her story speaks to anyone who seeks self-improvement through education and hard work, and, most particularly, to you. I hope that Admiral Hopper's voyage will inspire you as much as it has inspired me.

Grace Murray Hopper was born in 1906 into comfortable circumstances on the Upper West Side of New York City. Her father was a Phi Beta Kappa graduate of Yale College and a successful insurance company executive. Her mother was a housewife with a passion for puzzles and mathematics. Both parents encouraged their daughter's intellectual pursuits. Grace was an avid reader, and she took an early interest in building. She spent many hours as a child assembling things from the nuts, bolts, and metal pieces of her toy construction kit. Her passion for tinkering served her well in the 1940s, when her ability to diagnose mechanical failures and repair computers made a tangible difference in the nation's effort during World War II.

When time came for college, her father's alma mater was not open to her, so her sights were set on Vassar, one of the colleges that then attracted the most able young women in the country. To her dismay, young Grace failed the entry examination in Latin and had to take an extra year to remedy the deficiency before entering Vassar in 1924. She learned from this failure. She had no natural aptitude for grammar or spoken language, but she learned that languages (and much else) could be mastered by sheer determination and perseverance. Years later, she would dazzle audiences by writing in German left handed on the blackboard until she had filled the board to her left. Then she would switch the chalk to her right hand and proceed to fill the blackboard to her right in French!

At Vassar, Hopper pursued a double major in mathematics and physics. She considered preparing herself for a career in engineering, but she recognized that, unlike today, there was at the time virtually no place for women in engineering. So she planned on studying and eventually teaching mathematics. Upon graduation she won a fellowship to study at Yale, where she earned a master's degree in mathematics in three years. She then returned to Vassar to join the faculty and begin her teaching career while completing her Yale dissertation.

She soon became a legendary teacher, known for animating her mathematics courses with interesting and relevant practical applications. She audited courses in astronomy, biology, chemistry, geology, physics, philosophy, economics, and architecture, and drew on all these disciplines to develop unconventional and imaginative courses of her own. Whatever she taught, the enrollment quickly soared from ten or fewer to seventy-five. She broke down the barriers between disciplines and showed her students how mathematics could link one field to another. She became a highly effective public speaker, a talent that served her well later in her career. And she was regarded within Vassar as a skillful agent of change.

Well established at Vassar College by the age of 34, Grace Hopper could have contented herself with a life as a teacher, mentor, and campus leader for the next 40 years. But her modest personal demeanor notwithstanding, she desired more. She yearned to return to the study of advanced mathematics, and in the fall of 1941 she took a sabbatical to study partial differential equations at NYU with the famous mathematician Richard Courant, a refugee who had previously headed Germany's most prestigious mathematical institute. This proved another fortuitous choice, as her new knowledge of partial differential equations provided another major assist to the war effort just three years later.

The attack on Pearl Harbor radically changed Grace Hopper's life. By the time she finished up her NYU fellowship by the summer of 1942, she was determined to serve the nation, but the outlet for that service was not yet clear. As soon as an act of Congress authorized the creation of a women's corps in the Navy, Hopper was determined to join. Initially, she was rejected because of her age and diminutive size, but again, as she so often did, she persevered, finally convincing the Navy that her talent as a mathematician could be valuable to the war effort. She expected to become a code-breaker, but, to her surprise, she was assigned to the position of second in command of the Harvard Computation Lab under the direction of Howard Aiken in the summer of 1944. She arrived just in time for the installation of the first mainframe electromechanical computer, the Mark I, designed by Aiken and built by IBM.

Aiken was a visionary and a stern taskmaster; he had very high expectations for his subordinates but stood aloof. He was initially disappointed to learn that the Navy had assigned him a woman as his second in command. Again, Hopper persevered in the face of initial adversity. Because she worked so hard and was entirely loyal, she quickly earned Aiken's confidence. Aiken soon came to rely on Hopper's counsel and trust her completely. Because she was also a better communicator and a more accessible collaborator than Aiken, Hopper became the de facto leader of the team.

For Hopper and her small crew, the challenge was immense. Mark I was capable of making calculations in minutes that previously took teams of mathematicians weeks to perform. But for each new problem the machine had to be programmed, given coded instructions in zeros and ones that described the mechanical operations required to reach the solution. One tiny error in a program could bring the machine to a halt; but so could any number of sources of mechanical failure. Hopper's experience as a childhood tinkerer made her the lab's expert at diagnosing machine failures. Once, when she found that a moth had interfered with the machine, she coined the now widely used phrase "bug" to describe a programming error. She and her team were the first to talk about "debugging" computer programs.

It was easy enough, conceptually, to program the machine to calculate ballistics trajectories. But at least one problem was much harder: calculating the amount of explosive material needed to bring the fissile material in the first atomic bomb to critical mass. Hopper and her team worked on this problem with the brilliant mathematician John von Neumann, who developed the partial differential equations describing the implosion that could trigger a chain reaction. These equations were of a type that had never before been solved numerically. They required Hopper to call upon everything she had learned from her year of study with Courant in order to translate von Neumann's equations into a working computer program.

Working day and night under immense pressure for results, Hopper and her small team not only solved the problems they needed to solve, they also made substantial progress in conceptualizing how programs might be written most effectively. During the last year of the war, Hopper made the first of her several fundamental innovations in programming by inventing the "subroutine," a program that could be stored in the machine to handle operations that were required repeatedly, such as calculating a logarithm. The idea was a fundamental building block in the field of computer programming.

After the war, working for Remington Rand, she went a significant step beyond by inventing the "compiler," an invention that liberated programmers from having to be familiar with every physical operation of the computer. And then, most significantly, Hopper then turned her attention to developing a programming language that was close to ordinary language — a step that would make programming accessible to a much wider group. She led the development of COBOL, for many years the most successful and most widely used programming language for both business and military applications.

In 1967, after 18 years in industry she resumed active duty as a naval officer, and spent the next 19 years advising the Navy on its computing operations and serving tirelessly as its most effective recruiter, encouraging young men and women to enlist and learn computer skills. She was elevated to the rank of Commodore in 1983, and to Rear Admiral shortly thereafter. She retired from active duty in 1986, the oldest officer in the Navy. After she died in 1992, an aircraft carrier was commissioned in her name.

Grace Hopper was the kind of person we hope you will become: a leader, an innovator, a person of deep loyalty and commitment, a hard worker, and a creative force. Yale played only a small role in cultivating these qualities within her, but her brilliant career is a source of great institutional pride.

As you enter Yale College, with a new world all before you, I urge you to take inspiration from the story of Grace Hopper.

Pursue your passions as she pursued hers—from learning math to tinkering to forming and realizing a vision that computer programs could be written in ordinary language.

Give your curiosity free rein. Explore, as she did, every field of study that seems remotely interesting and find the connections among them.

Invest in acquiring skills—as she acquired languages, and math, and public speaking.

Stretch yourself beyond what is comfortable and familiar, as she did when she left Vassar to push herself to learn more advanced math and as she did again when she joined the Navy to serve her country.

Work hard and persevere in the face of initial adversity, as she did when she failed a college entry exam, when the Navy discouraged her from enlisting, and when the director of the Harvard Computation Lab expressed initial disappointment in her appointment.

Be creative without isolating yourself, as she did by pursuing radical innovations in computing while at the same time working effectively within organizations, being the glue that held teams of co-workers together.

Recognize that no one else can define the limits of what is possible for you, as she did when she chose to pursue an unconventional career before her time and against all odds.

You have come to a place that offers you extraordinary opportunities for self-discovery and self-improvement. May Grace Hopper's example inspire you to seize them.

Seeing the Big Picture

HERE AT Yale you will have the chance to expand your horizons, to widen your scope of vision, and to see the world from many perspectives. I want to encourage you, in every way that I can, to make the most of this rare and unique opportunity.

The simple truth is that *we* need *you*. In these times of great uncertainty, when we seem unable to deal with our gravest problems, we desperately need an infusion of broadly educated citizens and leaders to join the debates, raise the level of discourse, and move us in the right direction. We know all too well the missed opportunities of the past few years.

We entered 2009 full of hope that the world's nations could agree to save the planet from the scourge of global warming. But the U.S. Congress deadlocked in a struggle dominated by the parochial interests of various industries and regions and failed to act. Then, in Copenhagen, efforts to reach a global agreement were foiled when neither the United States nor the developing nations were willing to compromise for the good of all, and only the Europeans saw the big picture.

Freshman Address, August 27, 2011.

Consider our current economic condition. Since January 2009 it has been clear that there is only one way to prevent a deep and prolonged recession and avoid persistent high unemployment. We needed then, as we need now, a massive fiscal stimulus in the form of direct job creation, not tax cuts. And we needed, at the same time, to make a commitment to reduce the federal budget deficit dramatically over a period of years — not immediately, since that would prolong the recession, but predictably. We finally faced the question of deficit reduction this summer. But the ideological rigidity and parochialism of members of Congress moved the dialogue away from the big picture and paralyzed us with rigid and simplistic formulas — no tax increases, no increase in the debt ceiling, no cuts to Social Security and Medicare. After weeks of deadlock, we took only a tiny step toward solving the problem.

Last December, David Leonhardt, a member of the Yale College Class of 1994, identified with crystal clarity the issues we face in the form of a picture he published in the *New York Times* — a budget Sudoku. In this brilliant graphical display, he demonstrated that no combination of discretionary spending cuts could close the federal budget gap by 2020. The only way to do so involves some combination of reducing Social Security benefits, controlling Medicare and Medicaid costs, reducing defense spending, and raising taxes (or, at least, allowing the Bush tax cuts to expire). David's Sudoku allowed his readers to see the big picture clearly, and he was rewarded with the Pulitzer Prize.

I am going to make the audacious claim that David's Yale education has had a lot to do with his ability to see the big picture. He experienced, just as you will over the next four years, exposure to a variety of disciplines — in his case, mathematics, economics, politics, and history, as well as physics and art history. This broad education has allowed him to look beyond the small-mindedness of what politicians say to interpret the larger trends driving the economy and society. He also learned to write clearly, analytically, and forcefully. He mastered this essential tool not only through his English courses but also through his principal extracurricular activity as a reporter for and subsequently as editor of the *Yale Daily News*.

David Leonhardt is but one of many visible examples of the profound ways in which the liberal arts education you are about to experience can help you to develop the capacity to see the big picture. By sampling courses across a wide range of disciplines, you will learn to see problems from multiple perspectives. And by learning to think critically and analytically, you will become disinclined to accept simplified slogans as truth, more able to see subtle interconnections, more capable of forging solutions that embrace complexity without being overwhelmed by it. No matter what subjects you choose to pursue in depth, you will be required in your first two years to develop some breadth, and you will be challenged to think for yourselves — independently and analytically. In short, you will equip yourselves, in the words of Yale President Jeremiah Day, writing in 1828, with both the "discipline" and the "furniture" of the mind, rendering you capable of distinguishing clear and convincing arguments from doctrinaire assertions and unexamined prejudices. You will learn how to see the forest for the trees.

This capacity to see the big picture has been a characteristic of Yale graduates for decades, if not longer. In 1916, as America sat by watching a world war that many believed it would inevitably enter, a group of Yale College students came to realize that the new technology of aviation might potentially change the shape of warfare. While still in school, they convinced the Navy to constitute them as the first squadron of what became the Naval Air Reserve. In March 1917, these twenty-nine young aviators left school en masse and enlisted in the Navy, immediately comprising more than one-third of the military's qualified pilots. They made a substantial contribution to the allied war effort, because their Yale education helped them to see clearly what others could not.

Aviation has a role in the story of another Yale senior who was capable of seeing the big picture. Fred Smith, Class of 1966, had a vision that came to revolutionize the transportation of documents and small parcels. In the senior essay he submitted to the Economics Department, he laid out a simple idea: that shipments might be gathered from metropolitan areas all over the United States and flown in the evening to one central hub, where they would be reloaded onto planes headed to their destination metropolitan areas and flown out for delivery the next day. The oft-repeated story is that Mr. Smith earned a "C" grade for his efforts, and then went on, after serving in the military, to found a logistics company known as Federal Express. According to the legend, he saw the big picture, even if his economics professor did not. It is not true that he got a "C," though it makes the story better in the telling.

Lest you think airplanes always figure into the narratives of Yale graduates capable of seeing the big picture, let me give you two more stories. When Ruth DeGolia, Class of 2003, served as a summer intern in Guatemala, she came to recognize that the women in the rural villages in which she was working made weavings of unusual quality and beauty. But they sold for nearly nothing in local markets. Ruth encouraged these women to form cooperatives and market their wares over the Internet. She brought them fashion magazines to inspire them to weave woolens in patterns that would appeal to North American tastes. Today, the earnings of the cooperatives she helped to establish provide substantial support to public education, as well as access to electricity, clean water, and public health in more than thirty Guatemalan villages.

Just one more: David Levin (no relation) studied history and the history of education at Yale and designed and directed a tutoring program for New Haven schoolchildren. He then joined Teach for America and came to an understanding of why K-12 education was failing in our inner-city schools. In his big picture, students needed the discipline to focus on their work, the self-confidence to believe that they could succeed, and the motivation to recognize that their discipline would be rewarded with a better life if they managed to graduate and attend college. From this inspiration came the KIPP Schools, which David founded in partnership with Michael Feinberg, the graduate of another Ivy League school. KIPP has been a pioneer in urban education, demonstrating a model that truly works.

These stories inspire us with the achievements of those who started here just like you, with great potential, curiosity, open-mindedness, and a desire to make a difference in the world. The extraordinary resources of Yale College will give you the opportunity to realize that potential, to exercise that curiosity, to expand that mind beyond anything you can possibly now imagine, and to fulfill that desire to make a difference. If you stretch to your limits, and take courses and engage in extracurricular activities that broaden and challenge you, then you, too, will develop the capacity to see the big picture. We are counting on you. You are setting off on a grand adventure. Make the most of it!

THE WORTH OF THE UNIVERSITY

The University in Service to Society

MY SUBJECT this evening is how universities serve society. To answer the question, I will draw mainly on the experience of American universities, not because their contributions are unique or more important than those of universities elsewhere. I focus on the U.S. experience strictly because I know it best, and I do so in full recognition that some of the lessons learned in my country may not apply here in Greece.

Universities serve society in many ways, but I will focus on the contribution that they make through three activities in particular: research, education, and institutional citizenship.

First, by advancing knowledge of science, technology, and medicine, universities create the foundation for economic growth, material well-being, and improvements in human health.

Second, by educating students to be capable of flexible, adaptive, and creative responses to changing conditions, universities strengthen society's capacity to innovate.

And, third, by serving as models of institutional citizenship, universi-

Remarks delivered at Costis Palamas Hall, University of Athens, Greece, May 6, 2008.

ties contribute directly to social betterment and inspire their students to recognize an obligation to serve.

Let me discuss each type of service to society in turn.

University Research as an Engine of Economic Growth

In the modern economy, global competitive advantage derives primarily from a nation's capacity to innovate, to introduce and to develop new products, processes, and services. And that capacity depends in turn on the continued advance of science.

As the principal locus of basic research, universities play a key role in sustaining competitiveness and economic growth. Basic research, by definition, is motivated by curiosity and the quest for knowledge, without a clear, practical objective. Yet basic research is the source from which all commercially oriented applied research and development ultimately flows. I say "ultimately" because it often takes decades before the commercial implications of an important scientific discovery are fully realized. The commercial potential of a particular discovery is often unanticipated, and it frequently extends to many unrelated industries and applications. In other words, the development of innovative products and services that occurs today usually depends on advances in basic research achieved ten, twenty, or fifty years ago – most often without any idea of the eventual consequences.

The emergence of universities as America's primary basic research machine did not come about by accident. Rather, it was the product of a wise and farsighted national science policy, set forth in an important 1945 report that established the framework for an unprecedented and heavily subsidized system in support of scientific research that has propelled the American economy. The system rested upon three principles that remain largely intact today. First, the federal government shoulders the principal responsibility for financing basic science. Second, universities — rather than government laboratories, non-teaching research institutes, or private industry — are the primary institutions in which this government-funded research is undertaken. This ensures that scientists-in-training, even those who choose industrial rather than academic careers, are exposed to the most advanced methods and results of research. And, third, although the federal budgetary process determines the total funding available for each of the various fields of science, most funds are allocated, not according to commercial or political considerations, but through an intensely competitive process of review conducted by independent scientific experts who judge proposals on their scientific merit alone. This system of organizing science has been an extraordinary success, scientifically and economically.

The second and third of these central principles are worth emphasizing because of the impact they have on education as well as research. To isolate the nation's best scientists in research institutes, as was common in the Soviet Union and to some extent in China, deprives the nation of important benefits. It limits the exposure of students, especially undergraduates, to first-rate scientists and, often, to state-of-the-art equipment and methods, which tend to concentrate in the institutes housing the top scientists. Moreover, by removing many of the very best scientists from the university environment, the quality of teaching suffers and the curriculum is less likely to incorporate the latest advances and novel thinking.

Allocating research resources by means other than peer review of proposals submitted by individuals and groups also imposes a huge cost on national systems. In most European countries, political considerations dominate the process of allocating research funds to institutions. There is a powerful tendency toward spreading resources across a large number of institutions. And, even in Britain, where there is rigorous peer review, the bulk of grant funding is awarded by considering the quality of departments taken as a whole rather than judging the merit of specific proposals from individuals. This also tends to shave the peaks of excellence.

Ensuring that world-class science is conducted in universities should be an important objective of national science policy. The three principles I have identified — adequate government funding, co-locating advanced research and teaching in universities, and peer review that focuses on the merits of individual investigators — have helped the U.S. achieve excellent performance.

Educating Students for Innovation and Leadership

The knowledge created by the enterprise of academic science is by no means the only important contribution that universities make to the welfare of their societies. By educating students and preparing them well for service across the range of occupations and professions, universities contribute at least as much through their teaching as they contribute through their research. The very best of America's universities and colleges educate students to be creative, flexible, and adaptive problem-solvers, capable of innovation and leadership.

New scientific discoveries are made every day, and new theories displace old ones with relentless regularity. Many successful companies produce products or services based on technology or marketing strategies that did not exist a decade or two ago. And government officials, too, confront a world radically altered by changes in communications technology and new tasks that are dictated by increasing globalization. In such a world, knowledge of a given body of information is not enough to survive, much less thrive; scientists, business leaders, and government officials alike must have the ability to think critically and creatively, and to draw upon and adapt ideas to new environments.

The methods of undergraduate education used by America's most selective and distinguished universities and liberal arts colleges are particularly well suited to prepare students for a changing world. These institutions are committed to the "liberal education" of undergraduates. The premise underlying the philosophy of liberal education is that students will be best prepared for life if they can assimilate new information and then reason through to new conclusions. Since any particular body of knowledge is bound to become obsolete, the object of liberal education is not only to convey any particular content, but to develop certain qualities of mind: the ability to think independently, to regard the world with curiosity and ask interesting questions, to subject the world to sustained and rigorous analysis, to use where needed the perspectives of more than one discipline, and to arrive at fresh, creative answers. Society gains most from a pedagogy that seeks to enlarge the power of students to reason, to think creatively, and to respond adaptively.

What does this mean in practical terms? It means that, in the best universities and colleges, education is not a one-way street. Information is not simply conveyed from faculty to students and reproduced on examinations. Even as recently as the 1930s and '40s in the United States, in many college classes, professors spewed forth information in lectures, students copiously took notes, memorized them, and then "recited" them back to the professor when called upon in class. Today, students cannot simply rely on a good memory to succeed in college. Although lectures are still used in many courses, they are supplemented by other forms of pedagogy, and students are no longer encouraged to recite back what they hear in class or read in a textbook. Instead, students are encouraged to think for themselves — to offer their own opinions and interpretations in participatory seminars, writing assignments, and examinations.

The participatory seminar is now a fundamental part of most undergraduate and graduate programs at America's top universities and liberal arts colleges. The purpose of small seminars is to challenge students to articulate their views and defend them in the face of classmates and the professor, who may disagree. The format forces them to reason through issues and to think critically for themselves, not just repeat what a professor has told them or what they have read. Often these seminars are accompanied by in-depth research and writing assignments, where students are required to engage in independent study and write a paper articulating and defending their own conclusions.

Even most lecture classes for undergraduates have some form of discussion section attached to them, to give students the opportunity to discuss for themselves the materials being presented in lecture. Like the participatory seminar, these discussion sections consist of relatively small numbers of students, and, especially in the humanities and social sciences, they emphasize exchanging views and developing analytical skills, not memorization and recitation.

Professors also encourage critical thinking by the form of writing assignments they require and by the kind of examination questions they ask. Exams emphasize analysis and problem solving rather than description and memory. Many exam questions do not have a correct answer; they are designed to see how well a student can draw upon the facts and theoretical explanations at their disposal to fashion a coherent and defensible argument of their own.

This distinctive emphasis on critical thinking produces graduates who are intellectually flexible and open to new ideas, graduates equipped with curiosity and the capacity to adapt to ever-changing work environments, graduates who, in business, can convert new knowledge into new products and services and who, in government, can find innovative solutions to new challenges.

The University as a Local Institutional Citizen

I would like next to explore with you one more way in which universities can contribute to society—by being good institutional citizens both locally and globally. In both cases, acts of institutional citizenship make a direct contribution to human welfare, but they also contribute indirectly by modeling good citizenship for our students, thus helping to inculcate in them a sense of social responsibility.

When I became Yale's president in 1993, the city of New Haven, Connecticut, was deeply troubled. It was suffering from the absence of industrial investment and job creation, a partially abandoned downtown, blighted neighborhoods, and an unflattering external image. Ten years later, a feature article in the *New York Times* travel section called New Haven "an irresistible destination."

When I took office, we decided to develop a comprehensive strategy for civic engagement, create administrative infrastructure to support that strategy, and make a substantial, long-term commitment to its implementation. We recognized that the most enduring contributions we could make would require partnership with public officials and neighborhood interest groups in New Haven, but we knew this would take time to develop. To signal emphatically to both the university community and the city the seriousness of our commitment, we took two important unilateral steps during the first year of my tenure.

First, to demonstrate institutional endorsement of the prodigious volunteer efforts of our students, we established a program of paid summer internships to support the work of students in city agencies and nonprofit service organizations. Second, to stimulate immediately the process of strengthening neighborhoods, we announced what has become the most visible and successful of our urban initiatives: the Yale Homebuyer Program. The program, now widely imitated, subsidizes home purchases by our faculty and staff in the neighborhoods surrounding the campus. Of the more than eight hundred employees who have participated in the program over the last fifteen years, 80 percent were first-time homebuyers.

Another element of our strategy to become an institutional citizen was to accelerate Yale's effort to contribute to economic development through technology transfer. We sought out faculty with an interest in commercializing their results, used students at our School of Management to prepare business plans, drew upon Yale's extensive connections in the venture capital business to find financing, and helped to find real estate solutions in New Haven. We are seeing results. More than forty new companies have been established in the greater New Haven area, most of them in the field of biotechnology. These firms have attracted over $2.5 billion in capital.

The development of a strong biotechnology industry in and around New Haven augurs well for the long term, but it did little to address the immediate needs of the low-income, inner-city neighborhoods that surround our campus. To build trust and credibility, it was essential to establish working partnerships with grassroots organizations and community leaders. Neighborhood partnerships also provided an opportunity to coordinate the enormous talent and energy of our student volunteers and focus on a common purpose.

For example, we worked closely with community residents on plans to develop a large vacant site that sits directly between the University and a new, very attractive low-rise public housing project developed under a federal grant that we helped the city secure. We have built a facility that incorporates a community center, with a computer cluster for schoolchildren and heavily used meeting space for community organizations. We are now in the process of relocating the outpatient health care facility that serves our faculty, staff, and students to the site, where we will engage the neighborhood in numerous health outreach programs.

The University as a Global Citizen: Leading by Example

Let me point to one final example of institutional citizenship. The problem of global warming cries out for a multinational solution: reducing carbon emissions in a way that is equitable and efficient. Developing nations like China and India fear that serious limits on greenhouse gas emissions will unfairly constrain their future growth. Skeptics in the U.S. fear that controlling carbon will impose a large cost on our economy as well. Yet if we collectively fail to take action, future generations will likely face much larger costs from economic dislocation and environmental destruction.

Universities have an important role in the effort to curtail global warming. Much of the work on climate science that has led to the detection and understanding of climate change was done within our walls, and we have been at the forefront of modeling the economic, social, and environmental impact of rising global temperatures and sea levels. We will also participate in developing carbon-free technologies such as solar, wind, and geothermal power, as well as in finding more efficient ways to use carbon-based fuels.

More recently, universities have begun to play a different role, taking the lead in setting standards for carbon emissions that are substantially more restrictive than those adopted by national governments. In 2005, Yale made a commitment to reduce carbon emissions to 10 percent below the 1990 level by 2020, which translates to a 43 percent reduction in our 2005 carbon footprint. This is a reduction in the range of what will be needed to keep global temperatures from rising more than 2 degrees centigrade by the end of the century. It is an ambitious goal. If the nations of the world were to negotiate a reduction of this magnitude, we would be taking a giant step toward saving the planet.

We have made this commitment because we believe that in so doing we are being faithful to our mission as a teaching institution. We are leading by example. We have encouraged our sister institutions in the Ivy League to join us in setting a specific goal for reducing carbon emissions. And we are working on eliciting similar commitments from our nine partners in the International Alliance of Research Universities and from the thirty-four Chinese universities with which we have been working on curriculum reform and other issues over the past four years.

We have no illusion that the collective action of universities will have a measurable impact on global carbon emissions. But we do hope that our action will inspire others to believe that significant carbon reduction is feasible and not exceedingly costly. In leading by example, we hope to make a global carbon compact more likely.

Conclusion

Our efforts to mobilize students and faculty in support of our local community, as well as our efforts to mobilize the global community of universities to demonstrate that greenhouse gas reduction is feasible and affordable, flow naturally from the mission and purposes of our institutions. On our campuses we are devoted to the development of full human potential of our students and faculty. But many outside our walls lack the opportunity to flourish. Locally, our neighbors face more limited opportunity than we. Globally, future generations are threatened by the possibility that climate change will leave them with greater burdens than we ourselves must manage. In both cases, we, with the privilege of education, can help. We can contribute through our citizenship, as well as through our research and teaching, to the betterment of society.

Why Colleges and
Universities Matter

THREE YEARS after the onset of the Great Recession, even as the economy recovers, we remain in a state of deep national anxiety. Nearly 16 percent of the workforce remains unemployed, underemployed, or discouraged from seeking employment.[1] Families across the country are worried about their financial security and the prospects for their children. State governments, along with the federal government, which faced structural deficits even before the recession, must now deal with the painful necessity of reducing spending and increasing taxes despite the unpopularity of both sets of measures.

With every category of discretionary public expenditure under serious scrutiny, it is incumbent upon us to make the case for higher education with renewed vigor. To us, the case seems obvious; we take for granted that there is no more important investment in the future of our nation. But elected officials, and many of our fellow citizens, do not

Remarks delivered at the annual meeting of the American Council on Education, March 6, 2011.

1 Bureau of Labor Statistics, *Current Population Survey* (Mar. 5, 2011).

share our experience and do not necessarily share our conclusions. We need to persuade them why colleges and universities matter. And so my task this afternoon is to articulate, in a language that people can understand, the case for public support of higher education.

As committed educators, we know that the most profound consequence of education is one that we cannot "sell" easily to state or federal legislators or other elected officials. From our experience in the classroom, from the light in our students' eyes as they first comprehend a difficult idea, we know that education improves the soul. It empowers young people with the capacity to enrich their lives spiritually and materially, to educate their own children, and to become better citizens.

But the elected representatives who control the resources that support our institutions demand more concrete answers. So here are three claims that they can more easily advance and defend.

First, the basic research done in our universities has been for six decades and still remains the principal driver of U.S. economic growth and advances in human health.

Second, our diverse array of educational institutions — private and public, two-year and four-year, selective and less selective — educates a broad and diverse workforce suited to an immense variety of occupations and roles, and gives the U.S. economy unparalleled flexibility in adapting to changes in technology and market conditions.

Third, our colleges and universities are the nation's principal avenue of upward social mobility, delivering more than any other institutions on the promise of making America a land of opportunity.

Let me elaborate in turn the argument for each of these claims.

Universities as Engines of Innovation

Among fully developed economies, global competitive advantage derives primarily from a nation's capacity to innovate: to introduce and develop new products, processes, and services. This has been the foundation of America's economic leadership in the period following the Second World War. And it will continue to be a basis for American economic strength in the highly globalized economy of the twenty-first century.

Innovation in the economy requires perceived opportunities in the marketplace, but it rests on the underpinning of advances in basic research. The commercial potential of a particular discovery is often unanticipated, and often extends to many unrelated industries and applications, as was the case with the laser. When the argon-ion gas laser was invented at Yale in the 1960s, its inventor, William Bennett, had not the remotest idea that the laser he invented would be used thirty-five years later to perform surgery on his detached retina.

The contributions of university research are embedded in our daily lives. The Prius that I drove to the airport this morning uses lithium-ion batteries that were conceived in the 1970s by Stanley Whittingham, then a postdoctoral fellow at Stanford, and developed throughout his research career at Exxon and Binghamton University. Whittingham's idea was further refined by John Goodenough at the University of Texas, Austin, who made important advances in cathode design. Additional discoveries by Goodenough and Yet-Ming Chiang at MIT improved the performance of the lithium-ion battery, and made it a viable candidate to power electric vehicles.

University research also played a significant role in the discovery of the antiretroviral drugs that have made HIV a chronic, instead of a fatal, disease. William Prusoff and Tai-shun Lin of Yale demonstrated Zerit's effectiveness against HIV in 1994. A group of faculty at Emory — Dennis Liotta, Raymond Schinazi, and Woo-Baeg Choi — identified the drug that became Emtriva. Abacavir was invented at the University of Minnesota. Epivir was invented at McGill University in collaboration with IAF Biochem; subsequent research was conducted at Emory before the drug was brought to the market, and faculty at Yale first showed its effectiveness against hepatitis B. The active involvement and collaboration of universities in HIV drug development was no accident; it built upon years of basic research into retroviruses at these same institutions.

In 2007 two researchers based at European universities won the Nobel Prize for their 1988 discovery of giant magnetoresistance. This advance in basic research led to a new technology called spintronics (spin-transport electronics) that has found its first application in computer hard drives. Spintronics led to a disk reader that is orders of magnitude more sensitive than previous designs, opening the way to disk drives that store information much more densely, and thus more cheaply. This has accelerated exponential growth in storage capacity, enabling an entirely new frontier — computing in the "cloud."

There are many more examples like these. The first working quantum computer was built at Yale two years ago. It holds the promise of orders of magnitude increases in computing speed and power, although it is likely to be at least twenty years before a full-scale, commercially viable quantum computer is built. Another example: the 2010 Nobel Prize in Physics was awarded to two scientists at the University of Manchester for discovering the properties of graphene, a super-strong material comprised of a single layer of carbon atoms, which may in due course become the medium that replaces silicon as a semiconductor.

Our elected officials need to know that the scientific discoveries that will shape the future of our economy still emanate from our research universities. And, as two of the last three examples illustrate, this country has no monopoly on these discoveries. We need to generate our share of them, and that will require sustained funding.

As a corollary to the arguments for supporting basic research, we should also point out that, thanks to the incentives created by the Bayh-Dole Act of 1980, our universities are now more actively involved in stimulating commercial innovation than ever before. The National Science Board reports that articles written by faculty account for 64 percent of the papers cited in patent applications in 2008, up from 58 percent in 1998.[2]

In advancing the argument that university research is a fundamental driver of commercial innovation, we need to remember that Congress did not give us property rights over inventions funded by federal agencies for the purpose of enhancing our revenues. The purpose of the Bayh-Dole Act was to ensure that there was adequate incentive to commercialize the fruits of publicly funded research, so that socially valuable ideas would not lie fallow. This lesson of history is too often forgotten as universities pursue legislation and lawsuits designed to strengthen their intellectual property rights. Congress did not intend to confer upon us the right to maximize profits; it gave us private property rights for a public purpose – to ensure that the benefits or our research are widely shared. To emphasize this point, a small group of universities and organizations – Boston University, Brown, Harvard, Penn, and Yale – adopted in 2009 a Statement on Global Access to Medicines, which committed them to ensuring that developing countries would have low-cost access to drugs based on patents we license to pharmaceutical companies. A total of twenty-five organizations have endorsed this statement.

Colleges and Universities as Educators of a Diverse and Flexible Workforce

I have thus far illustrated some of the arguments we might make to increase public support for research. We also need to make the case for our educational mission. I would suggest that we emphasize two particular themes: first, even though we see the need for improvement in this dimension, our institutions do the important work of meeting the

2 National Science Board, *Science and Engineering Indicators* (2010).

workforce needs of a rapidly changing economy, and second, access to colleges and universities is today the principal means of upward social mobility.

Many of America's colleges and universities practice a method of education that is especially conducive to preparing graduates for our world of dynamic, constant change. What we call "liberal education" has two distinctive features that are not yet widespread around the world. First, most of our undergraduates are exposed to a wide variety of disciplines and hence develop the capacity to see the world from multiple perspectives. Second, the pedagogy of liberal education, at its best, encourages students not to reproduce what they learn in lectures and textbooks, but to think for themselves.

One of the great virtues of American higher education is its diversity. Some of our institutions offer broad, liberal education, and thus serve well those who go on to become scholars, teachers, scientists, professionals, managers, civil servants, and leaders in every sphere. But the dynamic economy also requires a workforce with the skills for an immense variety of roles. Hence, many of our four-year institutions and nearly all of our two-year institutions offer a rich set of vocationally oriented options to students. Next year, just two city blocks from the edge of the Yale campus in downtown New Haven, Gateway Community College will open a brand-new campus. Gateway's curriculum could hardly be more different from Yale's, and yet it plays an extraordinarily valuable role in preparing the Connecticut workforce. It offers associate's degrees in automotive technology, computer networking, exercise science, hotel-motel management, retail management, and a wide array of health care support vocations. Like many of our two-year colleges, Gateway's curriculum responds rapidly to changes in the local economy and to the needs of employers. About fifteen years ago, when Yale began to take an active interest in locating spinoff biotechnology companies around our campus, Gateway responded immediately by creating an associate's de-

gree program in biomedical engineering. The flexibility and responsive-
ness of our community colleges is a tremendous asset for the nation.

Colleges and Universities as Avenues
of Upward Social Mobility

I have to this point elaborated upon two reasons why colleges and universities matter: through their research they are engines of innovation
and economic growth, and they educate a diverse and flexible workforce
for a dynamic economy. Let me turn now to the third reason, well known
to you, but inadequately appreciated by our elected officials and fellow
citizens: in the United States today, there is no more effective instrument
of self-improvement than our colleges and universities.

The evidence is powerful. It is clear that lifetime earnings rise with
each year of schooling beyond high school, and this premium has grown
over time. In 1973 the median earnings of a student graduating from a
four-year college were 40 percent higher than a high school graduate;
by 2008 the earnings premium from four years of college had increased
to 66 percent.[3] Similarly, the median earnings for recipients of master's
degrees were 97 percent higher than those of high school graduates, and
median earnings for professional degrees were 174 percent higher. College graduates are also much less likely to be unemployed. Throughout
the current recession the unemployment rate of college graduates aged
twenty-five and older has remained at or below 5 percent. It is currently
4.3 percent, compared to an unemployment rate of 9.5 percent for high
school graduates.[4]

These figures reflect fundamental shifts in the economy. Unlike previous industrial revolutions, such as the assembly line, which devalued

3 College Board, *Education Pays* (2010).
4 Bureau of Labor Statistics, *supra* note 1.

individual skill, the onset of the information age has put a premium on skills. In addition, the globalization of commerce has put pressure on wages paid for manufacturing jobs that do not require a college education. Consequently, over the past three decades the inflation-adjusted median income of households with a bachelor's degree or more rose steadily while the inflation-adjusted median income of households with no more than a high school education has remained more or less flat since 1980.[5]

In addition to increasing expected incomes, higher education promotes upward mobility, and thus enables the realization of the deeply rooted American belief that individuals can improve their circumstances.

Ron Haskins of the Brookings Institution has offered compelling evidence that college creates the opportunity to break out of poverty. Of the adults who are born into families in the lowest 20 percent of the income distribution, those who do not attend college have only a 14 percent chance of making it to the top 40 percent of the income distribution. Those who complete college, however, have a 42 percent chance of reaching the top 40 percent of the income distribution.[6]

Equally convincing evidence comes from the record of highly selective colleges and universities, all of which offer very generous need-based financial aid. When asked, ten years after graduation, only 5 percent of Yale alumni report that at the time they attended college, their families had much higher incomes than the average of their class. If we exclude that group, the remaining 95 percent of alumni divide roughly evenly among those whose family incomes were higher than average, average, and below average. And yet ten years after graduation the average in-

---

5 Ron Haskins, "Education and Economic Mobility," in Haskins, Julia B. Isaacs, and Isabel V. Sawhill, eds., *Getting Ahead or Losing Ground: Economic Mobility in America* (Brookings Institution, 2008).
6 *Ibid.*

comes earned by alumni in each of these three groups was almost exactly the same! In other words, except for the very wealthiest, all graduates of Yale faced identical earning opportunities after graduation.

Conclusion

I hope you will forgive me, an economist, for emphasizing the economic reasons why colleges and universities matter. We are all well aware that these are not the only reasons. I mentioned earlier that education is good for the soul. It is also true that college graduates are healthier; they smoke less, weigh less, and exercise more than their contemporaries who did not complete college. They are more likely to take their children to a library, and to read to their preschool children on a daily basis. They are more likely to undertake voluntary service, and, when they volunteer, to spend more time at it. They are also more likely to vote.[7]

These are all important reasons why our governments, state and federal, should support the enterprise of higher education. But at a time of economic duress, it seems to me that the economic arguments are the most salient. Our colleges and universities – through the research we do, the flexible workforce we educate, and the social mobility we provide – contribute powerfully to the economic well-being of the nation. We need to make these arguments understood by state and federal legislators, by governors and the White House, and by the public. Unless we do, we will have little chance of maintaining and increasing federal support for research, Pell Grants, and student loans, and little chance of reversing the deeply distressing trend toward reduced state government support for our extraordinary public colleges and universities. We all know that our arguments are compelling, and that they have never been more important. Now is the time to get out there and make the case.

7 College Board, *supra* note 3.

Universities and Cities

IN 1826, David Hudson founded a school in what had been known as the Western Reserve of Connecticut. He brought to the task the ideas and ambitions of the Connecticut institution he took as his model. For even in those early years of the Republic, Yale aspired to become something more than the collegiate school founded in 1701 to educate the young Puritans for "service in Church and Civil State." Under the leadership of Timothy Dwight, Yale had begun the transition from college to university — opening a medical school and appointing the nation's first professor of natural science and its first professor of law. In the wake of these developments, Hudson's "Yale of the West" was established in the state of Ohio.

Today, I am honored to have the opportunity to bring to Cleveland some of the new ideas and ambitions of Case Western's mother institution, as you formally charge a Yale graduate with the responsibility

Remarks at the Inaugural Colloquium, Case Western Reserve University, January 30, 2003.

of leadership. I bring sincere congratulations to Ed Hundert and warm greetings to Mayor Jane Campbell.

From the late nineteenth century through the mid-twentieth, industrial firms, financial institutions, and public utilities were typically the largest employers in most of our cities. In recent decades, however, as manufacturing jobs migrated out of cities and as banks and public utilities consolidated, universities and their associated medical centers have grown to become the largest employers in a surprising number of our cities. I am not talking simply of New Haven, Cambridge, Columbus, Ann Arbor, and Bloomington; I am referring also to Philadelphia, Boston, San Francisco, and Birmingham, Alabama.

With this increased local prominence comes increased responsibility. As President Hundert has recognized in recent speeches, a large university contributes to the wider community's well-being by its very presence — by attracting external research funding and creating jobs, by purchasing locally provided goods and services, by bringing to the community highly educated citizens who tend to care about, and contribute to, the quality of the city's schools and cultural life. But as President Hundert has noted, these passive contributions are not enough. By adopting active strategies for civic improvement, by becoming engaged institutional citizens, we can make a major difference in the quality of urban life. Such engagement is consistent with the goals of institutions that have for centuries educated students for public service. It also benefits universities to the extent that an improved quality of urban life helps to attract the best students and faculty from around the world.

My task this morning is to relate to you the story of Yale's partnership with the city of New Haven. Over the past decade this partnership has contributed substantially to the renaissance of a city that was suffering from the absence of industrial investment and job creation, a partially abandoned downtown, blighted neighborhoods, and an unflattering external image. In the two years before I became president, a student was murdered on our campus and a major national magazine conveyed the impression that violent teenage drug gangs ruled the streets. By contrast, last year, a feature article in the *New York Times* travel section called New Haven "an irresistible destination."

Outsiders have long regarded the presence of Yale as one of the city's major assets, but, except for episodic engagement, the University's contributions to the community did not derive from an active, conscious strategy of urban citizenship. It is true that our students, for more than a century, have played a highly constructive role as volunteers. Even a decade ago, two thousand students volunteered regularly in schools, community centers, churches, soup kitchens, and homeless shelters, but these volunteer efforts were neither coordinated nor well supported institutionally. When I became president in 1993, there was much to be done to transform Yale into an active, contributing institutional citizen.

So much, in fact, that I decided that we needed to develop a comprehensive strategy for civic engagement, create administrative infrastructure to support the strategy, and make a substantial, long-term commitment to its implementation. Then I started by recruiting leadership, and I was fortunate to have near at hand the perfect entrepreneur to jump-start our efforts. Linda Lorimer had served Yale in several administrative positions prior to leaving in 1987 to become the president of Randolph-Macon Women's College. While serving there, she was elected to the Yale Corporation, our governing body, and thus she remained intimately familiar with the University. She agreed to resign her position on the Corporation, return to Yale as Vice President and Secretary, and work with me to develop a comprehensive strategy for urban partnership.

We began by taking an inventory of the extensive volunteer effort already undertaken by more than one hundred groups around the campus. By compiling and publishing this information we hoped to make the city more aware of Yale's involvement, but also to understand for ourselves where we already had a foundation upon which trust could be built and collaboration expanded. In a city with only one wealthy institution, and one that historically had been indifferent to local conditions, we had generations of distrust to overcome.

Within weeks of taking office in 1993, Linda Lorimer and I, along with two outstanding assistants, were hard at work talking with and listening to our neighbors – the newly elected Mayor, John DeStefano, members of the Board of Aldermen, leaders of the business community and clergy, the school superintendent, principals, and leaders of neighborhood organizations. We have kept these channels of communication open ever since, maintaining the spirit and practice of honest and open dialogue, which is essential to enduring partnership.

From these early conversations and our survey of campus resources and existing interventions, we developed a strategic framework that we believed most appropriate given the particular needs of New Haven and the particular capabilities of our university. Other city-university partnerships will develop different priorities, but an overarching strategy is necessary to ensure that efforts are not dissipated.

In New Haven, we determined that we could make a constructive contribution in four areas that cried out for attention. These have remained our areas of focus throughout the past decade.

The first area of focus was economic development. We had considerable faculty strength in the biomedical sciences, but no track record of encouragement or support for the transfer of technology to local businesses.

The second priority was strengthening neighborhoods. Here we believed that increasing the rate of home ownership could improve the stability of neighborhoods and the commitment of its residents, and that the University, with 10,000 employees, had the leverage to help. We also believed that as an educational institution, we had human resources that could provide help to the public schools.

The third area of focus was to increase the safety, appearance, and vitality of our downtown. We believed that this would greatly improve perceptions of the city and also directly benefit the university community, since we are located in the heart of downtown New Haven.

Finally, we focused on the image of the city, recognizing that improvement in the physical and material conditions of the city and its citizens were not in themselves enough to change perceptions of the outside world. We needed to communicate as well.

At the beginning we recognized that most enduring contributions to the improvement of New Haven would require partnership with our neighbors, but these would take time to develop. To signal emphatically to both the university community and the city the seriousness of our commitment, we took three important unilateral steps during the first year of my tenure. First, to provide appropriate support for the implementation of our strategies, we established an Office of New Haven and State Affairs. Second, we established the President's Public Service Fellowship — a program of paid internships to support student work in the city that attracts hundreds of applications every year for about 45 positions. Third, to strengthen neighborhoods we announced the Yale Homebuyer Program.

The Homebuyer Program offers all Yale employees a substantial subsidy for purchasing a home in New Haven, where housing prices had been in decline for five or six years and there was a high vacancy rate even in the nicest neighborhoods. The subsidy was initially $2,000 per year for ten years. From April 1994 through December 1995, we offered the subsidy to our employees for a home purchase anywhere within the city limits. By the end of 1995, nearly 200 employees had participated, and in the city's two upper-middle-class neighborhoods prices had completely stabilized and vacancies disappeared. At this point, we removed the subsidy from the high income neighborhoods, focused on the lower-income neighborhoods surrounding the University, and increased the subsidy to $7,000 on closing and $2,000 per year for each of the next nine years. To date, more than five hundred employees have purchased homes under the program.[1] Over the last seven years, 80 percent of the participants were first-time homebuyers, and 55 percent were members of minority groups.

The Homebuyer Program is an expensive proposition. We have committed over $12 million to date, and the annual cost of the program exceeds $1 million. Not every institution can afford an investment of this magnitude, but many employers can create programs tailored to their resources and the needs of their communities. Two other New Haven nonprofits – the Hospital of St. Raphael and the Mary Wade nursing home – now provide a one-time $5,000 cash incentive for home purchases, and the University of Pennsylvania and the University of Southern California have developed programs appropriate to their local circumstances.

Before discussing in some detail the four main elements of our strategy, I have one more observation about leadership. As a strategy unfolds, the skills needed for effective leadership may change. We recognized this after about three years. Linda Lorimer was an ideal start-up entrepreneur. She built bridges to every local constituency, developed an effective staff, and initiated scores of collaborative projects with neighborhood organizations and downtown leaders. By 1996, however, as our efforts to generate start-up companies were just beginning to show signs of life and when a large parcel of downtown real estate became available, it was clear to us that we needed an experienced urban developer on the team. Serendipitously, it was just at this moment that Bruce Alexander, an active Yale alumnus who developed Baltimore's Inner Harbor and New York's South Street Seaport, took early retirement from the Rouse Company. Our initial effort to recruit him for full-time service failed, but he

---

1 By the end of 2012, more than one thousand Yale employees had purchased homes under the program.

agreed to come to New Haven on a volunteer basis a few days each month to help us with our very complicated negotiations to acquire the major downtown parcel. After a year and a half of volunteer service, he was hooked. Linda Lorimer moved on to other important assignments, and Bruce became Yale's first Vice President for New Haven and State Affairs.

One more thought on the subject of leadership. In recruiting new deans as well as directors of major enterprises, I have made community outreach an explicit goal and a criterion against which performance is measured. The consequence is that our museums, the library, the athletics department, and every one of our ten professional schools has an expanded program of outreach.

Let me now take a few moments to sketch what we have been able to accomplish in each of the priority areas we first identified a decade ago: economic development, neighborhood improvement, downtown revitalization, and improving the city's image.

In many communities around the country, the scientific research undertaken by universities has been a powerful engine of local economic development. Without critical mass in electrical engineering and computer science, Yale — and consequently New Haven — missed out on the technological revolution that spurred the development of Silicon Valley and Boston's Route 128. But Yale has impressive strength in biomedical sciences, and thus in 1993 we had tremendous unexploited potential to build a biotechnology industry in and around New Haven.

In prior years, however, the University had taken a relatively passive attitude toward the commercialization of its science and technology. Again, leadership was the answer. We recruited Greg Gardiner, a senior technology executive at a major pharmaceutical company, and provided him with the resources to recruit a very able staff. Within two years, our Office of Cooperative Research was transformed from a relative laggard to a national example of best practice in the area of technology transfer.

The results have been impressive. Twenty-five new biotechnology companies have been established in the greater New Haven area, seventeen within the city limits. These firms have attracted over $1.5 billion in capital, and together they now employ 1,300 people.[2]

One of the major constraints in the initial years of this economic development effort was real estate. We worked closely with state and city officials to revive a long moribund Science Park at the factory location abandoned two decades ago by the Olin Corporation. Once the initial, publicly funded facilities had been fully leased, and it was clear that Yale was continuing to generate two or three new companies each year, private capital moved in to develop one million square feet of new space.

With respect to the low-income neighborhoods surrounding the campus, we chose first to work in the Dwight neighborhood, to the west of our campus, where, for several blocks, both students and community residents live side by side in low-rise apartments and multifamily houses. Beyond the transition area, the neighborhood becomes more homogeneous, a traditional inner-city neighborhood, but with an excellent housing stock with the potential for improvement.

With a representative of our Office of New Haven Affairs serving as a crucial liaison, we mobilized faculty and students from the schools of architecture, law, and management to help neighborhood residents develop a comprehensive plan for neighborhood revitalization. We sought and won a sizeable federal grant to allow implementation of this resident-led plan that supports job training, housing improvements, and a neighborhood elementary school. With the assistance of our Law School's clinical program and another federal grant we helped to secure, a new

---

2 In the ten years since this speech was delivered, those original twenty-five companies have raised an additional $2.5 billion, and twenty-seven new ventures have been established in the New Haven area, with initial investment of more than $500 million.

community development corporation was formed. Among the results of our collaborative efforts in the Dwight neighborhood are an addition to the neighborhood elementary school designed by Yale architecture students, the first new urban supermarket in the state of Connecticut in a generation — an effort facilitated by the work of management school students, an extensive literacy program staffed by undergraduate volunteers, community gardens planted with the assistance of Forestry School students, and improvisational children's theater programs mounted by Drama School students.

We are also working extensively in the Dixwell neighborhood northwest of campus, where we have rehabilitated a substantial number of residential properties we lease to graduate students, setting in motion a process that has encouraged other neighbors — including participants in our Homebuyer Program — to invest in the upgrading of their own homes. Recently, we have worked closely with community residents on plans to develop a large vacant site that sits directly between the University and a new, very successful low-rise public housing project developed under a HOPE VI grant. We will use a portion of this site for a new headquarters for the University Police, which will provide safety and security to those nearby, and we will incorporate in the new facility a community center, with a computer cluster for schoolchildren and a meeting room for community organizations.

Complementing our neighborhood efforts are some very substantial public school collaborations. At the Hill Regional Career High School over 200 students participate in eight science courses taught by members of our medical and nursing school faculties, and 65 students live on campus during the summer to study science and work in laboratories. At the Cooperative Arts and Humanities Magnet High School, students from our School of Music play an active role in the instructional program. We also take pride in the twenty-five-year-old Yale–New Haven Teachers Institute, an innovative program now being disseminated nationwide, where professors work during the summer with public school teachers as partners in curriculum development.[3]

As a final component of our neighborhood outreach, we have endeavored to make our campus more accessible to local schoolchildren. In addition to opening our museums to school visits, which has been the practice for generations, we now make our extensive athletic facilities available to hundreds of children enrolled in the National Youth Sports Program during the summer, and we host a citywide science fair each year.

Over the last decade we also have made major investments to develop the downtown retail districts. To the immediate west of campus, there is a student-oriented retail strip on Broadway. We worked with the city to improve the streetscape and pedestrian amenities. We assembled the key properties, renovated them, and recruited an attractive mix of national and mostly local retailers. We have maintained high standards for facades and signage, required our tenants to remain open during the evenings to give life to the street, and supported the development of local, minority-owned businesses. When I first recruited Bruce Alexander he asked me what kind of stores I wanted for Broadway. As a father of four, I replied, "J. Crew." Bruce went to J. Crew, and they announced that they had no interest in New Haven. Five years later, J. Crew opened on Broadway.

We have also worked to redevelop the central business district to the south of campus – the Chapel/College Street district. Early on, we helped at the Mayor's request to organize downtown property owners into a special service district, paying extra taxes for increased city services – cleaner streets, better lighting, more policing. Then, as I mentioned, a

---

3 In 2010, Yale made a very significant commitment to public education by funding New Haven Promise, a program that is providing college scholarships to every graduate of New Haven public and charter schools with at least a 3.0 grade point average and a 90 percent attendance record.

large, centrally located group of properties became available in the mid-1990s. The Mayor came to us with the request that the district be owned and managed as a unit, either by us or by a developer we helped to locate. We took on the challenge, investing in the upgrade of some twenty individual properties with retail on the ground floor and residential space above. Now the revival of the downtown is well under way, and private capital is flowing in to renovate retail space for new restaurants and to convert abandoned or under-occupied commercial buildings to residential apartments. Today, much of the central business district is a twenty-four-hour community with safe streets and many new restaurants, clubs, and retailers.

Finally, I turn to the question of New Haven's image. The city has long been a center for arts and culture, but for most of the region and the nation this has been a well-kept secret. In fact there is no other city of New Haven's size in the Western Hemisphere that can match its array of two major repertory theaters, three symphony orchestras, two world-class art museums, and a major natural history museum. Now that the downtown has been revitalized, marketing New Haven has become a major community priority.

About eight years ago, thanks to the efforts of two indomitable women of our community and with the support of the city, the University, and the Southern New England Telephone Company, we inaugurated an annual summer Festival of Arts and Ideas. This has become a major regional event, drawing organizations like the Royal Shakespeare Company and the Metropolitan Opera to New Haven. Thirty thousand people attended the Met's performance on the town green last summer. To publicize the Festival, the supporting program of summer concerts sponsored by the city, and the other cultural attractions of New Haven, we worked with the Mayor to fund a major regional marketing campaign. It is bearing fruit. I quote this year's Lonely Planet guide to New England: "Bravo, New Haven. Much maligned for decades as a stagnant urban seaport, this city of 123,000 souls has risen from its own ashes to become an arts mecca. The city's center is a tranquil core: the New Haven Green, decorated with graceful colonial churches and venerable Yale University. Scores of ethnic restaurants, theaters, museums, pubs, and clubs dot the neighborhood."

All collaborations require willing partners. We have worked hard to win the trust and confidence of community organizations and their leaders. This was not easy, because we had decades of bad feeling and resentment to overcome. It was not easy for New Haven's elected leaders to embrace the University. Yale-bashing had long been a winning political strategy.

We were especially fortunate to initiate our efforts just as John De-Stefano was elected as the Mayor of New Haven. He has courageously made the leap of faith toward partnership with us. We don't always see eye to eye; we have had some public disagreements and even more private disagreements. But the Mayor has recognized the enormous potential in mobilizing the University in support of civic objectives. Without his leadership, our efforts would have fallen short.

We have learned many lessons over the past decade. Here are some of the things that I believe a university must do to have a substantial impact on its local community:

- Urban partnership must be a clearly articulated institutional goal and widely understood to be a presidential priority.
- Recruit outstanding leadership and provide administrative resources sufficient for the tasks to be undertaken.
- Understand the University's existing points of contact with the community. These can provide a strong foundation for new initiatives.
- Develop and maintain honest and open channels of communication with all urban constituencies.

- Formulate a comprehensive strategy of engagement, tailored to match the University's capabilities to the city's needs.
- Encourage investment by state and local government through a willingness to co-invest.
- Share credit with elected officials and community leaders.
- Have patience. Elected officials and neighborhood groups will sometimes need to distance themselves and demonstrate their independence. Give your partners room.

Universities are uniquely poised to strengthen urban America. As large employers seeking to attract students and faculty from afar, they have compelling practical reasons to do so. But our efforts also flow naturally from our mission and purpose. On our campuses we are devoted to the full development of human potential, and we provide extraordinary resources to facilitate such development in our students and faculty. Outside our walls, many of our neighbors lack the opportunity to develop their own potential. To the extent that we can help those without privilege access such opportunity, we will help to insure the health of our democracy. Our responsibility transcends pragmatism. We must help our cities become what we aspire to be on our campuses — a place where human potential can be fully realized.

Harnessing the Wind

SEEKING INSPIRATION for this magnificent occasion, I turned to a captivating book published last year, entitled *The Boy Who Harnessed the Wind*. It tells the story of William Kamkwamba, a young boy from a tiny village in Malawi. From an early age he took apart radios and tried to figure out what made them work. Later, at age fourteen, after a devastating famine left his family too poor to pay school fees, he studied alone in a small public library that was stocked with books donated by the government of the United States. There he devoured an elementary textbook called *Explaining Physics* that helped him to understand conceptually what he had discovered inductively by tinkering with radios. Then, providentially, he stumbled upon a book called *Using Energy*, which illustrated how a windmill could be used to generate electricity. Scavenging parts from a junkyard, persuading friends and relatives to part with bicycle frames and copper wire, William built a windmill, so that he could read after dark. Later he built another windmill to power a water pump that insured his family against another famine.

Remarks on the Award of the Queen's Anniversary Prizes for Higher and Further Education, Guildhall, London, February 18, 2010.

William Kamkwamba's moving and inspirational story is a perfect tale for our age, and for this occasion. It shows us how education, science, and technology can improve the material conditions of life and uplift the human spirit. Through study, imagination, resourcefulness, and stubborn persistence William harnessed the wind, and in so doing created a better life for himself, his family, and his village. The institutions we honor tonight have in similar fashion harnessed the wind. They have drawn upon and advanced human knowledge of nature and culture, and reached out to the world around them, using that knowledge to improve the material and spiritual conditions of citizens both near and far.

Two of the many lessons taught by William Kamkwamba's story seem worthy of note this evening.

First is the importance of access to education. During and after the Malawi famine of 2002, William's family could not afford to pay the tuition to send him to secondary school. It took unusual determination and dedication on William's part to overcome this handicap by studying independently in the village library. By contrast, in the United Kingdom, thanks to massive government investment, access to free secondary education is ubiquitous, and access to tertiary education has increased dramatically. Of the relevant age cohort, nearly 60 percent pursue higher and further education, compared to only 15 percent four decades ago. Like the United States, the United Kingdom is fortunate to have a rich diversity of institutions that serve the wide range of society's needs for higher and further education — from the education in the liberal arts that inspires future scholars, government officials, and business leaders to the training that imparts essential skills to nurses, technicians, and office workers. The full spectrum of institutions that participate in strengthening the nation are represented and recognized here tonight, and we celebrate the contribution of them all.

The second lesson of William's story is that knowledge can have powerful practical consequences. We see this illustrated abundantly in the work of the institutions we honor tonight. From the management of chronic pain, to increasing crop yields, to combating climate change, the research and educational programs of the twenty-one institutions represented here are having an important influence on the world outside the academy. Indeed, each of the citations published on the website of the Royal Anniversary Trust refers to the public impact of the work being recognized. Even the outstanding archaeology done at the University of Reading is cited for the help it provides to law enforcement agencies, and the impressive array of African, Asian, and Middle Eastern languages offered by the School of Oriental and African Studies is cited for its contribution to social cohesion across the country.

It is laudable that the work of colleges and universities advances the nation's social and economic agenda. But, if I may be so bold, is there not a danger that too much weight is being accorded to immediate social benefit? The purposes of institutions of higher and further education go beyond immediate practical impact. Whether students study cooking at Thames Valley University or read "Greats" at Oxford, it is immensely valuable to awaken in them passions that will enliven and motivate them, and to develop in them a capacity to continue to learn throughout their lifetimes. Such outcomes will, of course, have societal consequences in some ultimate sense, because the success of our democracies depends upon having citizens with a capacity to learn and adapt. But learning cannot and should not be justified entirely on grounds of social impact. Learning enriches the human experience, and as educators we should not lose sight of this.

This danger is manifest also in the current discussion of the proposed new criteria for assessing government-sponsored research. The new Research Excellence Framework puts 25 percent weight on the impact of research on the economy, society, culture, public policy, or quality of life. The higher education funding councils recognize the difficulty of identifying such effects, and they are running a pilot exercise this coming summer to test the new approach. They propose, for example, that every unit seeking funding should conduct case studies of the consequences of their past research. Recognizing that the effects of research are rarely immediate, the funding councils suggest that units look back ten to fifteen years to identify the sources of impacts that can be observed today.

Such an approach to assessment may well miss more than it harvests. Most fundamental advances in science do not yield practical results in ten to fifteen years. The time lag is usually much longer, and consequences are rarely foreseen at the time of discovery. Putting too much weight on the immediate, even the intermediate-term practical impact of research will distort the progress of science, technology, and humanistic research in this country. The United Kingdom has 1 percent of the world's population, 12 percent of its scholarly citations, and 40 percent of its top five universities. Underweighting the importance of fundamental science and curiosity-driven research across the spectrum of human knowledge may jeopardize this enviable position.

William Kamkwamba's achievement had a powerful impact on his tiny African village. And there is no doubt that at a certain point he became aware of the potential practical consequences of the knowledge he had acquired. But his initial interest in electricity was not spurred by a practical objective. He simply wanted to understand how his radio worked. And his interest in the physics books he found was not motivated by a desire to provide electric power for his family and his village; he was motivated by intellectual curiosity pure and simple. In seeking practical outcomes from our institutions of higher and further education, whose work has so much value, let us not neglect the spark—the desire to understand—that makes all else possible.

Rethinking College Admissions

INDEPENDENT SCHOOLS, though few in number compared with their public counterparts, play an important role in shaping the landscape of American education. For more than a century, they have been at the forefront of pedagogical innovation and educational reform. Today they provide a vastly disproportionate flow of students to the most highly selective colleges and universities. Although they educate only 2 percent of the nation's high school students, independent schools nonetheless provide between one-quarter and one-third of the matriculants at highly selective universities.

Independent schools strive to create environments in which learning is valued and teachers are respected. They strive also to educate the whole child, recognizing that extracurricular activities, athletics, and the arts play an important role in the development of children. As a parent of four children educated in outstanding independent schools and as a former trustee who once led the search for a new head of one of these schools, I know firsthand about the astonishing devotion of teachers

Remarks at the Annual Meeting of the National Association of Independent Schools, New York City, February 26, 2003.

and school administrators to their important work. I also know about the sacrifices made by so many parents, who send their children to independent schools at great expense, because they want a superior education for their children. And having spent all day Sunday helping with the food concession as my daughter's school hosted the Western New England Prep School Swim Championships, I also know how parents are called upon to serve independent schools in many ways, to participate in the rich experiences the schools provide to children, and to help the schools succeed in their important work.

Now, I am well aware that I was invited here tonight to speak about college admissions. But before I do, I want to remind the parents among you that the purpose of an independent school education is not admission to college. It is instead to develop in students the ability to read intelligently and critically, to write clearly, to comprehend basic mathematical ideas, to appreciate the process of scientific inquiry, to work independently, and to work with others. In short, it is to encourage students to love learning and to provide them with the equipment to continue to learn and grow throughout their lives, on their own and in their communities, so that they will be prepared to be informed, responsible citizens of our democracy.

From this perspective, college is just another step on the path to lifelong learning and responsible citizenship. We like to think that we contribute value added, and I believe that we do. But we build upon foundations that are laid down at home and at school. The stronger those foundations, the more easily we can accomplish our task.

There is no doubt that the interest in attending highly selective colleges and universities has increased in recent years. Applications to Yale averaged about 11,000 per year in the early 1980s, rose to about 12,500 per year in the late 1980s, then slumped in the early 1990s before rising back to that level in the late 1990s. In the last three years, however, applications have surged from 13,000 to 17,600. The pattern differs at other schools, but a common feature is that applications today are at least 50 percent higher than they were ten or twenty years ago.[1]

The competitive pressures are intense, too intense in my view. There are more than 3,000 colleges and universities in America, and there are a great many that provide outstanding educational opportunities. Our national obsession with rankings has given much too much weight to those institutions that rank high in the survey conducted annually by *U.S. News and World Report.* Surely, some of the data reported in the survey, such as faculty-student ratios and the percentage of classes with small enrollments, are facts worth knowing in selecting a school. But these and other data elements are simply weighted arbitrarily and added up to produce a ranking that is in itself not very informative. Indeed, the raw differences among the top three schools, and then among the next ten or fifteen, are miniscule. None of us, parents or administrators, should take them too seriously.

Colleges and universities vary on many dimensions. Among these are size, location, areas of academic strength, the nature of the residential experience, the nature and variety of extracurricular opportunities, campus culture, and proximity to off-campus cultural resources. There is rarely one "best fit" for any high school graduate. A number of schools would normally be well suited to the personality and interests of any particular student. It is a mistake to think that only one school will do, and a bigger mistake to think that failure to gain admission to one's first choice is a defeat.

Independent school administrators sometimes voice the concern that their children are at a disadvantage in competing for admissions to selective institutions. I don't believe that the numbers support this claim. As I mentioned before, independent schools educate fewer than 2 percent

---

1 By 2012 applications to Yale College had grown another 65 percent, to more than 29,000 annually.

of America's high school students. Yet, at Yale, they produce approximately 20 percent of our applicants, 30 percent of those offered admission, and 33 percent of those who matriculate. These percentages were the same in 1980 as they are today. As these numbers imply, the admit rate for independent school students is significantly higher than for the remainder of the applicant pool. We value these students. They are well prepared, and they perform well at Yale.

Still, the purpose of the admissions process—at Yale, at many other colleges, and at many independent schools—is to admit a class that makes the most of our capacity to contribute to the larger society. We aim to prepare those who will serve by becoming leaders in scholarship, business, the professions, religion, the arts, and public life. None of these objectives is best realized by admitting a class that is homogeneous in background or interests. You won't become a better lawyer if all your undergraduate classmates are interested only in law; nor will you become a better doctor if all your classmates are the product of a single region of the country, a single income stratum, or a single religious background. We all learn from encountering difference, and for this reason alone we would seek a diverse class, absent any other social imperatives.

Thus, without quotas, formal or informal, we seek to admit classes that are diverse with respect to region, interests, and experiences. We seek those with special artistic and athletic talent, as well as those who have displayed the promise of leadership through entrepreneurship, volunteer service, or political involvement. We seek increasingly students from abroad, in part because the presence of international students in today's more closely connected world creates a richer experience for students from our own country. And we are hopeful that the Supreme Court will tell us that we can continue affirmative efforts to identify and admit students of diverse racial backgrounds.

We continue to seek racial diversity for two fundamental reasons. First, as I indicated, students of all races benefit from exposure to one another. This is more than an article of faith. There is ample evidence from surveys of our graduates that diversity among classmates is highly valued by members of all racial groups and is perceived as enhancing the preparation of all for living in a multiracial society. Second, there is convincing evidence, presented most thoroughly by William Bowen and Derek Bok, that since the 1960s the admission of increasing numbers of racial minorities, especially African Americans, to highly selective colleges and universities has opened career opportunities and has had a significant and positive impact on the creation of a substantially larger minority middle class, whose members participate in civic life to the same extent as their white counterparts. Today, African Americans are better represented in the leadership ranks of business and every profession, and in civic and charitable organizations, in no small measure because of the opportunities to attend the finest institutions of higher education that have been extended over the past thirty-five years. Today, for much the same reasons, most independent schools seek racial diversity in the composition of their student bodies, just as we do.

I come at last to the issue that has given me my fifteen minutes of national media attention. Well, actually, it has been almost fifteen months and I am still cited from time to time. I refer of course to my heterodox view of the process of early admission to selective colleges and universities.

I spoke up on this subject for two reasons. First, I believe that the early admissions process and binding early decision programs in particular do not serve the interests of high school students. And, second, I believe that binding early decision programs undermine one of the principal goals of the admissions process in those schools offering need-blind admissions and full, need-based financial aid. That goal is to broaden access so that the finest institutions of higher education are available and affordable for those who qualify for admission, regardless of the ability of parents to pay.

For several decades prior to the last one, most selective schools offered non-binding early admission programs (now called "early action"), by which offers of admission were extended in December to some of those who applied early. The students were not bound to accept these offers; they could apply elsewhere on the regular timetable and notify all schools of their decision by May 1. Only a small fraction of students applied early, and typically we admitted no more than 10 or 15 percent of a class by this route. In the late 1980s several schools found it to their advantage to introduce binding early decision programs, where students had to commit in advance to accepting an early offer of admission. This helped the schools that initiated such programs, by letting them identify students who clearly viewed them as their school of choice. It also helped those students who had a clear first choice. But still, only limited numbers were involved.

Through the early 1990s, one school after another hopped on the early decision bandwagon, and the numbers began to rise. Today, most highly selective schools admit anywhere from one-third to nearly two-thirds of their entering classes early. And among the most selective schools, only a few — notably Harvard, MIT, Chicago, and Georgetown — still had non-binding early action programs as of last year. Within the past year, after the very favorable public reaction to the views I expressed in a *New York Times* interview, Beloit College, the University of North Carolina, Yale, and Stanford have all reverted from early decision to early action.

There are at least four problems with the current system of early admissions. All of these problems would substantially disappear if all forms of early admissions were eliminated; they would be significantly mitigated by replacing early decision with early action.

The first of these is the current system encourages many students to form a view of their first-choice college too early in their high school careers. Those of you who work with high school students know even better than I how rapidly many of them are growing and changing throughout their high school years. A student's interests, friendships, and activities may change substantially in the last year of high school. It is not in a student's best interest to expect him or her to visit colleges in the junior year and to come to a first choice early in the fall of the senior year. Most students would benefit from having until May 1 to decide which among several colleges that admit them would be the best fit for them.

Second, the current system encourages students to introduce strategic considerations into selecting a first-choice college, instead of relying entirely on his or her personal preferences. School heads and college counselors, under pressure from parents and prospective parents to produce a good record of early placement, encourage students to come to a first choice, which, more often than not, means making a commitment to a school with a binding early decision program. And many students are discouraged from applying to their true "first choice," because a well-meaning counselor reckons that the probability of admission is very low.

Third, the current system disrupts the senior year of high school, especially in independent schools where a large fraction of seniors apply early. Most fundamentally, because the college admissions game is played all year long, it dominates the entire year in the minds of students. If no admissions took place until April, there would be more time for high school. Instead, in December, a certain fraction of the class receives good news. But, unless the counselors are much too conservative and aim nearly everyone too low, a comparable number of students are deferred or rejected. This splits the class into those who are eligible for early senior slide, and those who have to live with disappointment and anxiety for the next four months. And there is yet a third group, those who didn't apply early, who often come to feel that they missed out on an important part of the year's experience.

Finally, a system in which most schools have binding early decision programs works profoundly to the disadvantage of students needing financial aid. If such students are admitted to an early decision school, they must either accept the aid package they are awarded or decline the offer of admission. They are not allowed to wait until April to compare the aid package with those offered elsewhere. Thus, students seeking financial aid disproportionately pass up the opportunity to apply early. And this has consequences, because – as counselors understand and as a recent study by Chris Avery, Andrew Fairbanks, and Richard Zeckhauser[2] confirms – the probability of admission, for any given individual, is substantially higher in the early round, especially at early decision schools. In sum, early decision programs will tend to diminish the fraction of a collegiate student body on financial aid.

The first three features of the current system that I mentioned have adverse consequences for high school students, but they don't necessarily weigh heavily in the consideration given to reform by colleges. From the point of view of the college, early decision programs have two attractions. First, because the yield on early applicants is predictable, early decision enhances a school's ability to shape a diverse class with many attributes and talents represented. Second, it guarantees that a substantial fraction of the student body will enter with a positive attitude, having chosen their school, instead of viewing it as the best of the available default options.

The fourth feature of the current system is not only adverse to some students, those needing financial aid; it also undermines the commitment of colleges and universities to increase access. The steady lowering of barriers with respect to religion, race, gender, sexual orientation, nationality, and economic status has made America's selective colleges and universities increasingly a beacon of hope – the custodians of a promise that unbounded opportunities are available to those who excel regardless

2 Christopher Avery, Andrew Fairbanks, and Richard Zeckhauser, *The Early Admissions Game: Joining the Elite* (2002).

of background. Early decision programs work against this trend. They are biased in favor of the affluent, a bias that subverts an important public purpose of the admissions process.

The problems I have identified would more or less disappear if all early admissions programs were abandoned. I am not suggesting that the pressures to get into selective colleges would disappear, but students would have more time to decide and they would have less reason to engage in strategic behavior. The integrity of the senior year would be restored, and students with financial need would no longer be disadvantaged. Unfortunately, it is not so easy to get from here to there, unless all colleges and universities moved simultaneously in this direction. There are a number of colleges firmly wedded not simply to early admissions, but to their binding early decision programs. In such an environment, any single school opting to abstain from early admissions while others persisted would run the risk of losing qualified applicants who simply could not or would not wait.

Thus, at Yale this year, we chose a less risky course. We announced that we will return to the regime that prevailed until 1995: a regime of non-binding early action, where applicants attest that they are seeking early admission to one school only. This approach, were it to prevail everywhere, would substantially mitigate (though not eliminate) the pressure to choose a college too early, since one's first choice would not be binding. It would somewhat mitigate (but not eliminate) the consequences of behaving strategically. For example, if one applied early to one's second choice, because the odds of admission were high, one could still apply later to one's first choice. The disruption of the senior year would be only slightly mitigated, but, importantly, the disadvantage to students with financial need would be eliminated. Those admitted early could wait to compare their aid offers with those of other schools, and thus there would be no disincentive to making an early application.

You might ask, why allow non-binding applications to go to only one school? The answer is simple. If everyone switched to early action and allowed multiple applications, there would be an inevitable pressure for everyone to make all their applications early, and the whole system would be deprived of using evidence of a student's senior year performance. If we are going to move toward one common admissions cycle, it would be far preferable, from the perspective of both the high schools and the colleges, to have those decisions made in April rather than December.

What will happen next? I wish I knew the answer. I hoped that the announcement of our new policy in November would encourage other early decision schools to follow as they came to realize that their policies were perceived as unfriendly to high school students and high schools. In fact, only Stanford followed, announcing their move to early action six hours after our announcement. I still believe, however, that early action serves the interest of students better than early decision, for the reasons I have given. If you share this view, you can help. If members of the National Association of Independent Schools were to convey to the remaining early decision schools that they strongly favored early action, it would help to move a number of schools in the right direction.

Let me close where I began. You represent a group of exceptional schools that educate thousands of exceptional children. We admire the quality of education that you provide, and your students will continue to fare well in the admissions process. But you, and here I mean both schools and parents, can play a role in reducing the pressure that we put on our children. We are trying to do our part, although we recognize that we could lighten up in our intense efforts to recruit the students we admit. But you could lighten up, too. Acknowledge that there are many fine choices for your children and that no one school is a perfect fit. Let your children explore the options and do not rush them to a premature decision. And urge those colleges that retain early decision programs to abandon them. This will not take all the pressure out of the college admissions process, but it will help.

RIGHTS AND RESPONSIBILITIES:
WORDS FOR GRADUATES

Plates

1. Camille Pissarro, *Louveciennes*, 1871. Private collection.

2. Paul Cézanne, *Louveciennes,* c. 1872. Private collection.

3. Camille Pissarro, *The Côte des Boeufs at L'Hermitage*, 1877. © National Gallery, London / Art Resource, NY.

4. Paul Cézanne, *Orchard, Côte Saint-Denis, at Pontoise (The Côte des Boeufs, Pontoise)*, 1877. Museum of Fine Arts, St. Petersburg, Florida. Private Collection TR 1976.4066.7.

5. Earth from the lunar orbit of Apollo 8, December 24, 1968. Courtesy of NASA.

Reviving Public Discourse

WHEN YOU entered Yale four years ago, I offered some reflections on the letters exchanged by John Adams and Thomas Jefferson in the last fourteen years of their lives. You probably do not recall, but I suggested that there were many lessons to be learned from reading this extraordinarily rich and erudite correspondence. Though very different in temperament, these two founding fathers shared a vigorous passion for lifelong learning, a capacity for independent thought, and a friendship rooted in mutual respect and admiration. I urged you to use your time at Yale to develop the qualities of mind and character that would make these traits your own.

Inspired by passionate and committed teachers, you plunged into your studies deeply and seriously. I hope that you will never lose the curiosity and the open-mindedness that you have exhibited in the Yale classroom, and that, like Adams and Jefferson, you will never cease to question, learn, and grow.

As for your capacity for independent thought, look around. As any bulletin board on campus demonstrates, there is an astonishing range

Baccalaureate Address, May 21–22, 2005.

of viewpoints and activities here. The vigor of debate in student publications and the lively discussions you have had in seminars provide ample proof that you can think for yourselves.

And then there is the building of enduring friendships, so long a hallmark of Yale College life. For this, it might seem that you needed no special inspiration, just a unique residential system and a spirit of community that made it easy to form deep bonds. But the formation of enduring friendships required more than a supportive environment; you had to work at it, work at the self-understanding that is a prerequisite for any deep relationship. You should take pride in this, as you treasure, for a lifetime, the "friendships formed at Yale."

If you are leaving here with a passion for learning, a capacity for independent thought, and deep friendships rooted in self-understanding, then you have accomplished much of the work of a college education. But now, as you graduate, I want to set one more goal for you, one for which your Yale experience has prepared you well. I want to urge you to take a role in public life, to take responsibility as citizens in a world that has changed dramatically in the short time you have been here.

That the world has changed came shockingly to our attention only ten days after we met here in Woolsey Hall for your Freshman Assembly. Many of the changes wrought by September 11 will be enduring, but the altered geopolitical landscape is not what I intend to talk about today. Instead, I want to challenge you at a more personal level to do your part as citizens to improve the quality of civic discourse in the United States and around the world. In particular, I want to talk about two disturbing trends in contemporary political discourse in democratic nations: oversimplification and polarization. The strength of our democracy and the wisdom of our collective choices will depend on the efforts of your generation to reverse these trends.

Consider the U.S. presidential debates of 2004. Following the advice of the experts, the candidates reduced every issue to a formula. Proud as we were that both candidates were Yale graduates, think how often the same phrases were invoked over and over again. "Staying on message" was the name of the game. There was no real debate, no progression in the argument. Neither we nor the candidates learned much from the interaction, as we would in a normal conversation, when one person responds to, criticizes, or builds upon the ideas of another.

It was not always this way. Go back and read the Lincoln-Douglas debates. Here was true engagement, detailed and sophisticated argumentation on the most vexing question in American history: the question of slavery. Even the Kennedy-Nixon debates, the first to be televised, were much deeper and more penetrating than what we have come to accept as inevitable today.

Public discourse is not only oversimplified, it is polarized as well. In the last presidential election, the candidates were more deeply divided on foreign policy, economic policy, and moral or lifestyle issues than at any time in recent memory. For the first time in generations, the prevailing wisdom of the pundits was that the candidates had to secure the base within their own parties rather than win the swing voters in the middle. And so, compared to any election since at least 1984, the Republicans moved more to the right and the Democrats more to the left, with each party seemingly speaking to those on its flanks rather than those in the middle.

The tendency to oversimplification and polarization leads us to represent too many important public choices as false dichotomies. I am an economist, and so I ask your indulgence if I illustrate this point with examples from the realm of economic policy.

The public debate suggests that we must choose between a flat tax and a progressive income tax filled with loopholes that advantage special interests. Isn't there an obvious middle ground: a progressive income tax with fewer loopholes?

We are presented with a choice between preserving the current Social

Security system—which is headed toward bankruptcy—and creating a system in which individuals maintain their own retirement accounts and make their own investment decisions. But why can't we create more incentives for private savings while preserving the social insurance or safety net features of Social Security?

We are asked to choose between protectionism that slows worldwide economic growth and a passive acceptance of the dislocations caused by free trade. Can't we maintain free trade and design more effective programs to assist and retrain those displaced?

We need to talk sensibly about the policy choices that confront us. There are plenty of good ideas that are not that complicated. But we need to raise the level of discussion beyond sound bites.

Your Yale education has prepared you to help. You have not been shy about expressing your opinions here. Do not lose the habit. As citizens, here in the United States and elsewhere, you will need to engage to improve the quality of public discourse. Insist on an end to oversimplification and polarization. Write letters, join organizations that advocate for your beliefs, participate in local politics, and, above all, use the critical faculties you have developed here to raise the level of discussion.

Many of you have become well practiced in civic engagement during your time here. You have worked to improve New Haven's neighborhoods, helped to raise the standard of Yale's environmental practices, sought the return of ROTC, and won national recognition for combating hunger and homelessness. You have given time to tutoring and coaching young people in the community. Seventy of you gave a summer to work on community service projects sponsored by Dwight Hall, the President's Office, and local Yale clubs around the country. You have written opinion pieces of every persuasion for student newspapers and magazines. At one student journal of international affairs, the *Yale Globalist*, the editors are developing a network linking similar magazines on campuses around the world. This effort to promote reasoned dialogue among students on a global scale exemplifies the kind of project any one of you might undertake to raise the level of public discourse.

Maintaining your admirable engagement with civil society in the years ahead in the manner that I am suggesting will require your determination and courage. In the next few years, as you are struggling to succeed in new jobs or graduate studies, it will be easy to turn inward. There will be more than enough to keep you occupied. But when I award your degrees at Commencement, here is what I will say: "By the authority vested in me, I confer upon you these degrees as designated by the Dean and admit you to all their rights and responsibilities." Three centuries of history have defined these responsibilities to include rising to the challenges of the day and making a contribution to civil society — from the four Yale graduates who signed the Declaration of Independence, to those who fueled the abolitionist movement two and three generations later, to those who fought to preserve our freedoms in two world wars, to those who led the way in extending those freedoms to all in the civil rights efforts of the past half century.

Whatever your passion may be — saving the environment, alleviating poverty, conquering infectious diseases — we can make little progress in a democratic society without intelligent public discussion of the issues. By pursuing your passion and doing your part to improve public discourse, you can make a difference.

In one of his last letters to Adams, Jefferson, the eternal optimist, wrote: "I shall not die without a hope that light and liberty are on steady advance." Adams, by contrast, was skeptical. He believed that tyranny was as likely to emerge from free elections as from a seizure of power. He saw checks and balances, and an educated and informed public, as critical to the survival of liberal democracy. He would not be surprised by the current impoverishment of political discourse, but his response would be clear. He would appeal to education as the solution.

We are fortunate that, on the question whether liberal democracy would survive, Jefferson has had the better of the argument for these past two hundred years, at home and around the world. It is our responsibility as educated citizens — your responsibility — to keep it that way.

Women and men of the Class of 2005: As you go forth from here with a passion for learning, a capacity for independent thought, and deep and enduring friendships, never forget your obligations to serve responsibly those around you, to engage in civic life, to demand reasoned public discourse from others, and to set a standard with your own. The continued flowering of the freedoms you have so vigorously exercised in this place depends upon your engagement and your vigilance. Lead on.

Curiosity, Independence, and Public Service

FOUR YEARS ago, in this very hall, I welcomed you to Yale. I began by telling you about Yale's tradition of pioneering new fields of study, its magnificent collections, its extraordinary faculty and their scholarly accomplishments. Then, as one example of Yale scholarship, I cited Edmund Morgan's just-completed biography of Benjamin Franklin. I identified several of Franklin's personal qualities and suggested that during your time here you might find them worthy of emulation. To remind you, these particular virtues were curiosity, independent thinking, and devotion to public service. I thought I would return to these themes today, in part to reflect on how you have practiced these virtues here at Yale, but more importantly to suggest how these traits of Franklin might serve you well in the years ahead, and enable you to contribute significantly to the well-being of our globally interdependent human society. Returning to Franklin seems altogether fitting and proper this year, as we celebrate the 300th anniversary of his birth.

Baccalaureate Address, May 20–21, 2006.

First among the virtues I cited was curiosity. Franklin wondered where the air that went up chimneys came from, and why oil droplets held their shape on solid surfaces but spread to a thin film on water. When crossing the Atlantic, he charted the location of the Gulf Stream and designed new hulls, riggings, propellers, and pumps for sailing vessels. He advised Robert Fulton on adapting the steam engine for use in ships, and he figured out which materials conduct electricity and which do not. He rarely sat in meetings without doodling, and sometimes he designed elaborate math puzzles.

As far as I can tell, you have not been lacking in curiosity. More than three-quarters of you decided on a major different from the one you announced as your intention during the summer of 2002. And I would venture to say that most of you have discovered new passions that will last a lifetime. Seventy of you have served as docents or assistants in the University Art Gallery or the Center for British Art, and hundreds more have taken classes in these two extraordinary museums. Three hundred of you worked in science, engineering, or medical laboratories on research projects with faculty guidance. And well over four hundred of you went overseas for study or work internships. These are only a few of the ways you have exercised your curiosity; the years ahead will offer you many more opportunities.

Independent thinking was the second of Franklin's traits I encouraged you to emulate. I expect that you would agree that we have encouraged you to think independently here at Yale. From the papers you have written, the exams you have taken, and the seminars you have attended, you know that the teachers you have most admired did not encourage you to recite back their opinions. They wanted you to question everything and think for yourself. Clearly the students most praised by the faculty were not those most adept at simply remembering what they read. Instead, they were the students with interesting and original ideas about what they read, or what they learned in the lab. I would imagine that you, too, have admired most those classmates whose ideas challenged you to think again.

Encouraging your curiosity and independence, along with originality and open-mindedness—these were the goals that Yale set for you, and they are the major objectives of undergraduate education not only at Yale but at other leading American colleges and universities as well.

Interestingly, the power of the American approach to higher education has only recently been recognized by other nations for what it is: a central reason for the economic strength of the United States and its dominant position in global markets for the past sixty years.

The secret is simple. Economic leadership in the modern world does not depend on abundant natural resources, although oil-producing states experience waves of prosperity at times like the present one. Nor does economic leadership today depend on an abundance of cheap labor, although the combination of cheap but literate labor and the elimination of barriers to trade and investment can produce dramatic growth, as we have seen in China for the past quarter century. Rather, sustained worldwide economic growth depends on advances in science and technology, and thus global economic leadership depends on a nation's capacity to innovate.

Other nations have begun to understand the links between higher education, innovation, and economic success. In China, Japan, and elsewhere, universities are abandoning their traditional pedagogy and seeking to encourage curiosity and independent thinking, in order to develop scientists, engineers, and entrepreneurs who have the creativity and capacity for innovation that is required to compete effectively in the knowledge-based industries that will drive the twenty-first-century economy.

Let's turn now to the third of Benjamin Franklin's admirable traits— his devotion to public service. He served as the first postmaster of the American colonies and subsequently devoted twenty-five years to service as an ambassador abroad, first for the commonwealth of Pennsylvania, later for the confederated colonies, and ultimately for the new United States of America.

You have already shown an interest in service here at Yale. More than four hundred of you participated as tutors or mentors in the New Haven public schools, and many more of you have involved yourselves in other community service activities of the widest variety. Contrary to the prevailing perception that your generation is disengaged from public issues, many of you worked as volunteers in the 2004 elections, and more than one hundred of you served as interns last summer in Washington, D.C. Some of you took up important causes here on campus — urging the University to strengthen its commitment to protecting the environment, to refrain from investment in companies contributing to the Darfur genocide, and to increase the financial aid available to low-income families.

I want to encourage you to stay engaged with public issues, and to consider public service. Many important issues will fall to your generation for resolution. Can we sustain the health and well-being of an increasingly aging population? Can we live in peace and prosperity as emerging nations rise to share center stage with America? Can we reduce greenhouse gas emissions and avert the environmental catastrophe toward which we seem headed? To secure the future for yourselves and your children, your involvement with these issues is essential.

In Franklin's generation, as in Jefferson's and Hamilton's, public service attracted citizens of the highest caliber, the most highly educated and the most morally principled. The questions facing us as global citizens today are no less weighty than those confronting America's founders. The world needs your commitment to public service. We at Yale expect it.

You may not have thought about your education this way, but the economist in me hastens to point out this fact: other people have made a big investment in you. I refer not only to your parents, whose sacrifice, despite our strong financial aid program, was considerable. I refer also to the generations of Yale alumni who have supported half the cost of your education through their gifts to Yale's endowment and through their annual donations to the alumni fund. The thousands of alumni who have made your education possible did not invest only for the pleasure of seeing you lead fulfilling and rewarding private lives. They also invested because they expected, and continue to expect, that, like Yale graduates who preceded you, you will make valuable contributions to the wider society – by advancing science, scholarship, the arts, and the professions, and, above all, by taking responsibility for the future, by serving as leaders in your communities, in the nation, and around the world.

On Monday, I will confer upon you the degrees in Yale College as recommended by your Dean and admit you to all their "rights and responsibilities." This ancient and idiosyncratic formulation is not an accident. In modern democratic societies we are accustomed to speaking about rights, but at the moment of your commencement we remind you that with rights come responsibilities. Take note that we speak of "rights and responsibilities," not "rights and privileges." Attending Yale College was a privilege; being a graduate of Yale College is a *responsibility* – a responsibility to share the fruits of your education with a wider humanity, through leadership and service.

Women and men of the Class of 2006: Never cease to exercise your curiosity. Seek out new experiences; approach them with an open mind, and form your own independent judgments. And, as the qualities of mind that you have developed here propel you past obstacles and setbacks to personal fulfillment, never forget that you have a broader responsibility. You are among those who can help to make this world a better place. Rise to the challenge.

Journeys

THREE YEARS before you arrived here, on the eve of this university's three hundredth birthday, we took the bold step of declaring that Yale would transform itself into a truly global institution in its fourth century. You and your successors deserve no less. Like your predecessors, you will lead lives of consequence, but unlike them, you enter a world that has become increasingly interdependent economically and geopolitically. The world, and not merely this nation, will be the stage on which your lives and your careers play out.

Many of you have been the beneficiaries of our recent efforts to internationalize the University. We have strengthened the curriculum in international studies and extended to international students our policy of awarding full need-based financial aid to all students admitted to Yale College. The year you were admitted, we announced our intention to offer to every undergraduate an overseas experience, and, a year later, we introduced a new financial aid program to ensure that every student would have sufficient resources to spend a term or summer abroad.

Today, the fruits of these initiatives surround us. Since the year 2000,

Baccalaureate Address, May 26–27, 2007.

we have added forty-seven new scholars in international studies to the Faculty of Arts and Sciences, and the number of international applicants to Yale College has more than doubled. You are the first class in Yale's history in which the number of nations represented equals the number of states of the union; you come from fifty nations and fifty states. And you are the first Yale class in which a majority took advantage of overseas study programs, independent research grants, or work internships.

Dean Salovey and I have just returned from an extraordinary journey to China. We led a delegation of one hundred Yale students and faculty, invited by China's President Hu Jintao as a gesture of friendship when he visited our campus a year ago. The invitation was no accident. Yale has a long association with China, dating back to 1850 when the first Chinese to study in a Western university enrolled in Yale College. And today we have the broadest and deepest set of collaborations and programs in China of any Western university.

On our first evening in Beijing, we were received by President Hu in the Great Hall of the People and treated to an exquisite banquet. In the days that followed, the "Yale 100" met with top government officials, visited four universities, dined with families, explored a rural village, and saw many of China's most significant historical sites – the Forbidden City, the Great Wall, the ancient Terra Cotta Warriors and bronze chariots of Xi'an, and the soaring postmodern skyscrapers of Shanghai. We witnessed the sunset from a pavilion in the northwest corner of the Forbidden City, overlooking dozens of fifteenth-century buildings as if we ourselves were the dinner guests of some bygone Ming emperor. We were accorded an extraordinary level of respect and visibility; the visit of the Yale 100 was reported daily in the press, and, for the first two days, we were the top story on the evening news. Eighty-five members of our delegation had never before been to China, but after this magnificent introduction I imagine that most will return.

In a curious way, this trip, which provided such a rich education for faculty and students alike, reminded me of the experience that all of you have had during your time here in New Haven. Just as you were challenged by new ideas in the classroom, those encountering China for the first time were challenged by a relentless barrage of new ideas and new experiences. And just as you found in your first weeks and months in New Haven, prejudices were shattered, and preconceptions were replaced by observation and analysis. As one Yale student walked with my wife Jane along Chang'an Avenue, twelve lanes wide, after lunch with Chinese students at an elegant hotel adjacent to a shopping mall filled with boutiques representing the finest French, Italian, Japanese, and American designers — he remarked, "I thought that China was still a backward country, where everything would be primitive and disorganized, and that the Olympics next year would be a fiasco." Of course, China is still an emerging economy with many challenges, but the next day, with the rest of us, he gaped in awe at our close-up view of the magnificent new Olympic stadium, perhaps the most beautiful sports arena constructed in modern times. Similarly, many of our faculty, expecting China's universities to be miles behind Yale and its peers, were amazed by the state-of-the-art new laboratories at Tsinghua and Fudan Universities, and our Deputy Dean of our School of Management, who is in the midst of planning a new campus, said, upon seeing Tsinghua's new business school, "Let's just hire their architect and get started!"

As impressed as we were by China's rapid development, the trip also gave us some proud and poignant moments, as we heard about Yale from the perspective of the Chinese. An undergraduate at Peking University, Zhang Xinyue, spoke to our group, describing her experience at Yale last summer in terms that I am sure resonate with your own. "The experience," she said, "opened a door to a wider mind and a brighter future. . . . Yale is a place [that] encourages independent thinking and [the] courage to pursue dreams. . . . Yale students believe in a better world, and they are making efforts to achieve that." She went on to conclude, "Yale is not only a name. It is a kind of spirit handed down from generation to generation. Yale not only provides knowledge, it gives you confidence, courage, and a caring heart. The Yalies care about life, their nation, and the whole world." Zhang Xinyue's emphasis on the importance of independent thinking was echoed by both her university's president and the Vice Minister of Education, who recognize that encouraging the free inquiry that has been the essence of your experience here at Yale is the surest way to realize the full potential of China's human resources.

It was not only the new ideas and experiences we encountered that reminded me of your journey through Yale. Our students and faculty were also exhilarated by making new friends within the group, just as you were when you first met your Yale classmates. Our group, in its way, resembled your class. We were a diverse assembly—two or three students from each residential college, two from each professional school, a half dozen from the Graduate School of Arts and Sciences, and about three dozen faculty and staff from all over the University. Very few people knew more than two or three others. Yet, just as you did in your first days at Yale, most discovered new friends with whom they shared a lot, as well as those whose perspectives and interests differed sharply from their own.

Remember how amazed you were to discover the astonishing talents of your otherwise unpretentious and friendly classmates? I was reminded of this when I happened to overhear a fragment of conversation between a student in the directing program at the Drama School and a professor in the School of Music. The student-director said, "I am considering doing a production next season about a musician, so I need an actor who can really play an instrument, preferably the cello." And the music professor gave this astonishing reply: "There are *two* brilliant cellists on this trip, one of whom is standing next to you!" The cellist in question was a six-foot, three-inch young man who might easily have been mistaken for a varsity football player. China's modernity was not the only stimulus that shattered our preconceptions on this trip! The wealth of talent and human potential throughout this university never ceases to astonish me, and I am sure that each of you will leave here with vivid memories of extraordinary people, many of whom will remain your lifelong friends.

As remarkable as the development of modern China is, all is not bliss. There are many paradoxes. What appeared to us as rampant capitalism is still officially described as "socialism with Chinese characteristics." And even as students and university leaders advocate freedom of inquiry and independent thinking, one very successful Chinese businessman—a capitalist through and through—told us that he thought the Communist Party had become too democratic and too prone to compromise in the face of public opinion, rather than simply "doing the right thing." Chinese citizens remain subject to arbitrary arrest and detention, and, though the press is noticeably freer than it was a few years ago, the Internet is heavily censored. Still, there have been some major achievements in advancing the rule of law. Recently, private citizens have won court judgments against the state. And, as a powerful example of how we all might use our education to advance the public good, the Vice President of China's Supreme Court, a graduate of the Yale Law School, told us how he, amazingly, introduced into the Chinese courtroom the practice of cross-examination!

Some of China's problems are unique, but some are so inextricably bound up with those facing the United States that neither nation can succeed without the other. Protecting our environment is one such example. Global warming cannot be avoided unless both China and the United States take dramatic action. Yale is doing its part, with its commitment to reduce greenhouse gas emissions. But it will fall to your generation, acting as global citizens in concert with your counterparts in China and around the world, to show the way.

Women and men of the Class of 2007: Everywhere you go, you will

148

encounter new experiences and new people, some of whom will become fellow travelers on your journeys. If you leave here, as we know you will, with open minds and generosity of spirit, you will find every one of life's journeys a new adventure – not unlike your four years at Yale College, but rather just like it. And on every journey, you will need to employ the powers of critical thinking you developed here to learn as much as you can, and the passion and empathy you displayed here to give to others more than you take. As you go forth from here, I urge you to use your natural gifts and the education you have been given to seek fulfillment in your own lives, and to seek the betterment of life for all with whom we share this small and shrinking planet.

Life on a Small Planet

I GRADUATED forty years ago and three thousand miles away, in 1968, a year marked by urban riots, two tragic assassinations, an unpopular war in Vietnam, and defeated revolutions in France and Czechoslovakia. In the wake of this turmoil and strife, there appeared at the end of that year images so astonishing that they remain imprinted in memory. They were straightforward photographs, taken with a Hasselblad camera, neither edited nor manipulated to achieve emotional effect. Yet they elicited the most powerful emotions. They were stunningly beautiful, hopeful, and profoundly humbling all at once.

I refer to the first photographic images of the earth taken from the vicinity of the moon by the crew of the Apollo 8 spacecraft (plate 5).

Here we were in a world torn by conflict between two warring ideologies, led by nations with nuclear arsenals sufficient to destroy each other many times over, our security in the hands of leaders on both sides who preached and practiced the doctrine of Mutually Assured Destruction. Forty percent of the world's inhabitants were in poverty, major cities were choked with air pollution, and the opportunities available to women

Baccalaureate Address, May 25, 2008.

and people of color were starkly limited. And yet here was this extraordinary image reminding us that we all lived on one small, fragile planet — a beautiful, pristine jewel from the distance of 240,000 miles, as Milton somehow imagined three centuries earlier when he described "[t]his pendent world, in bigness as a star of smallest magnitude."[1]

We have come a long way toward making this fragile planet a better place. The Cold War is over. The fraction of humanity in poverty has declined from 40 percent to less than 20 percent. Through strict controls on the emission of sulfur dioxide, nitrous oxides, and particulates, we have dramatically improved air quality in the cities of Europe and the United States. And the opportunities for women and people of color, in this country at least, have increased to an extent barely imaginable forty years ago. Certainly, no one in 1968 was imagining that a woman and an African American would be among the leading contenders for the presidency of the United States.

But most of these results — the collapse of the Soviet Union, the abatement of pollution, and the advancement of the rights of women and minorities — were achieved by work within nations rather than through cooperation among nations. A major exception is the reduction of global poverty, which is in substantial part a consequence of the steady liberalization of international trade and investment through global agreements in the Tokyo and Uruguay rounds.

Small as the world appeared in 1968 from 240,000 miles away, today the world is much smaller. The revolution in communications technology has brought us closer together. Information, images, and capital flow instantaneously across national borders, and the flow of people and products is faster and more voluminous than ever before. Our economies have become much more interdependent, and, increasingly, the problems that beset us will require global rather than national solutions.

1 John Milton, *Paradise Lost*, book ii, line 1051.

A simple case in point is the current crisis in credit markets. A generation ago, the U.S. Government could have managed the situation in isolation. Today, to be successful, the Federal Reserve Bank needs either tacit or explicit cooperation from the European Central Bank and the Chinese Government.

As you go forth from this place that has been your home for four years, you will inherit this shrinking planet. It will be yours to take care of for the next forty years and more. You are, fortunately, far better prepared for this task than my generation was. The Yale College Class of 1968 had only nineteen students from outside the United States; they represented thirteen countries. Your class has one hundred and six students from outside the United States, representing forty-one countries. As best we can tell, fewer than one hundred students in the Class of 1968 benefited from a Yale-sponsored experience overseas or an independent junior year abroad program. In your class, nearly *seven* hundred have had such an experience. You have also had access to a curriculum far richer in its coverage of the languages, culture, society, politics, and economics of other nations.

Yale has offered you this richer curriculum, increased the representation of international students, and created hundreds of new opportunities for overseas study, research, and work internships because the demands of twenty-first-century citizenship compel these initiatives. Like generations of your Yale College predecessors, you have developed a capacity for close reading, critical and independent thinking, clear and effective writing, and quantitative and scientific reasoning. But a complete twenty-first-century education requires one essential new skill: the capacity for cross-cultural understanding. To be adequately prepared for life in a highly interdependent world, you need the ability, which I trust that you have begun to develop here, to recognize and appreciate that those from other nations and other cultures see the world differently, hold different assumptions, and often reach different conclusions even when presented with the same facts. Only with this capacity for cross-cultural understanding will you achieve your full potential in the inevitably global careers you will pursue and in the contribution you will make to the greater society.

This last point is particularly salient for those of you who are Americans. This nation has suffered through much of its history from isolation and insularity. Too often, our leaders have been insufficiently aware of the effects of America's actions on the rest of the world, and insufficiently mindful of how America is perceived throughout the world. Your generation will have an opportunity to remedy this historic deficiency, in an era in which international cooperation is needed more than ever if we are to continue to make progress toward a better life for all.

Stepping up to the responsibilities of global citizenship is probably not the first thing on your mind this weekend, as you reflect upon the passage of these four years, as you think about the friendships you have made, the teachers you have encountered, and the good of this place that you will take along with you. At this moment, your thoughts of the future are probably a mix of excitement and anxiety as you contemplate the next step in your education, or your first job, or whether you will get a first job.

But your Yale education has equipped you for more than your next step; it is yours for a lifetime. And its aim has not been merely to prepare you for successful careers and personal fulfillment, but to prepare you for lives of service. Your service might begin with private acts of generosity and kindness. But it extends to the practice of civic virtue that was identified as the purpose of a Yale College education in our founding charter of 1701. And civic virtue, envisioned as distinctly local three centuries ago, must embrace the global as well as the local in the shrinking world we inhabit today.

The challenges of global citizenship are many: to extend the benefits of health and prosperity to those without them, to reduce the threats from terrorism and the proliferation of weapons of mass destruction, and to preserve the capacity of the earth's resources to sustain its inhabitants in peace, health, and prosperity.

As you leave Yale College, I hope you will carry with you, as part of your commitment to global citizenship, a recognition that the burden of ensuring the well-being of future generations falls on you. In your homes, workplaces, and communities, as well as in your involvement in public life, I hope you will remember to seek an appropriate balance between present and future. I urge you to live in better harmony with this small planet's resources than prior generations have. And I urge you, as global citizens, to promote the prosperity and improved health of your own generation in a manner that is sustainable, in the sense that future generations will have at least as much opportunity to enjoy the fruits of the environment and the fruits of their own potential as we ourselves enjoy.

Women and men of the Class of 2008: this small planet is yours to make better. In the words of the prophet Isaiah: may you go out in joy and be led forth in peace. And, if you serve, as I trust you will, as faithful stewards of this small and fragile planet, may the mountains and hills burst into song and may all the trees of the field clap their hands.

The Economy and the Human Spirit

WHEN I welcomed you four years ago, you were exhilarated but apprehensive, excited to be taking on a new challenge, but more than a little intimidated — awed by the imposing architecture of this place, by the grandeur of this hall, by the rumble of its great organ, and by the dazzling accomplishments of your classmates, who all seemed to you to belong here, even if you were not quite sure about yourself. Now, appropriately, you feel as if you own the place; every corner of your college, every face in the dining hall, is familiar to you. You have made close friends, and you have memories you will never forget. While all this happened to you, the world around you was flourishing. And Yale was flourishing, too — building and renovating at an astonishing pace, adding new international programs, and enhancing financial aid to make the whole experience a lighter burden on your families.

Who would have imagined, four years ago, that the world economy would collapse? As you leave here, it is hard not to think about this un-

Baccalaureate Address, May 23–24, 2009.

happy reality. So, as an economist and as your president, I would like to offer a perspective on what has happened and what it means for you.

The world economy is a mess. Specifically, the collapse of the housing market in the United States has been followed domestically and globally in rough order of succession by the collapse of key financial institutions, the stock market, the commercial paper market, interbank lending, consumer spending, the financing of consumer credit, capital investment, and the commercial real estate market. In the United States, we have experienced the sharpest reduction in gross domestic product in five decades, and the ride is not yet over. As many of you know all too well, jobs are scarce. Within the past year, the unemployment rate has increased from 5.0 percent to 8.9 percent, and, unfortunately, it is more likely than not to exceed 10 percent before declining again.

How did we get here? Not, I believe, because of any inherent flaws in the nature of the market system. This is a very important point. Indeed, the ascendancy of markets, the relative demise of centrally planned economies over the past thirty years, the opening of nations to freer international trade and investment, and the rapid advance of science and technology have led to unprecedented levels of global economic growth. Even in the midst of this downturn it is crucial to remember that more people, both in absolute terms and as a percentage of the world's population, have crossed the poverty line in the past thirty years than in any previous period of history.

The cause of the current crisis is less fundamental: we accumulated too much debt – mortgages, credit card debt, corporate debt, debt to support financial speculation, and government debt.[1] From January 1981,

---

1 Surprisingly, government debt is only 16 percent of the total national indebtedness. The balance is the sum of private household, corporate, and financial sector debt.

when Ronald Reagan took office, to September 2008, the ratio of total national debt — public and private — grew steadily from 160 percent to nearly 360 percent of gross domestic product.[2]

As we have seen all too painfully, when individuals have lots of debt, declining asset prices trigger delinquencies, defaults, housing foreclosures, personal bankruptcies, corporate bankruptcies, and bank insolvency. Financial institutions lack the capital and the confidence to make new loans. Consumers and businesses reduce their spending. Company profits and stock values fall. Output and income decline, and wealth evaporates because the promise of future earnings that supports the valuation of assets is no longer credible. This is where we are now, with our national wealth — personal and institutional — down by more than 25 percent. Virtually every family in this hall has felt the impact of this disastrous sequence of consequences.

How did it happen that we accumulated so much debt? In my view, the fault lies with those responsible for the regulation of credit in the United States. It makes little sense to blame bankers, mortgage originators and re-packagers, or hedge fund managers for taking excessive risk in a lax and permissive regulatory environment. Individual restraint cannot control the aggregate amount of credit in the economy. This is the role of the Federal Reserve, other financial regulatory agencies, and ultimately the Congress. But these regulators were captured by an ideology

---

2 For ninety of the one hundred and ten years between 1870 and 1980, the ratio of total debt to gross domestic product was roughly 150 percent. In the boom years of the 1920s that preceded the Great Depression, debt of all kinds, private and public, rose to the unprecedented level of 180 percent of GDP, only to settle back to 150 percent after the Second World War. (The ratio of debt to GDP actually increased from 180 percent to 300 percent between 1929 and 1933, not because debt was rising, but because gross domestic product declined by 44 percent.)

of overconfidence in the efficacy of the unfettered "free" market. Instead of tightening credit as the economy boomed, we relaxed conventional regulatory requirements and failed to regulate the new forms of credit created by the use of derivatives. The story is as simple as this.

History teaches that all credit expansions are followed by recessions or depressions. It also teaches that recovery follows recession. The right mix of government policies can make recovery happen faster.[3] But in the end, fast or slow, we will recover, as long as the market is allowed to direct the creative and productive forces embodied in emerging technologies and in our educated citizens, including you, in particular. It will get better. It is just a question of when.

Meanwhile, you may be wondering why *you* had the bad luck to graduate *now*. I know that the process of finding a first job has been more difficult and stressful for you than for your immediate predecessors, and I know that many of you do not yet have definite plans for the year ahead. But do not be discouraged. There are exciting opportunities waiting for you, and little reason for despair. I want to reassure you and your parents that the investment of time, energy, and money that you have

3 See the May/June 2009 issue of the *Yale Alumni Magazine* for some of my views on this subject. The essential points are these: (1) government fiscal policy should focus on job creation, not tax cuts and benefit increases, at a time like now when most people's marginal propensity to spend from additional income is low; (2) jobs can be created quickly by increasing employment on infrastructure projects (highways, schools, etc.) that are *already under way* all around the country rather than earmarking "shovel-ready" projects in the districts of influential members of Congress; and (3) instead of buying the toxic assets of troubled banks through a cumbersome mechanism that may not succeed in properly capitalizing the banks, the government should reorganize these banks and spin off their viable commercial banking functions into separate entities that could promptly resume the normal flow of credit.

made in your Yale education will be abundantly repaid. It will be repaid in a material sense; it will reward you with personal fulfillment, and, most important, it has prepared you for lives of service to family, community, the nation, and the world.

To put matters in perspective, remember that you came here to reflect on the world around you, to expose yourselves to new ways of thinking, to encounter brilliant teachers, to make use of extraordinary library and museum resources, to develop the capacity to think critically, to express yourselves clearly, and to find, both in the classroom and in extracurricular pursuits, the passions that motivate you. You have done all this and more. By encountering classmates from all 50 states and 41 nations, you have learned to appreciate the diversity of human talents and perspectives. Thanks to Yale's extensive array of international programs, the great majority of you have had a chance to experience life in a different culture. You are not just four years older; by virtue of what you have learned about the world around you and about yourselves, you are immensely more capable of taking on life's challenges. You may doubt my conclusion at this bittersweet moment of separation. But believe me, you are ready to leave.

Now, let us think of the exciting possibilities that are open to you.

Let us start by noticing that there has been a dramatic change in our national agenda, the most significant change of course in nearly thirty years. Whatever your political persuasion, if you care about health care, education, or the sustainability of the planet, now is the time to get involved. Think about opportunities to engage with these issues — either in government or in the private sector, whether for-profit or nonprofit. The years immediately ahead are going to have consequences for a long time to come.

Some of you are already responding to this call. The number of you enlisted to serve in Teach for America, the largest single employer of

Yale College graduates, has more than doubled in the last two years. In America's schools, there are promising signs of reform all around, led by the spectacular success of new approaches that instill confidence and a drive for achievement in the most disadvantaged of our youth. Whether it is the charter school models introduced by organizations such as KIPP in New York City and Achievement First here in New Haven, or public school reforms associated with a wide array of family services as in the Harlem Children's Zone, we are seeing powerful evidence of improved performance. As the new administration and some of our largest foundations continue to embrace these new ideas, more opportunities will arise to engage you. You might think about following in the footsteps of Yale graduates David Levin, the co-founder of KIPP, or Dacia Toll, the co-founder of Achievement First, and contributing to the renaissance of primary and secondary education in the United States.

Or think about helping to address the challenge of global warming. In America and elsewhere around the globe, there is going to be massive public and private investment in new energy technologies. This will create tremendous opportunities, not only for those of you interested in science, engineering, or public policy, but also for those of you interested in business, where you might help launch entrepreneurial "cleantech" start-ups, or make established businesses greener and more socially responsible. In this arena you might take as your model Yale graduates like Frances Beinecke, executive director of the Natural Resources Defense Council, or Kevin Czinger, whose company, Miles Electric Vehicles, is one of several hoping to be first to the market with an all-electric car suitable for highway driving and daily commuting.

Or perhaps, as America adopts a new and more collaborative approach to foreign policy, you might think about building a career that contributes to greater international cooperation and understanding. Legions of Yale graduates before you have pursued this noble calling: from

Sargent Shriver, the founder of the Peace Corps, to Joseph Reed, long-time Under-Secretary-General of the United Nations, to career diplomats like John Negroponte, to our current Secretary of State, Hillary Rodham Clinton. Perhaps the Peace Corps, the military, or the Foreign Service would be a good first step toward such a career.

I was vividly reminded of the abundance of opportunities before you just two months ago, when I convened a group of Yale alumni in Silicon Valley to advise me on how the University might take better advantage of new media in carrying out its educational mission. Around the table were Yale graduates who have been instrumental in the founding and development of companies such as Microsoft, Palm, RealNetworks, Electronic Arts, and Facebook. Having come to California fresh from a series of gloomy meetings with Yale graduates in the New York financial community, I was astounded by the unbridled optimism of those in the new media and technology business. The prospects for investment, they told me, have never been better. The cost of launching a media business, thanks to the development of widely available software platforms and tools, is lower than ever, and the possibilities for creative engagement with the user community are unprecedented. So in addition to contemplating a contribution in education, or energy and sustainability, or foreign relations, you might also think about new media, where Yale graduates have helped to create entirely new forms of enterprise that did not exist a generation ago. You can do the same.

I cite these specific paths not to limit your imagination, but to encourage you to recognize that opportunities are everywhere. The education you have acquired here has given you the breadth and flexibility to take on the widest array of challenges, and it has given you the depth and rigor to make a meaningful difference wherever you choose to apply your talent.

In 1930, at the darkest moment of the Great Depression, the economist John Maynard Keynes wrote:

We are suffering just now from a bad attack of economic pessimism. It is common to hear people say that the epoch of enormous economic progress . . . is over; that the rapid improvement of the standard of life is now going to slow down . . . . ; that a decline in prosperity is more likely than an improvement. . . .

I believe that this is a wildly mistaken interpretation of what is happening to us. We are suffering, not from the rheumatics of old age, but from the growing-pains of over-rapid changes. . . . The increase of technical efficiency has been taking place faster than we can deal with . . . ; the improvement in the standard of life has been a little too quick.[4]

Keynes went on to predict that the standard of living in advanced capitalist countries would increase by a factor of four to eight over the next century. He was right; in the nearly eighty years since 1930, the per capita gross domestic product in the United States, adjusted for inflation, has increased by a factor of six.

Keynes' source of confidence about the future was a belief in the power of creativity and innovation, expressed through the efforts of free, well-educated individuals to apply scientific knowledge and human ingenuity to the development of new technologies, new products, and new services to improve material well-being.

The potential for material advance is no less abundant in the United States today than it was in Keynes' Britain of eight decades ago. And, what is even more abundant today is the potential for moving beyond material advance to a better quality of life for all — toward a healthier

4 John Maynard Keynes, "Economic Possibilities for Our Grandchildren," *The Nation and Athenaeum* (Oct. 11, 1930), reprinted in Keynes' collection, *Essays in Persuasion* (1931).

population, a cleaner environment, a better educated and wiser citizenry, a more peaceful world.

Women and men of the Class of 2009: You have within you the creative potential to make a better world for us all. The world is all before you. Choose your direction, and prove that this time of crisis is also a time of opportunity. You can do it. Yes, you can.

Reclaiming Politics

UNDERSTANDABLY, YOU may be uncertain and a bit anxious about what lies ahead. But, if history is to be trusted, you will find many paths open to you. Because of the talent you possess, as well as the intellectual and personal growth you have experienced here, you will find, with high likelihood, success in your chosen endeavors.

Perhaps I am overconfident about your prospects for personal fulfillment and professional success, but I do not think so. If you will concede my point for the sake of argument, let me ask the next question, one so deeply rooted in Yale's mission and tradition that for most of you, fortunately, it has become ingrained. And that question is: how can I serve? How can I contribute to the well-being of those around me, much as you all have done in building communities within the residential colleges and volunteering in so many valuable roles in the city of New Haven? Now is an important time to be asking this question. Let me suggest why, and then let me suggest an answer.

Aristotle tells us that we are by nature political animals. But one wonders whether he would recognize the species that we have become.

Baccalaureate Address, May 22–23, 2010.

Eighteen months ago, the United States elected a new president who was prepared to address, intelligently and collaboratively, the most pressing problems confronting the nation – education, health care, climate change, and improving America's image in the rest of the world. Late in the election campaign, the financial crisis intervened, and economic recovery and financial sector reform were added to this ambitious agenda.

What has happened since does not inspire great confidence in the capacity of our system to deal intelligently with important problems. We legislated a stimulus package that was less effective than it should have been, and far less effective than the corresponding measures undertaken in China. Fifteen months later, unemployment in the United States is still 9.9 percent. After months of stalemate, Congress enacted a health care bill that extends care to millions of uncovered individuals and families, but takes only the most tentative steps toward containing the escalating costs that will create an unsustainable burden of public debt within the next decade or two. We failed to address climate change in time to achieve a meaningful global agreement in Copenhagen. And, although financial sector reform now seems to be a possibility, the debate has been replete with misunderstanding of what actually went wrong and a misplaced desire for revenge.

Why is this happening? Let me make two observations, and then trace their implications for how you might conduct yourselves as citizens and participants in political life. First, contemporary political discussion is too often dominated by oversimplified ideologies with superficial appeal to voters. And, second, political actors in the United States give too much weight to the interests of groups with the resources to influence their reelection, and too little attention to the costs and benefits of their actions on the wider public.

In *The Federalist*, No. 10, James Madison addresses the second of these observations, in the context of the fledgling republic established by the U.S. Constitution. He notes that the tendency to pursue self-interest can never be entirely suppressed, but it can be mitigated by the proper design of political institutions. In contrast to a direct democracy where individuals would tend to vote for their own interests, a republican form of government, Madison argues, will have a greater tendency to select representatives who attend to the broader interests of the whole. He further argues that representatives in a large republic constituted of a wide range of divergent interests will find it easier to rise above parochialism than those in a smaller republic comprised of a small number of competing factions.

The protections that our form of government offers against ideology and faction have attenuated greatly since Madison's time, for at least two reasons. First, mass communication increases the opportunity to sway voters by appeal to simple formulations. Of course, the rise of mass communication could be a tool for raising the level of discourse through more effective education of the electorate. But it interacts with the second attenuating factor: that the money required to win elections through the media has created a dependence on funding from special interest groups. It is these interest groups who distort reasoned dialogue by sponsoring oversimplified messages.

It is easy to see how these developments have thwarted recent efforts to shape responsible public policy. For example, the interest groups opposing health care reform defeated efforts to contain costs by labeling them "death panels," and they defeated the creation of a new public vehicle for providing health insurance by insisting that we must "keep government out of the health care business," when in fact Medicare, Medicaid, and the Veterans Administration already pay nearly 40 percent of the nation's health care bill. I am not taking sides here, only pointing to the fact that intelligent debate on these subjects was crowded out by ideological distortion.

How can we create a national and global dialogue that transcends such oversimplification and parochialism? Let me suggest that we need each of you to raise the level of debate. You came here to develop your powers of critical thinking, to separate what makes sense from what is superficial, misleading, and seductive. Whether you have studied literature, philosophy, history, politics, economics, biology, physics, chemistry, or engineering, you have been challenged to think deeply, to identify the inconsistent and illogical, and to reason your way to intelligent conclusions. You can apply these powers of critical discernment not simply to fulfill personal aspirations, but to make a contribution to public life.

Every signal you have received in this nurturing community has been unwavering in its message that the growth of your competencies is not to benefit you alone. You have learned in your residential colleges that building a successful community has required you to respect and value one another, and, when appropriate, to moderate your own desires for the benefit of the whole. And so it should be in your lives after Yale. If you are to help to solve this nation's problems – or work across national boundaries to address global problems such as climate, terrorism, and nuclear proliferation – you will need to draw upon both these fruits of a Yale education: the capacity to reason and the ethical imperative to think beyond your own self-interest.

I know that many of you are taking advantage of these first years after graduation to take up public service, and I hope that even more of you will consider this path. There are plenty of jobs in the public sector for enterprising recent graduates; many are short-term, but others may lead to careers. Many of you have signed up to be teachers. Others will enter business or the professions. But whatever choice you make, you can help to strengthen the nation and the world, by treating our political choices not as triggers for an ideological reflex and not as opportunities to maximize self-interest.

To combat reflexive ideologies, you must use the powers of reason that you have developed here to sift through the issues to reach thoughtful, intelligent conclusions. To combat parochialism, you must draw upon the ethical imperative that Yale has imbued in you – an imperative that begins with the golden rule. Whether you serve in government directly or simply exercise your responsibilities as a citizen and voter, recognize that we will all be best served if we take account not merely of our own self-interest, but the broader interests of humanity. To move beyond ideology and faction, we need to raise the level of political discourse. You, as the emerging leaders of your generation, must rise to this challenge.

In first paragraph of *The Federalist,* No. 1, writing about the infant republic whose constitution he was endeavoring to defend, Alexander Hamilton asserts:

> It has frequently been remarked, that it seems to have been reserved to the people of this country, by their conduct and example, to decide the important question, whether societies . . . are really capable or not, of establishing good government from reflection and choice . . .

There is much in America's history of the past two and a quarter centuries that would incline us to conclude that Hamilton's question has been answered in the affirmative. Our institutions of representative government have proven themselves to be durable; the rule of law has prevailed, and the scope of personal liberty has expanded far beyond what the founders envisioned. But today, in the face of oversimplified ideology and the dominance of narrow interests, we must wonder again whether Hamilton's question is still open.

Women and men of the Yale College Class of 2010: It falls to you, the superbly educated leaders of your generation, to rise above ideology and faction, to bring to bear your intelligence and powers of critical thinking to elevate public discourse, to participate as citizens and to answer the call to service. Only with your commitment can we be certain that our future will be decided by "reflection and choice" in the broad best interest of humanity.

Taking Responsibility

I IMAGINE you are finding it difficult to believe that your time here has come to an end. Let me tell you from experience: your memories of Yale College, and the lessons you have learned here, will endure, but you have so many exciting possibilities ahead that the sense of loss you feel today will fade quickly. You have learned the value of seeing the world and the value of appreciating the differences among its peoples. You have worked hard. You have had fun. You have made friends for a lifetime. And you have come to know yourselves better than before — not only from the books you have read and the courses you have taken, not only from the overseas experiences you have had, but also from your endless discussions with classmates about your beliefs, hopes, and aspirations.

You have also learned something here about responsibility. You have lived in communities — communities formed by your suitemates, your entryway, and your college, as well as in communities defined as singing groups, chamber orchestras, dramatic societies, service organizations, publications, religious organizations, athletic teams, fraternities, sororities, and societies. Living in these communities and making them work

Baccalaureate Address, May 19–20, 2012.

has been a big part of your experience. You have learned that as gifted and talented as you are — and you are — it is not all about you. It is all about us. You have learned that making communities productive and a positive experience for all means taking account of the perceptions, feelings, and aspirations of others. Living in some of Yale's many communities has made you a better listener, more respectful of others, and better equipped to serve and to lead in the world beyond these walls.

And what of the world you are entering? There are big communities out there in which you will have roles, and, therefore, responsibilities. We are a global university, and each of you has a nation to which you now have an opportunity to contribute. Problems abound all around the world, and choices of direction are confronting every nation. Europe is debating austerity versus growth. In the aftermath of the Arab Spring, Middle Eastern and North African countries are testing whether democracy can thrive. China is struggling to find a way to distribute the fruits of increased prosperity more equitably, and to diminish the adverse environmental impact of rapid growth. The argument I wish to advance now applies equally to those of you with responsibilities as citizens of countries around the world, but I will focus on the United States, where all of you have chosen to attend school.

Surely you have noticed that there is a presidential election going on. But it does not seem to have captured the imagination of many of you, as elections have often in the past. Let me suggest why. Perhaps it is because the issues that truly matter for the nation and the world are not at center stage. And there are, for sure, issues that truly matter. How do we create a sustainable foundation for long-run prosperity, with good jobs created in ever-increasing numbers to spread the fruits of growth more equitably across the population? How do we provide high-quality and humane health care at a cost we can afford? How do we prevent the continued consumption of fossil fuels from warming our planet to the point that ecosystems are destroyed, food supplies are threatened, and rising sea levels force hundreds of millions to relocate? And, as a nation, how do we engage with a world in which the distribution of power and influence is inevitably becoming more multipolar?

It is not that these issues are being altogether ignored. For example, competing approaches to revitalizing the economy are very much the subject of debate, but the issues are typically broken into unconnected pieces and discussed in terms that reflect oversimplified ideological preferences rather than serious analysis. We talk about whether to increase the debt ceiling as if it were a religious issue, or whether to extend the tax cuts enacted a decade ago as if this were in itself the single question defining the proper role of government in the economy. Meanwhile, we ignore serious deliberation of how to undertake and finance, on a substantial scale, the investments in infrastructure, innovation, education, and training that *are* of fundamental importance to our future well-being.

The issue of climate change seems to have disappeared under the table, buried in an avalanche of know-nothing advocacy that disparages decades of disinterested scientific research. And the implications of a shift in the distribution of power among nations are simply not in the debate chamber. Instead, we talk of securing a new American Century, as if continued global dominance were a national objective. I do believe that America can prosper and lead in the twenty-first century. But the global landscape today is far different than it was in 1945, when World War II ended, or 1989, when the Cold War ended. We should be talking about how we might work effectively with other nations in the context of more widely shared power and responsibility.

I was poignantly reminded of the poverty of our current political discourse when, a couple of weeks ago, Yale Professor Steven Smith, who recently stepped down as master of Branford College, gave me a copy of his new edition of *The Writings of Abraham Lincoln,* published by Yale University Press.[1]

How utterly refreshing it is to read Lincoln's beautifully written, closely argued speeches and letters that grapple directly, deeply, and forcefully with the issues of his time. Of course, Lincoln's main preoccupation was with the subject of slavery, and he addresses that issue with a rigor and depth of argument that is simply unknown in American political discourse today. But he also touched brilliantly on other subjects of more direct relevance to our current situation. In a speech given in Milwaukee to the Wisconsin State Agricultural Association in September 1859, Lincoln addressed the full range of issues associated with deriving maximum social benefit from the development of what was then the nation's most significant natural resource – its fertile and abundant agricultural land.[2] Like so many of Lincoln's speeches, it is remarkable for displaying an extraordinary mastery of his subject matter. His discussion focused on the need for continued innovation as a means to greater productivity and prosperity. To enable such innovation, he stressed the importance of infrastructure in the form of access to adequate supplies of water, and he especially emphasized the need for education. Farmers, said Lincoln, need not only to be literate, but also to have a working knowledge of botany, chemistry, and the mechanical arts.

One might have thought that Lincoln's vision of increasing prosperity through investment in innovation, infrastructure, and education might have been set aside in the face of the overwhelming Civil War that confronted him within six weeks of taking office. But no, within a period of two years, working with Congress, Lincoln was able to enact legislation authorizing a transcontinental railroad; the Homestead Act enabling the

---

1   Steven B. Smith, ed., *The Writings of Abraham Lincoln* (2012).
2   Abraham Lincoln, "Address to the Wisconsin State Agricultural Society" (Sept. 20, 1858), in Smith, *op. cit.,* pp. 268–78.

establishment of farms across the western territories; and the Morrill Act granting land for the establishment of colleges to teach agriculture and the mechanical arts, colleges that subsequently became our treasured state universities.[3] These public investments were the foundation of late nineteenth-century America's prosperity.

We need to make such investments again today. We need to repair our crumbling physical infrastructure: our highways, ports, railroads, and airports, as well as waste and water management, traffic control, and communications systems. To make possible the flow of innovations upon which our economy depends, we need to maintain our commitment to investing in science. To equip our citizens with the skills required to be productive and competitive in a modern, technology-enabled workplace, we need to make large and well-directed investments in both basic K-12 education and in specialized technical training. The gap in earnings between the highly educated and the poorly educated has grown dramatically in the last three decades, and the earnings of those without a college education has not kept up with inflation. Educating our workforce is the most effective way to prevent rising income disparity.

By using the powers of reason and expression you developed here at Yale, by drawing upon your wide exposure to many disciplines and forms of discourse, each one of you has the capacity to make a difference in the quest to build a better world, for yourselves and for future generations. You can start by engaging in the public debate about the investments needed to secure our future and the perspective needed to operate effectively in a multipolar world. You can bring rigor and seriousness to the political dialogue, and insist that others do so as well by rejecting the superficial ideological slogans that are no substitute for true argument.

---

3 Lincoln also presided over legislation that protected the Yosemite Valley from development and ensured public access for recreational purposes.

And you can engage more directly in repairing the world through the career paths you choose and the organizations you join and support.

I am not saying that you all need to take up public service or teach school, although I hope and trust that some of you will. Instead, I am urging you to engage with the future by helping to raise the sights of your communities, as Yale graduates traditionally have, and not confine your activity merely to the private pursuit of health, wealth, and happiness.

This is where I started, by reminding you that Yale is not merely a place that enabled you to define and transform yourselves as individuals. It has been for each of you a network of many communities in which you were expected to participate and to which you were expected to contribute. The world outside is no different. We need you to engage, to consider the well-being of others as well as yourselves: we need you to take responsibility.

Lincoln closed his Wisconsin speech with a memorable passage, inspiring his audience in his inimitable and graceful prose not to accept the world passively, but to work actively toward its betterment. He said:

> Let us hope . . . that by the best cultivation of the physical world, beneath and around us; and the intellectual and moral world within us, we shall secure an individual, social, and political prosperity and happiness, whose course shall be onward and upward, and which, while the earth endures, shall not pass away.[4]

Women and men of the Yale College Class of 2012: You have expanded your own horizons, and you have sustained and improved the life of Yale's many communities. Now is the time to build flourishing lives for yourselves, and also to strive for the betterment of your communities—

4 Lincoln, *op. cit.*, p. 278.

local, professional, national, and global. Help these communities culti-vate the world around us and the worlds within us. Take inspiration from Lincoln and from your own experiences here at Yale, and make your course – and the course of those without the privileges accorded to you – onward and upward.

THE UNIVERSITY AS GLOBAL CITIZEN

The Lesson of 9/11

WHEN WE gathered ten years ago this evening, our community was shocked, filled with grief, frightened, and uncertain. At that moment no one knew for sure who had caused the tragedy, how many had died, or whether there were more attacks to follow. The members of our community reached out to one another in their grief and uncertainty. After the candlelight vigil here on the evening of September 11, Jewish and Muslim students came together. They invited the whole campus to another vigil three days later, where Jews and Muslims read words of comfort and hope from each other's sacred texts. We responded to terror with tolerance and mutual understanding.

Tonight, with the perspective of a decade, this remains the principal lesson of 9/11: that the best weapon in the war on terror is an open mind. History teaches us that extremism — a dogmatic insistence that one is in possession of the unique truth — leads to nothing but misery and suffering. In a characteristically brilliant essay, the British philosopher Isaiah Berlin identified for us the dangers of "the pursuit of the ideal." Those who adhere to rigid ideologies, to belief systems religious or secular that

Remarks on the 10th anniversary of 9/11, Cross Campus, September 11, 2011.

claim absolute certainty about what is right and wrong, are prone, indeed are almost inevitably drawn to persecuting, imprisoning, torturing, or murdering those who do not subscribe to their uncompromising orthodoxies. The fundamentalism at the root of 9/11 is not unique; it has many precursors — from the Inquisition to the witch trials of colonial New England, to the mass executions of Hitler and Stalin, to ethnic cleansing in Cambodia. Blind adherence to ideology, a conviction that one alone is in possession of the whole and genuine truth, is a recipe for disaster.

Historically, terror has been confronted with force, with results that are sometimes successful, sometimes ambiguous. Hitler was overcome after a stupendous sacrifice of human life. The leader of Al Qaeda has at last fallen and his organization has been weakened, but the consequences of two costly wars, fought by many brave Americans committed to freedom and openness, remain uncertain.

Here at Yale every day, in the classroom and outside, we confront fundamentalism and terrorism by other means. We challenge established beliefs; we encourage each other to find reasons for our beliefs; we confront closed-minded dogmatism with argument. This is the essence of liberal education: we encourage everyone in this community to engage the power of reason to examine all points of view, to shape arguments, to weigh evidence, and to develop independently a view of what is true and what is not. We encourage each other, in the words of Thomas Jefferson's advice to his nephew, to "fix reason firmly in her seat, and call to her tribunal every fact, every opinion."

Today, perhaps more than our Enlightenment forebears and our nation's founders, we recognize that truths so obtained are rarely if ever certainties; they are contingent and provisional, subject to revision if confronted by superior logic or disconfirming evidence. And because our truths are not certainties, we tolerate those who reach different conclusions. Toleration allows us to hear opposing views, and open-mindedness allows us to refine our views of what is true, and our views of how to live an ethical life.

If we are tolerant, we can live in peace and harmony with those we cannot persuade. If we are open-minded and reason independently and creatively, we can improve ourselves as ethical beings, and we can, if we choose, make the world a better place.

Freedom, toleration, and open-mindedness: these are the values of the University. These are the values that America at its best stands for. Even as we remember and honor the victims of the terror inflicted upon us ten years ago this day, let us commit ourselves to reject blind adherence to dogma and affirm freedom, toleration, and open-mindedness. Let us ever confront darkness and prejudice with light and truth.

Leading by Example

I AM greatly honored to participate in this distinguished series of lectures in preparation for next year's UN Summit on Climate Change. Because Yale is among Copenhagen University's founding partners in the International Alliance of Research Universities, I am especially delighted to have the opportunity to visit your campus and to advance our global collaboration.

There is no longer any doubt that we have a problem. The Fourth Assessment Report of the Intergovernmental Panel on Climate Change concluded last year that the evidence of global warming is "unequivocal."[1] The Panel, consisting of 2,500 leading climate scientists from around the world, determined with "very high confidence that the net effect of human activities since 1750 has been one of warming."[2] And it concluded

Remarks at the Climate Lecture Series, University of Copenhagen, January 20, 2008.

1 Intergovernmental Panel on Climate Change, *Fourth Assessment Report: Synthesis Report Summary for Policymakers* (2007), p. 1.
2 *Ibid.*, p. 4.

that "most of the observed increase in globally-averaged temperatures since the mid-20th century is very likely due to the observed increase in anthropogenic GHG [greenhouse gas] concentrations."[3] The Panel concluded that, in the absence of corrective measures, global temperatures are likely to rise between one and six degrees centigrade by the end of this century, with the best estimates ranging between two and four degrees. Even a one-degree increase in temperature will limit fresh water availability and cause coastal flooding in much of the world, but, as the Panel noted, economic, social, and environmental damages and dislocation will become much more consequential if global temperatures increase by more than two degrees.

I want to devote the first half of my remarks to the work that universities are doing to improve our understanding of global warming and what can be done about it. In particular, I would like to highlight the ongoing efforts to demonstrate that substantial reductions in greenhouse gas emissions are both feasible and relatively inexpensive. Then I would like to conclude with some reflections on what governments must do to secure the future of the planet. Designing a response to global warming is unusually complex, and the practical and political impediments are formidable. But these complexities and impediments are not an acceptable excuse for inaction. We need to address this problem now, for the sake of future generations.

The Role of Universities

So what roles should universities play in advancing sustainable development at the local and global levels?

First, universities must continue to advance the science of climate change and its consequences. We will make further investments in sci-

3 *Ibid.*, p. 5.

ence to refine our models of how climate change occurs and how it is likely to affect the economy and the environment. We will also sponsor policy research to illuminate the likely consequences of corrective actions. It is worth noting that nearly half of the 2,500 scientists and policy experts who constitute the Intergovernmental Panel on Climate Change are based in universities.

Around the world there are many significant university initiatives directed toward advancing the science of global warming. The University of Tokyo, for example, is committed to a major reorganization of its scientific effort to create an entire division of sustainability. This is an exciting interdisciplinary approach that holds great promise.

A second major area of university involvement is energy technology. MIT's president, Susan Hockfield, declared in her inaugural address that alternative energy technology would be her institution's foremost research priority. MIT is devoting significant resources to this vast area of research, which includes not only developing carbon-free technologies such as solar, wind, and geothermal power, but also finding more efficient ways to use carbon-based fuels through improved building materials and design, as well as improved vehicle and power plant technologies.

MIT is not alone. The University of California, Berkeley and the University of Illinois recently received a $500 million commitment to fund alternative energy research from British Petroleum—the largest corporate gift ever made in support of university-based research.

A third important role for universities is to educate students who will go on to be future leaders and influential citizens of the world. At Yale we take this part of our mission extremely seriously. We have greatly expanded our teaching programs in the environmental area. We now have over sixty courses available to undergraduates, who can choose either environmental studies or environmental engineering as a major subject. The study of the environment and sustainability is now embedded in the curriculum of our graduate schools of business, architecture, and public health. And our graduate School of Forestry and Environmental Studies, which offers an interdisciplinary curriculum spanning science and policy, has for decades produced some of America's most influential environmental leaders. Today, the heads of many of our leading environmental organizations – including Environmental Defense, the Natural Resources Defense Council, and Conservation International, among others – are graduates of the School.

Finally, universities can demonstrate to the world that substantial reductions in greenhouse gas emissions are feasible and not prohibitively expensive. This fourth role of universities interacts with the third. In our efforts to demonstrate best practices in limiting carbon emissions we are teaching our students – who are full participants in this campus-wide effort – how to be responsible citizens of the world. Together, we are learning how to balance near-term economic considerations against the long-term health of the environment and future human generations.

I would like to illustrate how universities can reduce their carbon footprints by using Yale as a case study. But before I do, let me briefly outline the broader picture of sustainability at Yale. We have a comprehensive sustainability framework that includes protection of natural ecosystems, conservation of our water resources, recycling of materials, and the use of natural, locally grown food in our dining halls. We aspire to leadership in all of these dimensions of sustainability, and we hope to inculcate in our students a lasting consciousness of what it means to live on a planet with finite resources in full awareness of how human action today affects the future of both humanity and the natural environment.

Our sustainability program at Yale, in short, involves educating the next generation of leaders in our society to live in better harmony with the planet than prior generations. Our aspiration is to promote growing prosperity that is sustainable, in the sense that future generations will have no less opportunity to enjoy the fruits of the environment or the fruits of their own potential than we ourselves have enjoyed.

How did Yale set out on this path? First, we have always had a strong presence at Yale of environmentally conscious scholars and students. Just before the millennium, we created a task force, the Advisory Committee on Environmental Management, led by faculty, which was asked to suggest improvements in Yale's environmental practices. We then launched a series of small environmental projects and ultimately created an Office of Sustainability.

One of the events that significantly influenced me toward taking bolder action was a report prepared by three undergraduate students. These students thoroughly documented Yale's environmental practices and pointed the way toward what might be done in the future to improve our policies. The student report appeared just as we hired Julie Newman as our first Director of Sustainability. We now had a vision, which I embraced, and a leader thoroughly up to the task of moving the university forward. Today, Julie Newman not only coordinates Yale's efforts, but she has assumed a position of leadership in sustainability practices across the university community – regionally, nationally, and globally.

Now I would like to describe Yale's efforts to reduce its greenhouse gas emissions. I'll start by noting that Yale employs more than 12,000 people, making us the second-largest employer in our home state of Connecticut. There are 11,000 students on our campus, and we have an annual budget of $2.5 billion. We are a large organization by any standard, large enough to be a model of responsible environmental practice for other universities and business organizations, large enough to demonstrate to political leaders that greenhouse gas reduction is feasible and affordable.

The centerpiece of our effort at Yale is our commitment to reduce the University's greenhouse gas emissions to 43 percent below our 2005 baseline by 2020, a goal within the range of estimates of what's required to keep global temperatures from rising two degrees centigrade. Our target is more ambitious than the goal adopted at Kyoto, but has a longer timeframe, 2020 rather than 2012.

The good news is that we've reduced our carbon emissions by 43,000 metric tons in the first two years of our program. That's a 17 percent reduction from our 2005 levels. This rapid process has given us confidence that we are going to achieve our reduction well before our 2020 deadline. We also have additional emissions-reducing projects currently planned for implementation within the next three years, the most important of which is a new co-generation plant on the campus of our School of Medicine. These projects will achieve an additional 17 percent reduction in our greenhouse gas emissions.

We plan to reduce our carbon footprint through a mix of conservation measures, the use of renewable energy on our campus, and direct participation in carbon offset projects. Some of the specific steps we have taken to reduce emissions are worthy of mention:

- In the last two years, we have retrofitted the heating, ventilation, and air conditioning systems in ninety of our roughly three hundred buildings. Heating and lighting is managed by automated controls.
- We have installed thermally efficient windows in many of our largest existing buildings, and in all of the new buildings we have constructed in the last decade.
- We have acquired new power plant equipment and modified some existing equipment to achieve substantial savings in fuel consumption. We are using a mix of conventional and renewable fuels in our power plant and our campus bus fleet.
- All of our new buildings, and even most of our renovations, have achieved a Silver rating or better from the Leadership in Energy and Environmental Design (LEED) Green Building Rating System. We are constructing a new home for our

School of Forestry and Environmental Studies that is designed to be carbon-neutral. It is truly a marvel of green architecture, and it will be the second new building at Yale to gain the highest rating, LEED Platinum. Only fifty-one buildings worldwide have thus far achieved this standard; eleven of them are on university campuses. We are currently exploring, along with several sister institutions, an alternative standard for new construction that focuses more directly than LEED on greenhouse gas reduction.

- In several of our existing and new buildings we have installed ground source heat pumps to help meet heating and cooling needs.
- We have reduced aggregate electricity consumption by 10 percent in our residential colleges each of the last two years, by sponsoring a competition between the colleges. Part of this reduction is attributable to more conscientious behavior in turning off lights and computers, but we have also distributed thousands of compact fluorescent light bulbs. We intend to achieve another 5 percent reduction in student electricity consumption this year.
- We are developing standards for the replacement of university-owned vehicles with hybrid models. As we replace the University's buses and trucks, we want to minimize fuel consumption and also use renewable fuels where possible.
- We are experimenting with solar and wind power as part of our effort. We are installing solar panels on a number of our buildings, both existing and new. And we are installing small wind turbines in the windiest sections of our campus.

Nearly all of these projects require up-front investment, but the good news is that most of the actions we have taken to date have brought sufficient energy savings to yield a positive economic return. Based on our experience, I am convinced that just about every large organization that carefully examines its energy sources and consumption will find many investments that have an economic payoff.

Nonetheless, some of the investments we are making, and some that we will make in the future, do incur some net economic cost. For example, our studies suggest that there is a significant premium associated with establishing LEED Gold as a minimum standard for new construction, relative to our current standard of LEED Silver. In part, this is why we are considering the development of an alternative standard more closely linked to carbon emissions.

Today, we usually pay a premium when we substitute renewable fuels for conventional fuels. That equation might change if there were a carbon tax to reduce greenhouse gas emissions. To evaluate such situations, we calculate what the net cost or savings would be in the presence of a $50 or $100 per ton carbon tax.

In some cases, we will invest to achieve carbon savings even at a modest net economic cost, in part to demonstrate the feasibility of new technologies and in part to encourage policy change that would price carbon correctly. Recognizing that some of the steps we are taking produce economic savings while others impose a cost, we believe that we can reach our greenhouse gas reduction goal at a cost of less than 1 percent of our annual operating expenses. Indeed, in our most likely scenario the net cost is closer to 0.5 percent of our operating expenses.

This is a price that we are more than willing to pay to achieve such a significant reduction in Yale's carbon footprint. I would ask each individual in this room the following question: would you pay a tax of 0.5 percent of income to save the planet? Perhaps I am an incorrigible optimist, but I believe that when asked this question most people would answer "yes."

I should mention that many of Yale's peer institutions also are aggressively reducing their carbon footprints. Cornell University, for example, has a project using lake water for campus-wide cooling, and the University of Pennsylvania has purchased wind power to meet 30 percent of its electricity needs. And I am delighted that the University of Copenhagen has committed to reducing its energy consumption by 20 percent in the next decade. By the end of this academic year, we expect that every one of our sister institutions in the Ivy League will adopt its own concrete and achievable greenhouse gas reduction goal.

Yale is also encouraging three groups of international universities to become leaders in reducing carbon emissions. The International Alliance of Research Universities, which includes Copenhagen, is working on defining common metrics and similar policy goals. At Davos later this week a group of more than twenty international universities will convene at the Global University Leaders Forum to discuss adopting a common approach to reducing greenhouse gas emissions. And next week, at the request of the Chinese Ministry of Education, Yale will conduct a workshop for officials from China's top thirty-four universities on environmental best practices.

As we consider the contributions that universities around the world might make in the effort to address climate change, we need to recognize that important differences in our histories and stages of development might dictate different goals. It would be unfair, for example, to expect universities in China and India to commit to reducing their greenhouse gas emissions to 10 percent below their 1990 levels, as Yale has done. Chinese universities have grown dramatically since 1990. National enrollments tripled between 1998 and 2003, and many individual campuses have more than doubled their size in the last decade. It seems unreasonable to expect institutions that have experienced two-, five-, or ten-fold increases in energy consumption since 1990 to turn back the clock. Nonetheless, these universities can still adopt ambitious programs to reduce emissions significantly below current levels.

I would hope that as universities around the world set aggressive goals for carbon reduction and pursue them successfully, our students, regardless of the degrees they earn and the career paths they choose, will leave with an appreciation of sustainability that will govern their behavior in the workplace and their lives as citizens.

But the ultimate test of our collective efforts will be in the sphere of national and international policy. Voluntary climate commitments alone will not suffice to achieve the greenhouse gas reductions needed to save the planet. At best, these voluntary efforts can help raise consciousness among citizens and demonstrate to policymakers the feasibility and cost-effectiveness of setting ambitious goals to reduce carbon emissions. It is to the broader questions of public policy that I now turn.

Public Policy

There is an emerging consensus that to keep global temperatures from rising more than 2 degrees centigrade, atmospheric concentrations of greenhouse gases need to be stabilized in the range of 450–550 parts per million, or "ppm." In a widely noted report circulated in late 2006, Sir Nicholas Stern, the distinguished British economist and Treasury official, concluded that to reach this objective, global emissions of greenhouse gases would need to be reduced somewhere between 25 and 75 percent by 2050, depending on whether we aim for 550 or 450 ppm. Even the more modest target is a tall order, because the economy will be three to four times larger in 2050 than it is today.

The magnitude of the problem highlights one important fact: the solution *must* be global. Given current levels of emissions in the United States and Europe, and the projected growth of the Chinese and Indian economies, we simply cannot make the reductions required on a global scale without the cooperation of the United States, the European Union, China, and India. If any one of these four economic powers refuses to participate in an international program to reduce carbon, we cannot succeed in stabilizing global temperatures. Any one holdout pursuing a business-as-usual strategy will make the cost of adequate global reduction prohibitive.

There is a broad consensus among economists that the most effective way to stop global warming is to ensure that decentralized decision-makers – consumers and business enterprises – pay a price for greenhouse gas emissions. This can be done either directly, by imposing a tax on carbon, or indirectly, by creating a "cap-and-trade" mechanism – that is, by imposing limits on total emissions and issuing tradable allowances. A tax or cap-and-trade scheme can be imposed either upstream (at the source where petroleum, coal, or natural gas is extracted or converted to fuel) or downstream (in power plants, factories, or motor vehicles where greenhouse gases are emitted). There is controversy about both issues, and as an economist I would enjoy exploring the nuances in depth, but in the big picture we can design either a tax or tradable allowance system more or less efficiently. And, while it matters, it does not matter that much whether we tax fuels or issue quotas at the source, or at the point of combustion and atmospheric release. What matters more is this: will we set taxes high enough or emissions quotas low enough to elicit a sufficient response? If we set a carbon tax that is too low, or set emissions "caps" that are too high, we will fail to arrest global warming, and we will fail to minimize the net economic, social, and environmental cost of rising global temperatures.

Before commenting on the big question, let me make a couple of additional observations. First, whether one sets taxes or emissions quotas, most economists favor gradualism for compelling reasons. Adjustment in the short run is much more costly than adjustment over a decade or two, when energy-inefficient capital equipment and motor vehicles can be phased out gradually in favor of more efficient alternatives. What is essential for the efficient operation of either a tax or a cap-and-trade regime is that individuals and businesses know what their taxes or allowances will be well into the future. A gradually rising tax on carbon or a gradually falling quota on carbon emissions that is credible will be sufficient to elicit socially optimal investment decisions, both in the deployment of existing technologies and in the development of new technologies. It is not necessary to impose high taxes or low quotas immediately.

Second, although there are good theoretical and practical arguments on both sides of the question, in the context of reaching international agreement, a cap-and-trade scheme may have a decisive advantage over a carbon tax. Developing countries will strongly resist a uniform global carbon tax, which they would perceive as placing upon them an unfair burden; yet different taxes across nations would distort investment incentives. By contrast, agreement on a global cap-and-trade system could take account of a country's stage of development by assigning more stringent reduction targets to developed countries and less stringent ones to developing countries. Regardless of the equitable adjustments made in distributing national quotas, as long as allowances are tradable internationally, a uniform price for carbon will result, creating a solution that would be both equitable among nations and efficient in the allocation of investment.

So, how high a carbon price do we need? To reduce annual global emissions 25 percent by 2050, the *Stern Review* finds that we would require a carbon tax (or a market price of tradable emissions allowances) in the range of $350–400 per ton of carbon by 2015, rising to more than $600 per ton by 2050. Fortunately, my Yale colleague William Nordhaus demonstrates that Stern's result should not be taken seriously; it is driven by a combination of extreme and internally inconsistent assumptions about the attitude of individuals toward risk and the rate at which the well-being of future generations is discounted. Nordhaus' own model indicates the same reduction in emissions can be achieved by a carbon price that rises gradually from $35 per ton in 2015 to about $100 per ton in 2050.

But can we be confident that a 25 percent global reduction in carbon emissions by 2050 is enough?[4] Martin Weitzman, the Harvard econo-mist, highlights this question by pointing out that we may be missing the boat if we set emissions goals and price carbon according to "expected" or "best-guess" scenarios when in fact there is a huge penumbra of un-certainty surrounding the quantitative effect of carbon emissions on temperature, and similar uncertainty surrounding the impact of rising temperature on human well-being and the economy. Perhaps, he sug-gests, we should price carbon as if we were taking out insurance against the most catastrophic scenarios, rather than paying for the "expected" or "most likely" consequences of global warming. This approach would yield a carbon tax significantly in excess of Nordhaus' range, though probably still below Stern's. The principle of gradualism, however, sug-gests that one would adjust slowly to paying high insurance premiums, and invest along the way in acquiring, through better science, knowl-edge that would permit a narrowing of the range of uncertainty.

Finally, there remains a key question: is the cost to society of reducing carbon emissions so high as to be politically infeasible? Our best eco-nomic estimates suggest that it will cost between 0.5 percent and 1 per-cent of global output to reach reduction goals in the neighborhood of 25 percent by 2050. Voluntary efforts at Yale and elsewhere are demon-strating that the low end of that cost range may be achievable. Again I ask: is a tax of 0.5 percent too big a price to pay to save the planet? I think not.

But there is an even more convincing refutation of the proposition that fighting global warming is too costly, and it is this: we have already

---

4 More recent evidence, including that discussed in the next piece in this volume, suggests that the answer is "no."

experienced something that looks very much like a carbon tax, and a very large one. In fact, we have demonstrated that we can absorb a carbon tax as high as the implausibly high one that Stern's model dictates. In 2002, the price of crude oil averaged $25 per barrel. Today it is close to $100 per barrel, an increase of $75 per barrel. If, counterfactually, the demand for crude oil were perfectly inelastic, a $600 per ton tax on carbon, the tax recommended by Stern in the year 2050, would increase the price of crude oil by about $70. And of course demand is not perfectly inelastic, so the actual effect of a carbon tax on the price of oil would be considerably below this level. A carbon tax at the more realistic level proposed by Nordhaus – $100 by 2050 – would increase the price of oil by less than $12 a barrel.

I am not saying that we already have a carbon tax, because a proper carbon tax would apply equally to coal, natural gas, and other sources of combustible carbon. But I am saying that we have over the past five years absorbed an increase in the price of oil more than six times larger than the increase we are likely to need to curtail global warming.

What have we learned from this "natural experiment" with oil prices? Let me note just two lessons. First, until the recent credit crunch in the United States – an event largely unrelated to the increase in oil prices – the world economy has prospered. Despite the fact that all are importers of oil, Europe and the United States have experienced robust growth since 2002 while China and India have shot out the lights. So it is clear that we have the capacity to absorb a carbon tax. Second, just as our economic models of climate change predict, investment in alternative energy technologies has accelerated dramatically in response to rising oil prices. Venture capital investment in clean technology in the United States has increased by a factor of eleven since 2003, and "cleantech" investment as a share of all venture capital funding has grown from just over 1 percent to 12 percent.

When the delegates to the United Nations Summit on Climate Change convene in Denmark next year, let us hope that they take inspiration from the work that is being done by universities around the globe to advance the science of climate change and its consequences, to develop new carbon-free and energy-efficient technologies, to educate the next generation to a new consciousness about sustainability, and to demonstrate to the world that reducing greenhouse gas emissions is both feasible and affordable. Let us also hope that they will absorb the lessons of the recent past and not shrink from their responsibility to reach a global agreement on carbon reduction that is meaningful and effective. Our future depends on what happens next year, here in Copenhagen.

Rising to the Challenge
of Climate Change

THIS GATHERING gives important testimony to China's concern for ensuring sustainable development for its citizens and China's growing sense of shared responsibility for the condition of our planet. China is making impressive investments to "Propel the Green Economy," most notably in the development of alternative energy technologies, but also in planning new cities in accordance with best practices of eco-friendly urban design.

The problem confronting us is even more serious than the public has understood. Earlier this month, the National Research Council of the United States — the research arm of our national academies of science, engineering, and medicine — released a new report on Climate Stabilization Targets. The report documents our best current understanding of the effects of various levels of greenhouse gas concentrations in the atmosphere on global mean temperatures, rainfall, crop yields, forest fires,

Keynote Address at the Eco-Forum Guiyang, July 30, 2010.

and sea levels. It is a disturbing picture, in part because the initial impact on temperature of reaching a certain level of atmospheric concentration, as measured in CO_2-equivalent parts per million (ppm), is only slightly more than half the eventual impact.

For example, it is expected that reaching a concentration of 550 ppm would be associated initially with a rise in global mean temperature of 1.6 degrees Celsius. But even if we were to succeed in stabilizing greenhouse gas concentrations at this level, the global mean temperature would continue to rise another 1.5 degrees over the next several centuries, until the total increase in temperature stabilized at 3.1 degrees higher than the starting point. Of course, all these numbers are surrounded with bands of uncertainty, but the basic conclusion is robust: the immediate impact of reaching a given level of atmospheric concentration is roughly half the impact that will be felt centuries later.

And here is a second disturbing conclusion: the National Research Council's assessment of the latest evidence and modeling indicates that emissions reductions in excess of 80 percent will be required to stabilize atmospheric CO_2 concentration at 550 ppm, or indeed at *any* level. Any lesser reduction in emissions would only slow—but not stabilize or reverse—the increase in atmospheric carbon concentration, and global temperatures would keep rising *forever*.

To grasp this, imagine a sink partially filled with water. Now imagine that the flow of water from the faucet is five times the volume of the water flowing through the drain. Clearly turning the faucet down a little will not suffice to keep the water level from rising, unless we turn the faucet down 80 percent, enough that the water flowing in does not exceed the water flowing out. Now equate the flow from the faucet with our best estimate of carbon emissions and the flow down the drain with our best estimate of the capacity of the land and the oceans to remove carbon from the atmosphere, and it becomes clear why, regardless of the current concentration of carbon, a reduction of at least 80 percent in emissions is needed to stop the level of atmospheric carbon, and consequently global temperatures, from rising indefinitely.

This news only heightens the tragedy of failing to come to a meaningful global agreement in Copenhagen. These efforts must continue. But, in the meantime, if we cannot act collectively, we need to act separately — not only as nations, but also as private citizens and organizations. Fortunately, on this front there is much good news. Despite the difficulty of mobilizing national governments to reach agreement, many are acting individually. As I mentioned, China's efforts in advancing clean technologies and low-carbon urban designs are notable. And so is the focus of many European nations and Japan on increasing energy efficiency.

But I want to highlight in particular how growing consciousness of the peril of global warming has influenced in encouraging directions the behavior of non-state actors, such as universities and business corporations. Many organizations are showing leadership, and their actions, taken collectively, demonstrate that we can make considerable progress toward a low carbon economy by employing best practices in the use of existing technologies, as well as by changing attitudes and behavior.

For universities, leading by example comes naturally. We are educational institutions, and what we do teaches lessons to our students. By moving aggressively to reduce the carbon footprints of our campuses, we teach our students that sustainability matters, and that they are responsible for the future of their planet. We also help to demonstrate to policymakers that significant reductions in greenhouse gas emissions are feasible and not prohibitively expensive.

Five years ago, Yale committed to reduce its carbon emissions 43 percent by the year 2020. We are on track. We have confidence that we will reach our target before 2020. Today, every one of our sister institutions in the Ivy League has adopted a greenhouse gas reduction goal, and many Chinese universities are making similar efforts to reduce their carbon footprints. The International Sustainable Campus Network and the Global University Leaders Forum are collaborating to disseminate best practices widely among the world's universities.

It should not be surprising that universities have taken the lead in voluntary efforts to reduce carbon emissions. As teaching and research institutions, universities are dedicated to public service. What is more surprising, and even more encouraging, are the efforts of for-profit business corporations in recognizing that good environmental citizenship can both save them money and win the loyalty of customers.

Many examples are highlighted in the popular recent book *Green to Gold*, written by Yale professor Daniel Esty and his colleague Andrew Winston. Esty and Winston document scores of cases where companies have been motivated to take aggressive action to not only reduce energy consumption and carbon emissions, but also to conserve water, use recycled materials, eliminate the use of toxic materials, and protect the ecosystem in other ways. Esty and Winston make the case that such actions are not only socially responsible; they are also good business. Some actions lead to considerable cost reductions, and others are rewarded in the marketplace by consumers who are increasingly willing to pay a premium for environmentally friendly products and reward companies with good environmental practices.

Some fuel-saving and carbon-reducing efforts are astonishingly simple, yet economically rewarding. For example, UPS, the world's largest package shipper, redesigned its truck delivery routes to eliminate *left turns!* By reducing idling time, the company saved over 3 million gallons of fuel annually. UPS's principal competitor, FedEx Corporation, retrofitted 95 percent of its branch offices with energy-efficient lighting and motion sensors. The savings in electricity consumption repaid the investment in less than eighteen months.

Even more interesting are the efforts of companies to position themselves as "green" and thus capitalize on a growing consumer preference for both green products and companies exhibiting good environmental practices. Some of these efforts — such as the attempt of BP to position itself as the most environmentally friendly petroleum company — have been undone by behavior that was inconsistent with the company's desired image. But other efforts have been very successful.

Perhaps most notable is the success of the Toyota Prius, the first widely marketed hybrid automobile. For a car of its size, weight, and amenities, the car carries a substantial price premium. Yet for its first few years in production, Toyota could not produce vehicles fast enough to satisfy the enormous consumer demand for a car that not only saved on fuel consumption, but also signaled that the driver cared about the condition of the planet. The success of the Prius bodes well for the potential of all-electric vehicles, which reduce carbon even more dramatically, and which will also necessarily be priced higher than vehicles of comparable size and features.

The private actions documented by Esty and Winston are inspiring, and reflect the direction of popular sentiment throughout the world. But the fact remains that we will not achieve the needed 80 percent reduction in carbon emissions without concerted action of the governments of the world's largest emitters. In the near term, imposing stricter standards on existing technologies, as China has done with electrical appliances and motor vehicles, will help. But new technologies will be absolutely necessary if we are to achieve reductions of 80 percent or more. And these new technologies are far more likely to emerge and be viable in the market if carbon is correctly priced to reflect its threat to human health and economic well-being. We need a global price on carbon.

Undoubtedly, universities and private companies will continue to demonstrate that significant near-term carbon reduction is both feasible and affordable, but their efforts only set the stage for what is ultimately needed: strong and decisive action by the governments of the world's largest economies. China and the United States must respond to this call, and lead the world to a sustainable future.

The American Research University
and the Global Agenda

I AM an economist by training and profession. Years ago, in addition to teaching survey courses in microeconomics and industrial organization, I also taught courses on such subjects as "The Political Economy of Oil" and "The International Competitiveness of U.S. Manufacturing," reflecting a long-standing interest in the politics and economics of world affairs. Now I see these issues from the dual perspective of international economist and university president.

I suspect that you are not often inclined to put universities and foreign policy into the same sentence. So let me offer you a provocative hypothesis: namely, that the American research university is a highly effective instrument of U.S. foreign policy. It would be an even more effective instrument if our political leaders understood fully what a unique and powerful asset our country has in its great universities. I am going to state the case in five parts.

First, America's power, both hard and soft, derives from the strength

Remarks at the Foreign Policy Association, New York, April 16, 2008.

of its economy, the current credit crunch notwithstanding. The strength of our economy depends in large part on our leadership in science, which in turn depends upon the strength of our research universities.

Second, the strength of our economy also derives from our capacity to innovate, which in turn depends upon the kind of education that America's top universities and liberal arts colleges provide.

Third, U.S. research universities are magnets for the most outstanding students from around the world. Those students either stay here or they go home. America wins either way. If foreign graduates stay, they strengthen the productive capacity of the U.S. economy. If they go home, they increase the capacity of their home economies, but they also serve as ambassadors for America and as advocates for openness, freedom of expression, and democracy.

Fourth, our nation's great universities are increasingly ensuring that American students gain exposure to the culture and values of another nation as a part of their educational experience. This offers the hope that our future leaders and engaged citizens will have greater global awareness in the future than in the past.

Finally, our universities have broadened the conception of what constitutes a "student." Today, we provide leadership education to specialized audiences around the world, to help them address challenges to global political and economic stability, public health, and the environment.

Let me discuss each of these points in turn.

Leadership in Science

For decades, America's competitive advantage in global markets has derived from its capacity to innovate – to develop and introduce new products, processes, and services. That capacity depends in large part on America's leadership in science, and the principal locus of scientific advance has been our research universities.

The emergence of universities as America's primary machine for scientific advance did not come about by accident. Rather, it was the product of a wise and farsighted national science policy, set forth in an important 1945 report that established the framework for an unprecedented and heavily subsidized system in support of scientific research that has propelled the American economy. The system entailed the federal government assuming responsibility for funding basic research, the colocation of advanced research and education in universities, and allocation of research funds by peer review. This system of organizing science has been an extraordinary success, scientifically and economically.

Oddly enough, for political and cultural reasons, no other nation has successfully imitated the U.S. system of supporting basic science, the source from which all commercially oriented applied research and development ultimately flows. In Europe, too much research has been concentrated in free-standing institutes rather than universities, divorcing cutting-edge research from training the next generation of industrial scientists and engineers. And, in the U.K. as well as continental Europe and Japan, most research funding has been allocated by block grants to universities or departments, rather than by the intensely competitive process of peer-reviewed grants to individuals and research groups. As a result, our lead in science has been maintained. Even today, more than 30 percent of scientific publications worldwide are authored in the U.S., and nearly half the world's Nobel Prizes in science go to Americans.

Our competitive advantage in emerging industries based on science — such as computers in the 1960s, software in the 1990s, and biotechnology today — should not be taken for granted. Yet federal funding in support of basic research has waxed and waned. The budget of the National Institutes of Health was doubled between 1998 and 2003, a 14 percent annual rate of growth. For the past five years, the NIH budget has grown at an annual rate of less than 2 percent, failing to keep up with inflation. This means that much of the young talent we trained during the boom cannot get funding today. What we need to succeed as a nation is a steady, predictable growth in basic research, at the rate of long-term average growth in GDP. If we don't do this, we are likely to lose our wide lead in biomedical technology, and we will fail to establish ourselves as the world leader in other major areas of emerging importance — such as alternative energy technologies.

Educating Innovators

Our hard and soft power in foreign affairs depends on the strength of our economy. And the strength of our economy depends not only on having scientific leadership, but also on our national capacity to translate cutting-edge science into commercially viable technologies. This capacity depends in turn on two principal factors: the availability of financial capital and an abundance of innovative, entrepreneurial human capital. Our highly decentralized financial system, despite its endemic cyclicality of which we are today painfully aware, has unique advantages in encouraging investment in innovation. Funding for start-up companies in the United States is more easily available, and more adequately supported by value-added services, than anywhere else in the world.

And, thanks to the kind of higher education we provide, the human capital required for innovation is more abundant and more effective in the United States than anywhere else in the world. Why? Because, at our best colleges and universities, we educate students to be creative, flexible, and adaptive problem-solvers, capable of innovation and leadership in science, business, and the professions. We are told constantly that China and India are training more engineers than we are. And it is true that we could and should invest more heavily in science, math, and engineering education at all levels to ensure that our graduates have the technical capacity to succeed. But if you look closely at China and India, you will see that their aspiration is to educate students who are more like ours — students with the capacity to think creatively and independently.

For the past four summers, I have led a workshop for the leadership teams of China's top universities. The number-one topic on their agenda is how to reform curriculum and pedagogy to reflect the best practices of American universities. Why? Because they see in the products of U.S. education, including those U.S.-educated Chinese who are coming to dominate their own faculties, greater creativity and an enlarged capacity for innovation. China's political leaders are encouraging this effort at university reform, because they recognize that creativity and the capacity to innovate are characteristics that China will need in order to compete when they can no longer rely on a steady stream of low-cost labor migrating from the countryside to industrial employment. It is a sad fact that China's leaders have a more sophisticated understanding of the decisive advantages of U.S. universities than our own political leaders.

Educating International Students

Nearly one-quarter of all students who leave their home countries for higher education abroad come to the United States, and our nation's share of the very best students is much larger. Only the finest universities in the United Kingdom offer serious competition to the best institutions in the United States, although in recent years Australia and Singapore have made significant efforts to compete for strong international students. These countries made substantial gains in the first years after the passage of the Patriot Act, when failure of the Departments of State and Homeland Security to adjust rapidly to new requirements rendered many thousands of students unable to secure visas in time for the start of the academic year.

The problem with student visas has now largely been fixed, thanks to a felicitous high-level intervention. But it is seldom appreciated in policy circles how much America gains from this inflow of international students. Nearly half of America's Nobel Prize winners in science have been foreign born. In the current debate about immigration policy, almost all the public attention focuses on the inflow of low-income immigrants from Mexico and the Caribbean. Outside Silicon Valley, Seattle, and Route 128, we hear too little about the difficulty our most technologically sophisticated companies are having in attracting sufficient highly skilled scientists and engineers. Much of the outsourcing of R&D undertaken by high-tech firms is not driven by cost considerations, as is the outsourcing in manufacturing, back office work, and call centers. Instead, much R&D outsourcing is forced by the absence of qualified, highly skilled engineers and scientists with graduate degrees.

The annual quota for H-1B visas, covering foreign students who seek to remain and work in the U.S. after graduation, has been fixed for years at 85,000, and the annual allocation is typically exhausted within days at the start of each year. Recently, a new rule has extended the period of stay under an H-1B to twenty-nine instead of twelve months. But the number of visas to be allocated has not increased. The demands of high-tech industry have been lost in the contentious debate about illegal aliens and the immigration of unskilled workers.

There is no doubt that our nation would benefit from retaining more graduate engineers and scientists, and for them there's a simple solution: scrap the H-1B visa and staple a green card to the diploma!

As I mentioned before, our universities serve the nation well not only by educating those who stay in our country, but also by educating those who return to their home country. It is true that in some cases, we would gain even more by retaining highly skilled graduates. But it is also true that those who return home typically serve as ambassadors for American values, or at least they understand them. I have already cited one example: the pressures for curriculum reform and critical thinking in China, along with pressures for greater freedom of expression on university campuses, are coming in large measure from those educated in the

United States. Again and again, I encounter international students at Yale who tell me that they have been astounded by the degree of openness and intellectual freedom they find in America. And when I travel abroad, I see senior leaders in influential positions whose views of the world have been transformed by their educational experience in the United States.

Sending Our Students Abroad

Increasingly, American universities are also encouraging domestic undergraduates to spend time in another country. Traditional junior-year abroad study programs remain widely available. They attract a large fraction of students at institutions like Dartmouth and Middlebury, but only a modest fraction of undergraduates at Yale. We have responded by offering every undergraduate at least one international study or internship opportunity either during the academic year or during the summer. And we provide the financial resources to make it possible. By mobilizing our alumni around the world, we have created a superb infrastructure of serious summer work internships in seventeen cities: Shanghai, Hong Kong, Singapore, Delhi, Accra, Cape Town, Kampala, Athens, Brussels, Budapest, Istanbul, London, Madrid, Buenos Aires, João Pessoa, Montreal, and Monterrey. In addition we send hundreds abroad every summer for immersion language courses or Yale summer school courses taught at partner institutions. We expect that an increasing number of institutions will follow our lead in making an overseas experience available to every student, and eventually in making an overseas experience a requirement for the bachelor's degree.

I believe that a twenty-first-century liberal education requires not simply the capacity to think critically and independently, but also the capacity to understand how people of different cultures and values think and behave. The world has grown smaller and nations have become more interdependent. Whatever profession they choose, today's students are likely to have global careers and deal regularly with collaborators or competitors who see the world differently. To be adequately prepared for such careers, exposure to another culture is necessary. And a single meaningful encounter with cross-cultural differences in one's formative years will typically make it possible to learn more easily from subsequent encounters with other cultures later in life.

I also believe that providing American students with a meaningful overseas experience is the best way to escape the insularity and parochialism that has too often influenced American foreign policy. With international exposure, our students will not only become better professionals, but better citizens. By getting more U.S. students abroad, our colleges and universities will create a more informed citizenry and one capable of thinking about foreign policy issues with greater sensitivity and intelligence.

Educating Leaders to Advance the Global Agenda

Our universities serve not only those students who enroll full-time in courses of study leading to undergraduate, graduate, and professional degrees, they are also increasingly engaged in the provision of short-term executive education. Many institutions, notably the Kennedy School at Harvard, make a substantive contribution to U.S. foreign policy by running short-term and even semester-length courses for foreign government officials. Recently, Yale has initiated a series of multidisciplinary programs for senior governmental officials from China, India, and Japan. To cover effectively the complexity of the most important global issues, we draw upon faculty from throughout the University – from our professional schools of law, management, forestry and environmental studies, and public health, as well as our departments of economics, political science, and history. The "students" in these programs typically

THE UNIVERSITY AS GLOBAL CITIZEN

have the rank of vice minister or, in the case of India and Japan, member of parliament.

Educational programs such as these have very high impact, because we are working with students who already occupy positions of significant power and influence. Even at America's finest universities, only a small fraction of our regularly enrolled students turn out to have a significant influence on the affairs of a nation or the world.

Such high-level programs have an effect similar to that of "track two" diplomacy, or informal interaction among senior government officials. Only here the contact is not government-to-government, but U.S. experts-to-foreign governments. Even if the views of our academic experts do not always align with the position of our government, the foreign ministers and parliamentarians who attend these programs leave with a deeper understanding of American perspectives.

Conclusion

Let me recapitulate. I have argued that America's universities are a highly effective instrument of U.S. foreign policy, because they:

- Have given America decisive leadership in science;
- Educate students to become leaders with the capacity to innovate;
- Educate international students who strengthen our nation by staying here or serving as ambassadors when they return home;
- Give U.S. students a deeper understanding of foreign nations and cultures; and
- Prepare international leaders to tackle the global agenda.

I hope that I have convinced you.

THE DEVELOPMENT OF
HIGHER EDUCATION IN ASIA

The Rise of Asia's Universities

I STAND before you this evening as a representative of the third oldest university in the United States, little more than 50 miles from the two oldest universities in the English-speaking world. Today, the strongest British and American universities — such as Oxford, Cambridge, and Yale, not to mention Harvard, Stanford, Berkeley, MIT, University College London, and Imperial College London — call forth worldwide admiration and respect for their leadership in research and education. Sitting atop the global league tables, these institutions set the standard that others at home and abroad seek to emulate; they define the concept of "world-class university." They excel in the advancement of human knowledge of nature and culture; they provide the finest training to the next generation of scholars; and they provide outstanding undergraduate and professional education for those who will emerge as leaders in all walks of life.

Seventh annual lecture of the Higher Education Policy Institute, delivered at the Royal Society, London, February 1, 2010. I am grateful to Thomas Kaplan for excellent assistance in research and many helpful editorial suggestions. A revised version of this lecture was published as an article in *Foreign Affairs*, May/June 2010, pp. 63–75.

But, as we all know at this, the beginning of the twenty-first century, the East is rising. The rapid economic development of Asia since the Second World War — starting with Japan, South Korea, and Taiwan, extending to Hong Kong and Singapore, and finally taking hold powerfully in mainland China and India — has altered the balance of power in the global economy and hence in geopolitics. The rising nations of the East all recognize the importance of an educated workforce as a means to economic growth, and they understand the impact of research in driving innovation and competitiveness. In the 1960s, '70s, and '80s, the higher education agenda in Asia's early developers — Japan, South Korea, and Taiwan — was first and foremost to increase the fraction of their populations provided with postsecondary education. Their initial focus was on expanding the number of institutions and their enrollments, and impressive results were achieved.

Today, the later and much larger developing nations of Asia — China and India — have an even more ambitious agenda. Both these emerging powers seek to expand the capacity of their systems of higher education, and China has done so dramatically since 1998. But they also aspire simultaneously to create a limited number of "world-class" universities to take their places among the best. This is an audacious agenda, but China, in particular, has the will and resources that make it feasible. This aspiration is shared not only by other nations in Asia but also by certain resource-rich nations in the Middle East.

Consider the following recent developments:

- In the Gulf States, hundreds of millions of dollars are being spent to open branches of top U.S. and European universities such as Cornell in Qatar and the Sorbonne in Abu Dhabi.
- This past autumn, the new King Abdullah University of Science and Technology opened in Saudi Arabia. Its

$10 billion endowment exceeds that of all but five American universities.

- In Singapore, planning is under way to build a new public university of Technology and Design, and a new American-style liberal arts college affiliated with the National University.
- In China, the nine universities that receive the most supplemental government funding to enhance their global competitiveness recently self-identified as the C9 — China's Ivy League.
- In India, the Education Ministry recently announced its intention to build 14 new comprehensive universities of "world-class" stature.

This evening I want to discuss the motivations for attempting to build world-class universities, the practical obstacles that must be overcome, and the potential consequences of success. Because the circumstances in the Middle East are very different, I will limit my attention to Asia.

There are other important trends that are changing the global landscape of higher education: the rapidly increasing flow of students across borders, the expanding number of satellite campuses being established by U.S. and European universities, the emergence of for-profit providers of both on-site and distance education, and the urgent need to strengthen higher education in the world's poorest nations, most notably in sub-Saharan Africa. I lack the time this evening to cover this entire terrain, so I shall confine myself to analyzing the prospects for and the potential consequences of developing world-class universities in Asia.

Asian Ambitions: Expanding Access to Higher Education

In the early stages of postwar Asian development, it was well understood that expanded access to higher education was a requisite for sustained economic growth. A literate, well-trained labor force was a key ingredient in transforming Japan and South Korea over the course of the past half century, first from agricultural to manufacturing economies and subsequently from low- to high-skill manufacturing. With substantial government investment, the capacity of the tertiary educational systems in both countries expanded rapidly. The gross enrollment rate, the ratio of students enrolled in tertiary education to the size of the age cohort, rose from 9 percent in Japan in 1960 to 42 percent by the mid-1990s. In South Korea, the increase was even more dramatic, from 5 percent in 1960 to just over 50 percent in the mid-1990s.[1]

In this earlier period, China and India lagged far behind. By the mid-1990s only 5 percent of college-age Chinese attended college, putting China on par with Bangladesh, Botswana, and Swaziland. In India, despite a postwar effort to create first a set of national comprehensive universities and later the elite and very small Indian Institutes of Technology, the gross enrollment rate stood at 7 percent in the 1990s.[2]

Speaking at the 100th anniversary celebration of Peking University in 1998, China's president, Jiang Zemin, publicly set his country's sights on greatly expanding its system of higher education, and his administration made it happen – faster than ever before in human history. By 2006, China was spending 1.5 percent of its GDP on higher education, nearly triple the share of GDP it was spending a decade earlier.[3]

The results of this investment have been staggering. Over the decade following Jiang Zemin's declaration, the number of institutions of higher

1 UNESCO, *1975 Statistical Yearbook* (Paris: UNESCO, 1976), p. 107; and World Bank EdStats, http://www.worldbank.org/education/edstats.
2 *Ibid.*
3 Tables 2-1 and 20-37, National Bureau of Statistics, *China Statistical Yearbook 2008*, and Tables 2-9 and 18-37, National Bureau of Statistics, *China Statistical Yearbook 1997.*

education in China more than doubled, from 1,022 to 2,263.[4] Meanwhile, the number of Chinese who enroll in college each year has quintupled — rising from 1 million students in 1997 to more than 5.5 million students in 2007.[5]

This expansion in capacity is without precedent. China has built the largest higher education sector in the world in merely a decade's time.[6] In fact, the increase in China's postsecondary enrollment since the turn of the millennium exceeds the total postsecondary enrollment in the United States.[7]

China still has a long way to go to achieve its aspirations concerning access to higher education. Despite the enormous surge, China's gross enrollment rate for tertiary education stands at 23 percent, compared to 58 percent in Japan, 59 percent in the U.K., and 82 percent in the United States.[8] Expansion has slowed since 2006, owing to concerns that enrollments have outstripped the capacity of faculty to maintain quality in some institutions. The student-teacher ratio has roughly doubled over the past decade.[9] But enrollment will continue to rise as more teachers are prepared, because the Chinese leaders are keenly aware of the importance of a well-educated labor force for economic development.

India's achievement to date has not been nearly so impressive, but its

4 Table 20-3, National Bureau of Statistics, *China Statistical Yearbook 2009*.
5 Table 20-6, National Bureau of Statistics, *China Statistical Yearbook 1999*, and Table 20-2, *China Statistical Yearbook 2008*.
6 Zhao Litao and Sheng Sixin, "China's 'Great Leap' in Higher Education," Background Brief No. 394, East Asian Institute, National University of Singapore, 24 July 2008, p. i.
7 UNESCO Institute for Statistics, http://stats.uis.unesco.org.
8 UNESCO, *2009 Global Education Digest*, p. 128–137.
9 Wu Bin and Zheng Yongnian, "Expansion of Higher Education in China: Challenges and Implications," China Policy Institute, University of Nottingham, February 2008, p. 11.

aspirations are no less ambitious. India is already the world's largest democracy. In two decades, it will be the most populated country in the planet, and by 2050, if growth can be sustained, it could become the second largest economy in the world. To sustain that growth, India's Education Minister, Kapil Sibal, aims to increase his country's gross enrollment ratio in postsecondary education from 12 to 30 percent by 2020. Sibal's goal translates to an increase of 40 million students in Indian universities over the next decade — perhaps more than can feasibly be achieved, but even getting halfway there would be a remarkable accomplishment.

Asian Ambitions: Building World-Class Universities

Having made tremendous progress in expanding access to higher education, the leading nations of Asia have now set their sights on an even more challenging goal: building universities that stand in competition with the finest in the world. This is a tall order. World-class universities achieve their status by assembling scholars and scientists who are global leaders in their fields. This takes time. It took centuries for Harvard and Yale to achieve parity with Oxford and Cambridge, and more than half a century for Stanford and the University of Chicago (both founded in 1892) to achieve world-class reputations. The only Asian university to rank in the top 25 in global league tables, the University of Tokyo, was founded in 1877.

Why do China, India, Singapore, and South Korea aspire so openly to elevating some of their universities to this exalted status? For two reasons, I would submit. First, these rapidly developing nations recognize the importance of university-based scientific research in driving economic growth, especially since the end of the Second World War. Second, world-class universities provide the ideal context for educating graduates for careers in science, industry, government, and civil society who have the intellectual breadth and critical-thinking skills to solve problems, to innovate, and to lead.

Let me expand on each of these points. Although China and India remain at a stage of development where they are able to compete effectively by deploying low-cost labor in manufacturing, their surplus agricultural labor will eventually be absorbed in cities — as it was in Japan and South Korea — and wages will begin to rise. At this stage, it will become impossible to sustain rapid economic growth without innovation, without being early to market with new products and new services, many of them the fruits of applied research based on underlying scientific advance.

To oversimplify, consider the following puzzle: Japan grew much more rapidly than America from 1950 to 1990, as its surplus labor was absorbed into industry, and much more slowly than America thereafter. Now consider whether Japan would have grown so slowly if Microsoft, Netscape, Apple, and Google had been Japanese companies. I think not. It was innovation based on science that propelled the U.S. to more rapid growth than Japan during the two decades prior to the crash of 2008. It was Japan's failure to innovate that caused it to lag behind.

The emerging Asian nations recognize, very explicitly in their national policy documents and plans, the link between building indigenous research capacity and economic growth in a post-industrial knowledge economy. And they also recognize that university-based research is the most effective driver of scientific discovery and ultimately, both directly and indirectly, of economically relevant new technologies. Hence derives their aspiration for research universities capable of working on the scientific and technological frontier — and not a moment too soon, in my opinion. At their current pace of urbanization, China will begin to lose its labor cost advantages in manufacturing in about two decades, and India will reach the same point a decade later. This gives both nations enough time to make significant progress in building the capacity to compete effectively on the frontier of innovation.

But it takes more than research capacity alone to develop a nation. It takes well-educated citizens of broad perspective and dynamic entrepreneurs capable of independent and original thinking. This is the second factor motivating Asia's ambition to build world-class universities. The leaders of China, in particular, have been very explicit in recognizing that two elements are missing in their universities – multidisciplinary breadth and the cultivation of critical thinking. Asian higher education, like its European counterpart but unlike America, has been traditionally highly specialized. Students pick a discipline or a profession at age eighteen and study little else. And, unlike the norms in elite European and American universities, pedagogy in China, Japan, and South Korea relies heavily on rote learning. Traditionally, students are passive listeners, and they rarely challenge each other or their professors in classes. Pedagogy focuses on the mastery of content, not on the development of the capacity for independent and critical thinking. The traditional Asian approaches to curriculum and pedagogy may be highly functional for training line engineers and mid-level government officials, but they are perhaps less well suited to educating elites for leadership and innovation.

It is curious that while American and British politicians worry that Asia, and China in particular, is training more scientists and engineers than we are, the Chinese and others in Asia are worrying that their students lack the independence and creativity to drive the innovation that will be necessary to sustain economic growth in the long run. They fear that specialization makes their graduates narrow and traditional Asian pedagogy makes them unimaginative. Thus, they aspire to strengthen their top universities by revising both curriculum and pedagogy.

Requisites for World-Class Universities: Research

Having discussed what is motivating the Asian quest for world-class universities, let us turn next to what needs to be accomplished. So the first question is: what does it take to build universities capable of world-class status in research? First and foremost, it requires the capacity to attract scholars and scientists of the highest quality. In the sciences, this means first-class research facilities, adequate funding to support research, and competitive salaries and benefits. China is making substantial investments on all three fronts. Shanghai's top universities — Fudan, Shanghai Jiaotong, and Tongji — have each developed whole new campuses within the past few years, with outstanding research facilities, located close to industrial partners. Research funding has grown in parallel with the expansion of enrollment, and Chinese universities now compete much more effectively for faculty talent. In the 1990s, only 10 percent of Chinese who received a Ph.D. in science and engineering in the United States returned home.[10] That number is now rising, and, increasingly, China has been able to repatriate mid-career scholars and scientists from tenured positions in the United States and the United Kingdom, who are attracted by the greatly improved working conditions and the opportunities to participate in China's rise. India, too, is beginning to have more success in drawing on its diaspora, but it has yet to make the kind of investment that China has made in improving facilities, research funding, and extra compensation for faculty of distinction.

Beyond the material conditions required to attract faculty, building a national capacity for first-class research can be greatly facilitated by an efficient and effective system of allocating research funding. The underlying principles for creating such a system were brilliantly articulated in a 1945 report entitled *Science: The Endless Frontier,* by Vannevar Bush, the Science Adviser to President Truman. The report acknowledges that the discoveries in basic science are ultimately the basis for developments in

---

10 National Science Foundation, *Asia's Rising Science and Technology Strength: Comparative Indicators for Asia, the European Union, and the United States,* 2007, p. 7.

industrial technology, but it notes that the economic gains from advances in basic science often do not accrue for decades and often yield results in applications that were entirely unanticipated at the time of the scientific breakthrough. When the properties of coherent light were first identified in the late 1950s, no one imagined that lasers would become useful in eye surgery decades later. Because the full economic benefit of a breakthrough in pure science can rarely be captured by the original inventor, private enterprises will typically have insufficient incentive to make many socially productive investments. Government must take the lead.

Bush's report established the framework for a national system of support for scientific research founded in three principles, which still govern today. First, the federal government bears the primary responsibility for funding basic science. Second, universities – rather than government-run laboratories, non-teaching research institutions, or private industry – are the primary institutions responsible for carrying out this government-funded research. Third, although the government determines the total amount of funding available in different fields of science, specific projects and programs are not assessed on political or commercial grounds, but through an intensely competitive process of peer review in which independent experts judge proposals on their scientific merit alone.

This system has been an extraordinary success, and for a number of reasons. It has the benefit of exposing postgraduate scientists-in-training – even those who do not end up pursuing academic careers in the long run – to the most cutting-edge techniques and areas of research. It allows undergraduates to witness meaningful science firsthand, rather than merely reading about the last decade's milestones in a textbook. And it means the best research gets funded – not the research proposed by the most senior members of a department's faculty, or by those who are politically well-connected.

This has not been the typical scheme for facilitating research in the

East. Historically, most scientific research in East Asia has taken place apart from universities – in research institutes and government laboratories. And in Japan, South Korea, and China, funding has primarily been directed toward applied research and development, with a very small share of total R&D funding devoted to basic science. In China, for instance, only about 5 percent of R&D spending is aimed at basic research, compared to 10 to 30 percent in most OECD countries.[11] Expressed as a share of GDP, the U.S. spends seven times as much on basic research as China.[12] Moreover, the use of peer review for grant funding in East Asia is inconsistent at best, completely absent at worst. Japan has historically placed the bulk of its research resources in the hands of its most senior investigators. Despite acknowledging several years ago that a greater share of research funding should be subject to peer review, only 14 percent of the government's spending on non-defense-related research in 2008 was subject to competitive review, compared to 73 percent in the United States.[13,14]

On the other hand, there is no doubt Asian governments have made increasing research and development a priority in recent years. R&D spending in China has increased rapidly over the last two decades, rising from 0.6 percent of the country's GDP in 1995 to 1.3 percent of GDP in 2005.[15] That is still significantly below the advanced OECD countries, but it is likely to keep climbing. The Chinese government has set a goal

11 OECD, *Main Science and Technology Indicators,* 2009, pp. 25, 29.
12 National Science Foundation, *Science and Engineering Indicators 2008,* p. 4-41.
13 Ministry of Education, Culture, Sports, Science and Technology, *White Paper on Science and Technology 2009,* pp. 116–117, 200; and National Science Foundation, *Science and Engineering Indicators 2010,* pp. 4-22 to 4-27.
14 For the purposes of this comparison, I consider federal research funding appropriated to the National Science Foundation, the Department of Energy, and the National Institutes of Health as being subject to competitive review.
15 OECD, *Main Science and Technology Indicators,* 2009, p. 25.

of increasing R&D intensity to 2 percent of GDP by 2010 and 2.5 percent of GDP by 2020.[16] And there is some evidence of the payoff from increased research funding. To give one benchmark, from 1995 to 2005, Chinese scholars more than quadrupled the number of articles they published in leading scientific and engineering journals. Only the U.S., the U.K., Germany, and Japan account for more publications.[17]

Requisites for World-Class Universities: Education

Having described what it takes to build world-class capacity in research, let us now turn our attention to what is required to transform education. As I mentioned earlier, Asia's aspiration is to develop graduates of elite universities who have a broad, multidisciplinary perspective on the world and who have the capacity to innovate. This has led officials in China, Singapore, and South Korea, in particular, to look closely at America's leading universities, which differ from Asian norms in both the structure of the curriculum and the practice of pedagogy.

Asian leaders are increasingly attracted to the American model of undergraduate curriculum, which typically provides students with two years to explore a variety of subjects before choosing a single subject on which to concentrate during their final two years. There are two principal rationales for this approach. First, significant exposure to multiple disciplines gives students alternative perspectives on the world, which both allows them to function more effectively in their chosen field and better prepares them to encounter new and unexpected problems. The second rationale is that students are in a better position to choose a specialization at age twenty than at age eighteen. I would not press these

16 OECD, *Reviews of Innovation Policy: China,* 2008, p. 111.
17 National Science Foundation, *Science and Engineering Indicators 2008,* pp. 5–38.

arguments too far in this forum, since it has not been my experience that the graduates of Oxford and Cambridge are too narrow by virtue of having specialized at age eighteen. But I have no doubt about the virtues of the American model. At its best, it produces strong results by effectively broadening the perspective of graduates.

That world-class universities must cultivate independent, critical thinking is a much less controversial point. In today's knowledge economy, no less than in the nineteenth century when the philosophy of liberal education was articulated by Cardinal Newman, it is not subject-specific knowledge, but the ability to assimilate new information and solve problems is the most important characteristic of a well-educated person. The Yale Report of 1828, a document with enormous influence on American undergraduate education, distinguished between the "discipline" and the "furniture" of the mind. Mastering a specific body of knowledge — acquiring the "furniture" — is of little permanent value in a rapidly changing world. Students who aspire to be leaders in business, or medicine, or law, or government, or in the academy need the "discipline" of mind — the ability to adapt to constantly changing circumstances, confront new facts, and find creative ways to solve problems.

The cultivation of such habits requires a pedagogy that encourages students to be more than passive recipients of information; rather, they must learn to think for themselves, and learn to structure an argument and defend it, or modify it in the face of new information or valid criticism. The Oxford-Cambridge tutorial is perhaps the paradigm of such pedagogy. But the tutorial system is almost unthinkably labor-intensive in an Asian, let alone an American, context. The American substitute has been the interactive seminar, where students are encouraged to take and defend positions in small groups, and to challenge, rather than blindly accept, the instructor's point of view. Even where numbers dictate reliance on large lecture courses, small discussion sections serve as a complement to the lectures. Examinations in top U.S. universities rarely call for a recitation of facts; they call upon students to solve problems they have not encountered before, or to analyze two sides of an argument and state their own position.

In Asia's quest to build world-class universities, there has already been dramatic movement in the direction of developing an American-style curriculum. Peking University introduced Yuanpei Honors College in 2001, a pilot program that immerses a select group of the most gifted Chinese students in a liberal arts environment. These students live together and sample a wide variety of subjects for two years before choosing a major field of study. Yonsei University in South Korea has opened a liberal arts college with a similar curriculum on its campus, and the National University of Singapore has created a University Scholars program in which students do extensive work outside their disciplinary or professional specialization.

For the past six years, the presidents, vice presidents, and party secretaries of China's top universities, those singled out for special support by the government, have met annually with Yale faculty and administrators in a weeklong workshop to learn about the practices of American institutions and share their own experiences with the reform of curriculum, faculty recruitment, and pedagogy. Although I do not claim a direct causal linkage, their progress toward curricular reform has been astonishing. At Fudan University, all students now take a common, multi-disciplinary curriculum during their first year before proceeding with the study of their chosen discipline or profession. At Nanjing University, students are no longer required to choose a subject when they apply for admission; they may instead choose among more than 60 general education courses in their first year before deciding on a specialization.

Changing pedagogy is much more difficult than changing curriculum. It takes increased resources to offer classes with smaller enrollments, but it also requires the faculty to adopt new methods. This is a huge challenge in China, Japan, and South Korea, where traditional Asian pedagogy prevails. It is much less of a concern in India and Singapore, where the legacy of British influence has created a professorate much more comfortable with engaging students interactively. The Chinese, in particular, are eager to tackle this challenge, but they recognize that the key to changing pedagogy is the growing representation in the professorate of those who have studied abroad and been exposed to methods of instruction that do not rely on rote learning. Increasing exchange opportunities, whereby Asian students study in the West and Western students spend time in Asian universities, will also help to accelerate the transformation.

Prospects for Success

As we can see, developing world-class universities in Asia will take more than money and determination. To create world-class capacity in research, resources must not only be abundant, they must also be allocated on the basis of scholarly and scientific merit, rather than on the basis of seniority or political influence. To create world-class capacity in education, the curriculum must be broadened and pedagogy transformed. These are all problems that can be solved with sufficient leadership and political will.

Another requisite for success is focus. Not every university can or needs be world-class. The experiences of the U.S., the U.K., and Germany are instructive. In the U.S. and U.K., higher education is a differentiated system of many types of institutions, of which the comprehensive research university is merely one. And within the set of comprehensive universities, government support for research is allocated chiefly on the basis of merit, which allows some institutions to prosper while others lag. In the U.S., fundraising reinforces this tendency to differentiation. Success breeds success, and, for the most part, the strongest institutions attract the most philanthropy. In Germany, by contrast, government policy has deliberately constrained institutions from achieving distinction. By opening enrollment, allowing the student-faculty ratio to rise everywhere, isolating the most eminent researchers in separate institutes, but otherwise distributing resources on the basis of equity rather than merit, the German government has destroyed the worldwide distinction its best universities once held. Only recently has Germany decided to focus resources on three universities in particular in order to make them more globally competitive.

Japan and South Korea have learned this lesson. Both have flagship national universities that are well supported: the University of Tokyo and Seoul National University. And in Japan at least two other public universities, Kyoto and Osaka, are not far behind Tokyo and well above the rest. China has this message, too. In 1998, it identified seven universities for disproportionate investment: Peking, Tsinghua, Fudan, Shanghai Jiaotong, Nanjing, Zhejiang, and Xi'an Jiaotong. And even within that set, the government has drawn distinctions, concentrating national resources on Peking and Tsinghua Universities in an effort to propel them into the worldwide top twenty. The Shanghai-based institutions — Fudan and Jiaotong — are making nearly comparable investments, thanks to generous supplemental funding from the Shanghai government.

India is the anomalous case. In the 1950s and '60s, it focused resources on establishing five Indian Institutes of Technology. These, and the ten more added in the past two decades, are outstanding institutions for educating engineers, but they have not been globally competitive in research. And India has made no systematic effort to raise the status of any of its fourteen comprehensive national universities, which are severely underfunded.

The current Minister of Education is determined to create world-class comprehensive universities. But the egalitarian forces that dominate India's robust democracy threaten to constrain the prospects for excellence, by spreading funding too thin and allowing considerations of social justice to trump meritocracy in selecting students and faculty.

Two years ago, the government announced that it would create thirty new world-class universities, one for each of India's states, clearly an unrealistic ambition. The number was subsequently reduced to fourteen, one for each state that does not yet have a comprehensive university, but even this target seems excessive, compared with China's focus on seven, and special focus on two within the seven.

Given the extraordinary achievements of Indian scholars throughout the diaspora, the human resources for building world-class universities at home are surely present. But it remains to be seen whether India can tolerate the large discrepancies in faculty compensation that would be necessary to attract leading scholars from around the world. Consequently, an alternative and potentially more promising strategy being pursued by the government is to allow the establishment of foreign universities and to create conditions under which private universities — foreign or domestic — can flourish.

In one respect, however, India has a powerful advantage over China, at least for now. The freedom of faculty to pursue their intellectual interests wherever they may lead, and the freedom of students and faculty alike to express and thus test their most heretical and unconventional thoughts — these freedoms are an indispensible feature of a truly world-class comprehensive university. It may be possible to achieve world-class stature in the sciences while constraining freedom of expression in politics, the social sciences, and the humanities. Some of the Soviet Academies achieved such stature in mathematics and physics during the Cold War. But no comprehensive university has done so in modern times.

There is one other potential obstacle to success in China, which is currently the subject of intense discussion: the unique way in which university leadership responsibilities are divided between each institution's President and its Communist Party Secretary, who serves as Chair of the University Council. Often the two leaders work together very effectively as a team. But there are concerns that the structure of decision-making limits a President's ability to achieve his or her academic goals, since the appointment of senior administrators — vice presidents and deans — is in the hands of the University Council, chaired by the Party Secretary, rather than the President. The issue of university governance is currently under review by China's Ministry of Education.

Conclusion: A Positive-Sum Game

The rise of Asia's universities is a natural manifestation of the more general phenomenon of globalization. As barriers to the flow of people, goods, and information have come down, and as the economic development process proceeds, the nations of Asia have increasing access to the human, physical, and informational resources needed to create institutions at the highest level of excellence. If the emerging nations of Asia concentrate their growing resources on a handful of institutions, tap a worldwide pool of talent, and embrace freedom of expression and freedom of inquiry, they have every prospect of success in building world-class universities. It will not happen overnight; it will take decades. But it may happen faster than ever before.

How should we in the West regard this prospect — as a threat or as an opportunity? I would argue forcefully that competition in education, like the phenomenon of globalization itself, is a positive sum game.

Consider the following example. One of our most distinguished geneticists at Yale and members of his team now split their time between laboratories in New Haven and Fudan University in Shanghai. Another distinguished Yale professor, a plant biologist, has a similar arrangement at Peking University. In both cases, the Chinese provide abundant space and research staff to support the efforts of Yale scientists, while collaboration with the Yale scientists upgrades the skills of young Chinese professors and graduate students. Both sides benefit.

The same argument can be made about the flow of students and the exchange of ideas. As globalization has underscored the importance of cross-cultural experience, the frequency of student exchanges has multiplied. As Asia's universities improve, so do the experiences of students who participate in exchange programs. Everyone benefits from the exchange of ideas, just as everyone benefits from the free exchange of goods and services.

Finally, increasing the quality of education around the world translates into better-informed and more productive citizens. The fate of the planet depends on our ability to collaborate across borders to solve society's most pressing problems – the persistence of poverty, the prevalence of disease, the proliferation of nuclear weapons, the shortage of water, and the danger of global warming. Having better educated citizens and leaders can only help.

Reform, Innovation, and Economic Growth in Japan

MANY REASONS are given for the slowdown of the Japanese economy that began in 1990. Some argue that macroeconomic policy was responsible; others cite a precariously weak financial system. As a microeconomist and longtime student of industrial innovation, I prefer another explanation. Although Japan led the world in process engineering and product quality control, its scientific and financial infrastructure did not provide Japanese companies and entrepreneurs with adequate fuel to drive the kind of radical product innovation in science-based industries that was responsible for the success of the United States economy in the 1990s.

Today, Japan is in the midst of restructuring the funding of its university-based scientific research, and it has taken a dramatically new approach to the governance of its universities. I believe that these changes, if carried through with sufficient vigor, hold great promise for strengthening the innovative capacity of the Japanese economy. In these remarks, I would like to explain why I hold this belief, an explanation

Remarks at the Japan National Press Club, November 29, 2005.

that will require first an examination of how universities function in the United States as a steady and reliable engine of innovation and economic growth.

It would come as a surprise to most Americans that Japan's universities and research-funding institutions are engaged in a period of intense reform. By standard measures of educational performance, and attainment, Japanese students are competitive with the best in the world. A recent study by the Organization of Economic Cooperation and Development in September 2005 confirmed that graduation rates among Japanese high school students are among the highest in the world, as is the percentage of those graduates who go on to complete a college degree or other postsecondary education course. Performance scores in mathematics, problem-solving, science, and reading for Japanese students are significantly ahead of their peers elsewhere, and the Japanese public and private financial commitment to education is also among the strongest. Taken together, the result has been that Japan has one of the best-educated workforces in the world, particularly in science and technology.

The superior education of the labor force and a large and well-trained pool of engineers contributed mightily to Japan's rapid growth from 1945 to 1990. In the early years, a high savings rate and a pool of low-wage, underemployed labor in agriculture fueled Japan's growth. By the 1970s and '80s, once its surplus labor was absorbed, Japan had developed a new source of competitive advantage that rested on superior education: it led the world in the engineering of manufacturing processes and the control of product quality. But Japan's leadership in process innovation and incremental product innovation did not prepare it for the IT revolution of the 1990s. With successive waves of radical innovation in software and communications technology, the U.S. gained a decisive advantage throughout the sector that dominates the world's most developed economies – the services. Today, Japan's capacity for radical product innovation in leading-edge technologies such as software and biotechnology is much weaker than the quality of its science and engineering workforce would lead one to expect. The recent reform efforts have begun to address this problem.

The Contribution of University Research to Innovation and Economic Growth

To understand how the current reforms might benefit Japan, it is instructive to examine the U.S. experience of the past sixty years. The Japanese slowdown of the 1990s, and the contrasting U.S. productivity surge, made clear what many commentators had missed in the 1980s: the source of American economic leadership is its capacity to generate advances in science and translate them into entirely new products, processes, and services. To underscore the point, America's lead is widest in those industries in which innovation is based on relatively recent scientific advance, such as pharmaceuticals, microprocessors, and software.

Historically, this source of global competitive advantage is new. Although commercial and industrial innovation have played an important part in determining world economic leadership since at least the opening of the Age of Exploration and surely since the first Industrial Revolution, innovation based on recent scientific advance emerged as a major economic force only in the second half of the twentieth century.

In fostering science-based innovation, the United States has drawn upon two national characteristics that have long been a source of advantage: the ready availability of capital and the relative absence of barriers to the formation of new firms. These institutional features help with the rapid translation of science into industrial practice. But the United States government also recognized, in the immediate aftermath of World War II, that public investment was essential to generate steady progress in basic science. Scientific discoveries are the foundation of industrial technology. But the economic consequences of these discoveries are rarely understood immediately and may take decades to be fully worked out. Thus, private firms have little incentive to undertake the long-term, unpredictable work of basic science. Government must take the lead.

The American system of scientific research rests upon three principles that have guided public policy since the end of World War II.

First, the federal government is the principal financial supporter of basic science. Second, universities – not government laboratories, non-teaching research institutes, or private companies – are the primary institutions where basic scientific research is conducted. And third, most federal funds are allocated through an intensely competitive process of peer review.

The results are clear. Over the past three decades the U.S. has been the source of about 35 percent of all scientific publications worldwide, and more than 60 percent of the world's Nobel Prizes in science have been awarded to Americans or foreign nationals working in American universities. It is clear that publicly funded basic science has been critical to technological innovation. A recent study prepared for the National Science Foundation found that 73 percent of the main science papers cited in industrial patents granted in the United States were based on research financed by government or nonprofit agencies and carried out in large part in university laboratories.

The deliberate decision to locate most fundamental research in universities rather than government laboratories or private research institutes has another equally significant benefit. It enables the next generation of scientists to receive its education and training from the nation's best scientists, who are required to teach as they pursue their own research. This model of graduate education enhances both the creativity of students and the vitality of the research enterprise.

Some of these well-trained graduate students become professors after they complete their degrees and postdoctoral study, thus ensuring that the academic research engine is continually replenished with new, skilled scientists. But the many who enter industrial employment after graduation take with them invaluable assets – state-of-the-art knowledge obtained by working at the frontiers of science and experience with the most advanced research tools and equipment.

They also take with them a particular way of thinking, a topic to which I turn next.

The Contribution of Liberal Education to Innovation and Economic Growth

Universities and colleges also contribute to economic growth through their teaching by engaging students in intellectual inquiry, encouraging them to question received wisdom, developing their capacity to think independently, and fostering their problem-solving abilities. It is not only the education of industrial scientists and engineers that has an impact on economic performance, but also the education of all those engaged in the business sector – executives, entrepreneurs, financiers, and consultants alike. In a rapidly changing world, students who aspire to leadership in business or government must have the ability to think critically and creatively.

American liberal arts education exposes to students to a variety of subjects and perspectives, giving them intellectual breadth as well as the depth that comes from concentration in a single discipline. Just as the largest social benefits derive from scientific research that is driven by wide-ranging curiosity rather than a particular commercial objective, so, I would argue, the largest social benefits derive from a pedagogy that enlarges the power of students to reason and think creatively rather than master a specific body of knowledge.

A distinctive emphasis on critical thinking produces graduates who are intellectually flexible and open to new ideas, graduates equipped with curiosity and the capacity to adapt to ever-changing work environments, graduates who can convert recently discovered knowledge into innovative new products and services. By producing thinking and engaged graduates capable of innovation, liberal education prepares students for the challenges that we cannot even imagine today, challenges we must address if we wish to continue to grow and prosper.

Recent Japanese Efforts to Reform Science Funding and University Governance

The reforms currently under way here have the potential to move Japan toward worldwide best practice, especially in the funding of basic scientific research. Since 2000, grant funding subject to competitive review has grown by 57 percent. And, at the Ministry of Education, Culture, Sports, Science, and Technology (MEXT), the largest funder of university-based research, the process of awarding grants has been transformed to resemble more closely the U.S. system of peer review. Centered in the Japan Society for the Promotion of Science (JSPS) since 1998, the Japanese approach to competitive research funding got off to a rocky start. Career public servants who were not themselves scientists controlled the process initially, and the reviewers were picked from a list of candidates nominated by academic societies. The results, reported in a 2003 study, were a dramatic skewing of grant recipients toward the most senior scientists, replicating the allocation produced by the traditional politics of the academy. Since one of the objectives of moving toward competitive review was to provide opportunity for young scientists to succeed strictly on the merits of their proposals, the JSPS system was quickly overhauled. Now government program officers are highly qualified scientists recommended by universities and research institutes, serving three-year terms. And the process now draws its external reviewers from a database of those in the nation's scientific community who have been most successful in winning grants and publishing papers.

Still, Japan has a long way to go. Only $4.4 billion, or 13 percent, of the government's $34.1 billion spending on research is subject to competitive review. In the United States, 73 percent of government research funding is subject to competitive review.

Over time, changes in the system of funding basic science could have a substantial impact on Japan's capacity for major science-based innovation in commercial products and services. But strengthening basic science alone is not enough to ensure success. The American experience suggests that two other factors are significant.

First, the Japanese financial system needs to have the flexibility to allow small, science-based start-up enterprises sufficient access to capital. According to a recent study, Japan ranks second to last among the twenty-seven OECD countries in venture capital investment as a percentage of GDP. And only 23 percent of Japan's venture capital is directed toward the leading science-based sectors — communications, information technology, and biotechnology. By contrast, more than half of U.S. venture investment is in these sectors.

Second, Japan needs to consider whether it wishes to reform the pedagogical practices of its leading universities to encourage its future scientists and business leaders to be more independent and creative. Interestingly, China is already moving in this direction — at least in the education of its elites. Two of China's leading universities have recently begun to abandon the completely specialized European model of undergraduate education in favor of the American model, with a year or two of general liberal arts education followed by concentration on a major subject. A larger number of China's top universities have radically changed their hiring and promotion policies in an effort both to improve the quality of the faculty and to speed the rate at which the system absorbs younger scholars trained in the United States. In addition, the presidents and senior academic administrators from China's leading universities have have shown keen interest in understanding how U.S teachers elicit participation in class discussion and stimulate independent thinking among their students.

The changes in the governance of national universities put in place last year provide an enhanced opportunity for Japanese universities to tackle the question of pedagogical reform. Under the new arrangements, with presidents selected by a board of directors divided between faculty and outsiders, the national universities will have considerably more flexibility to differentiate themselves from one another. Indeed, government funding will be tied to the success of each university's performance as measured against its independently formulated strategic plan. Thus far, discussion of possible reforms under the new governance regime has given more attention to personnel policies and criteria for evaluating individual and institutional performance than to pedagogical reform. But liberating universities from conformity with national regulations has substantially reduced the barriers to such reform.

It remains to be seen whether the recent changes in research funding and university governance will significantly enhance Japan's capacity to innovate. The reforms are moving in the right direction, and they have created the opportunity for a dramatic upgrade in the quality of scientific research and in the creativity of Japanese university graduates. Perhaps the challenge of China's rise will spur Japan to achieve the full potential that is latent in the recent reforms. Only time will tell.

The Role of Liberal Education
in China's Development

CHINA'S UNPRECEDENTED expansion of access to higher education advancement has been accompanied by an aspiration to make its leading universities competitive with the best in the world. Since 2004, with the support of the Ministry of Education, my colleagues at Yale and I have worked with the Presidents, Vice Presidents, and Party Secretaries from more than thirty of the Chinese institutions represented at this Forum in an annual workshop devoted to educational leadership and reform. From year to year, I have observed remarkable progress: making the procedures for faculty appointments and promotion more open and competitive, recruiting increasing numbers of outstanding scholars and scientists, expanding laboratory facilities and industrial partnerships, and, most germane to the subject of this week's conference, thinking about how to reform both curriculum and pedagogy to cultivate talent most effectively. The question we have spent the most time discussing, over these past few years, is the incipient restructuring of undergradu-

Remarks at the China–Foreign University Presidents Forum, Nanjing, China, May 2, 2010.

ate education in China, along lines inspired by the model of liberal education as practiced by both comprehensive universities and liberal arts colleges in the United States.

This morning, I would like to probe what this model has to offer China, and why experimentation with it, which has already begun in earnest, is worth pursuing. I say this in full recognition of the reality that a wholesale transplantation of ideas developed in a different cultural context is unlikely to succeed. To be successful, the reform of undergraduate education must be a process of adaptation and innovation appropriate to a Chinese context, not a direct adoption of models used elsewhere.

To understand why curricular and pedagogical reform may help to advance China's development, let me begin by talking about Japan. Twenty-five years ago, many commentators in the United States were extolling the virtues of Japanese management practices, worrying about Japan's large trade surpluses, and predicting that Japan would soon overtake the United States as the world's leading economic power. In the first four decades after the Second World War, Japan's productivity and GDP rose more rapidly than that of the United States; yet after 1990, Japan stagnated for fifteen years. Only in the middle of the last decade, before the financial crisis of 2008, did it resume a reasonable pace of economic growth.

What happened? The conventional story is that excessive corporate debt and a rigid financial system, hampered by an unwise deflationary monetary policy, put the brakes on Japanese growth. This is a partial truth, but if we end the explanation there we would fail to recognize a more profound underlying cause of Japan's slowdown.

In the 1950s and 1960s Japan's growth was propelled by the same fuel that drives China today: a high savings rate and a large pool of under-employed labor, which allows manufacturing to boom without driving up wages. By the 1970s, Japan had absorbed its surplus labor, and a new growth dynamic took over: attention to quality and efficiency in manufacturing. But Japan's edge did not survive the IT revolution of the 1990s. Innovation in software and communications technology gave the United States a decisive productivity advantage. Japan could not innovate fast enough, and it fell into a fifteen-year slump.

China's leadership has recognized the reasons for Japan's failure to innovate, and it is already taking steps to prepare China for a future, perhaps two decades away, in which it will no longer be able to compete globally and win on the basis of low labor costs. Understanding that China must learn to innovate, President Hu Jintao made innovation and creativity the centerpiece of his current five-year plan.

How do you make a country more innovative and creative? If we wish to learn from history, it would be wise to consider the principal factors that have contributed to America's decisive advantage in innovation, and then do something about each of them. Pursuing this exercise, the first requisite is for China to achieve world-class stature in basic scientific research, not just in applied engineering, because basic science is the ultimate source from which all applied technology flows. The second requisite is to develop a financial system with the flexibility to support high-risk start-up enterprises, which generate a disproportionate share of transformational innovations, and the third is for China's educational system to encourage its graduates to think creatively and independently.

China is addressing the first of these requirements aggressively. I will not dwell on this. You all know of the tremendous expansion of research facilities of leading universities, the effort to recruit scientific leaders from abroad, the expanded use of peer review in awarding research grants, and the very successful initiatives to locate R&D operations of major global companies in proximity to university campuses. As for the second requirement, China has already taken measures that Japan long resisted, by gradually opening its major financial institutions to foreign partnerships and encouraging the rise of venture-capital and private equity sectors. It is the third requirement for future economic development—the need for a curriculum and a pedagogy that foster creativity and independent thinking—that is of central concern today.

To develop an economy based on innovation requires well-educated citizens of broad perspective and dynamic entrepreneurs capable of independent and original thinking. China's leaders, as well as the university officials who have been participating with us in our leadership workshops, have explicitly noted that, in the past, two crucial elements have been missing from the undergraduate education provided in Chinese universities: multidisciplinary breadth and the cultivation of critical thinking.

Most Asian universities, like those in Europe but unlike those in the United States, have traditionally offered specialized undergraduate degrees. Students pick a discipline or a profession at age eighteen and study little else thereafter. And unlike in elite European and U.S. universities, pedagogy in China has relied historically on rote learning. Students too often tend to be passive listeners. In the classroom, they rarely challenge one another or their professors. Learning focuses more often than not on the mastery of content, rather than on the development of the capacity for independent and critical thinking.

The traditional Asian approaches to curriculum and pedagogy may work well for training line engineers and midlevel government officials, but they are less suited to fostering leadership and innovation. While U.S. and British politicians worry that China is training more scientists and engineers than the West, Chinese leaders and educators, as well as others throughout Asia, are worrying that their students lack the independence and creativity necessary for their countries' long-term economic growth. They fear that specialization makes their graduates narrow and that traditional Asian pedagogy makes them unimaginative. Hence, many of you here in China, as well as your counterparts in Singapore and South Korea, for example, have become increasingly attracted to the American model of liberal arts education.

As this audience knows, universities in the United States typically provide students with two years to explore a variety of subjects before choosing a single subject on which to concentrate during their final two years. The logic behind this approach is that exposure to multiple disciplines gives students the ability to cope with new and unexpected problems by examining them from a variety of different perspectives. Such multidisciplinary breadth is more likely to lead to creative solutions to new problems.

A business leader, for example, is more likely to succeed if he or she has had exposure to both the economic laws governing markets and the psychology of human behavior in organizations. And governmental leaders would be well served by the study of history and moral philosophy, as well as economics, psychology, and technology. Complex problems are most often solved by drawing on several branches of human knowledge, rather than just one.

Many of China's leading universities have already begun to move toward the American liberal arts curriculum. Peking University introduced the Yuanpei Honors Program in 2001, a pilot program that immerses a select group of gifted students in a liberal arts environment. These students live together and sample a wide variety of subjects for two years before choosing a major field of study. At Fudan University, all students now take a common, multidisciplinary curriculum during their first year before proceeding with the study of their chosen discipline or profession. At Xi'an Jiaotong University, students may earn both a bachelor's and a master's degree by following a "two-plus-four" course of study: two years of general, multidisciplinary education followed by four years of specialization. And here at Nanjing University, students are no longer required to choose a subject when they apply for admission; they may instead choose among more than sixty general-education courses in their first year before deciding on a specialization.

But even more important than multidisciplinary breadth is the ability to assimilate new information and use it to reassess old conclusions and develop new ones. Cultivating such habits requires students to be more than passive recipients of information; they must learn to think for themselves and to structure an argument and defend it or modify it in the face of new information or valid criticism. The Oxford-Cambridge "tutorial" system is perhaps the epitome of such pedagogy. The American substitute has been the interactive seminar, in which students are encouraged to take and defend positions in small groups and to challenge, rather than blindly accept, the instructor's point of view.

Changing the style of teaching is much more difficult than changing the curriculum. It is more expensive to offer classes with small enrollments, but small classes alone do not ensure that students are challenged to become more interactive in class. This requires faculty to adopt new approaches in the classroom, to encourage students to think for themselves, to argue with one another, and even to challenge the instructor's viewpoint. This has been a major challenge in China, despite the recognition by university leaders that a transformation of pedagogy would be a desirable outcome. Training teachers will help, but most likely the transformation of pedagogy will take time. Clearly, professors who have studied abroad and been exposed to interactive methods of instruction will be best equipped to revamp teaching. Increasing opportunities for Asian students to study in the West and for Western students to spend time in Asian universities will also help accelerate the transformation.

The benefits and risks of encouraging independent thinking are more or less self-evident. Fostering greater creativity among the highly educated will inevitably generate more innovation in the economy and thus promote prosperity. It may also lead to new approaches to pressing social problems such as inequality and environmental degradation. But the risks for China are equally evident. Those trained to think for themselves are likely to want greater voice in political affairs. Encouraging independence and creativity in the leaders of the next generation is likely to make China more democratic as well as more prosperous.

REFLECTIONS ON ECONOMIC ADVANCE
AND REFORM

Confronting China's Challenges

In April 2006, during his address at Yale University, President Hu Jintao invited one hundred Yale faculty members and students to visit China as his guests "to enhance mutual understanding between young people and educators of the two countries." Last week, in response to President Hu's generous display of friendship, I had the opportunity to lead a delegation of sixty-two Yale students and thirty-eight faculty and staff to Beijing and Xi'an. Most of our delegation had never been to China before; many had never been beyond the borders of the United States. All of us were awed by the remarkable progress China is making, and truly inspired by your nation's history, culture, and dynamism.

China's economic growth is impressive, and in its magnitude historically unprecedented. Since 1978 more people have been lifted out of poverty than over the entire course of the Industrial Revolution in Europe and North America between 1780 and 1850. To sustain rapid growth over the coming decades, however, China must confront some major challenges, and it is about this topic that I want to speak to you today. In particular, I would like to discuss three challenges to sustaining rapid

Remarks to the Asia Society of Hong Kong, May 23, 2007.

economic growth: the need to develop a more robust rule of law, the need to encourage the independent and creative thinking that supports innovation, and the need to mitigate the adverse environmental impact of rapid growth.

Establishing a Rule of Law

China's remarkable growth has been fueled, in substantial part, by opening the country to trade and foreign investment. Outside investors everywhere are most attracted to environments that offer stable and predictable business relationships, enforceable contracts, and freedom from arbitrary and unforeseen intervention by government. China's decision to enter the World Trade Organization signaled its awareness of these requirements by obligating itself to numerous conditions requiring reform of Chinese law.

China has made remarkable progress in the past decade toward establishing a rule of law. The reform of administrative law, enacted by the National People's Congress in 2004, has introduced increased regularity and new processes to the decision-making of government agencies. Some administrative decisions now require notices of rulemakings and the opportunity for public comment; many actions of government agencies are now subject to appeal and review by courts. Limited rights of private ownership have been established by law, and for the first time, individuals have been empowered and have, in a few cases, succeeded in defending their property rights against the state.

These changes are impressive, but not yet comprehensive. Despite steady progress in the spheres of commercial and administrative law, Chinese leaders are well aware that the judicial system is still incompletely developed, corruption is pervasive, and certain types of legal protection expected in modern commerce, such as enforceable intellectual property rights, are still for the most part absent. Freedom of expression remains unprotected, and arbitrary arrests and detention continue to inhibit China's development in the political sphere.

As China continues to grow, the demands for a stable and predictable rule of law will come increasingly not from outside investors, but from its own rising class of businessmen and -women. As Chinese companies develop valuable trademarks and media products, enforceable intellectual property rights will no longer seem like an unreasonable imperative proffered by the U.S. Government. China's leaders recognize that they will need to respond to the demands for an increasingly robust and pervasive rule of law, and take measures to reduce the corruption of government officials, or else the pace of investment and GDP growth will slacken.

The China Law Center at the Yale Law School, established in 1999 by former U.S. State Department official Professor Paul Gewirtz, is deeply engaged with China's courts, law schools, administrative agencies, and the National People's Congress on aspects of legal reform – bringing prominent U.S. officials, scholars, and judges into contact with their Chinese counterparts and encouraging their collaboration. Among the Center's most significant contributions have been working with the People's Supreme Court on the structure of the Chinese judicial system and working with the National People's Congress on the reform of administrative law.

Later this month the China Law Center, in collaboration with the China National School of Administration, will sponsor the third annual session of the China-Yale Senior Government Leadership Program, an intensive training program on how the "rule of law" functions in the United States. This program regularly attracts to Yale the most senior group of Chinese government officials to participate in executive education outside of China. Participants in the program have included Yale scholars from a variety of fields, two U.S. Supreme Court justices, current and former U.S. cabinet secretaries, the Governor of New York, the Secretary-General of the United Nations, and, last year, the President of the United States. At Yale, we consider our involvement with China's efforts to widen the rule of law to be one of our most significant global undertakings.

Innovation and Creativity

Twenty years ago, many commentators in the United States were extolling the virtues of Japanese management practices, worrying about Japan's large trade surpluses, and predicting that Japan would soon overtake the United States as the world's leading economic power. In the first four decades after the Second World War, Japan's productivity and GDP rose more rapidly than that of the United States; yet after 1990, Japan stagnated for fifteen years, only recently resuming a reasonable pace of economic growth.

China's leadership has recognized the reasons for Japan's failure to innovate, and it is already taking steps to prepare China for a future, perhaps two decades away, in which it can no longer compete globally and win on the basis of low labor costs. Understanding that China must learn to innovate, President Hu Jintao has made innovation and creativity the centerpiece of his current five-year plan.

China is investing heavily in science and higher education. Total central government expenditure on universities grew by a factor of seven between 1995 and 2002. To cite a couple of striking examples, Shanghai Jiao Tong University has built more than 275,000 square meters of state-of-the-art science and engineering labs on its sprawling new campus, while IBM, Intel, and Microsoft built major facilities in the adjacent industrial park. And Peking University's Institute of Microelectronics has built two state-of-the-art semiconductor fabrication lines, each employing a different advanced technology. No U.S. university has a comparable facility.

China's leading universities are also making a conscious effort to attract back the best of those who have gone abroad for Ph.D. study. For established faculty from the West, several top schools are now offering salaries and housing allowances designed to match the standard of living on U.S. campuses. Peking and Fudan Universities have established large laboratories for leading U.S. scientists of Chinese origin, in both cases Yale geneticists. This type of investment creates tremendous spillovers for China as it permits younger faculty and graduate students to work in close proximity with some of the best scientists in the world.

Even more interesting than China's investment in science is its recognition that its pedagogy needs to change. Some senior national leaders have come to believe that the traditional Chinese deference to the authority of the professor discourages independent thinking and thus potentially limits China's development as an innovator. These leaders note that the top colleges and universities of the West encourage their students to speak up in class, challenge their professors, and question conventional wisdom.

Through a series of annual workshops with the leaders of China's top universities, Yale has been deeply involved in the facilitation of discussion concerning curricular and pedagogical reform, as well as other best practices in higher education.

Reducing the Environmental Impact of Economic Growth

China's economic growth labors under a handicap that did not burden those nations that developed earlier. Western Europe, North America, Russia, Japan, and South Korea all achieved industrialization at a time when the environmental impact of growth was below the radar screen.

The impacts were severe, to be sure, but global awareness of these impacts was limited until, roughly, forty years ago. China, unlike its more developed neighbors, must make its transition from an agricultural to an industrial and eventually to a knowledge economy in an atmosphere of worldwide pressure to mitigate the adverse environmental consequences of growth. And it must do so with full knowledge of the adverse public health consequences of air pollution and contaminated water supply for its own citizens — consequences of which earlier industrializing nations were unaware, or could ignore.

The burden is huge. China will soon surpass the United States as the largest producer of the greenhouse gas emissions that are causing harmful climate change. To accommodate rapid growth, China is building coal-fired power plants at the rate of one per week, and it is expected to account for one-third of the worldwide growth in energy demand between now and 2020. As many as 500 million people will migrate from countryside to city by mid-century, and hundreds of new satellite cities will be built. It matters enormously for the future of the planet whether these cities are sprawling, automobile-dependent, and energy-inefficient, or alternatively, "smart" cities — dense and reliant on public transport.

It would be entirely unfair to place the full burden of mitigating environmental impacts on China and other emerging economies. The West must do its part. I agree entirely with the view of Professor Lu Zhi of Peking University, who, during a recent visit to Yale, stated that China's environmental dilemma is the world's dilemma, and that if we want China to change, we all have to change. The United States and the rest of the developed world cannot ask China and other developing countries to halt their economic and social progress because we have already filled the atmosphere with greenhouse gases and because we do not want competition for the natural resources on which we all depend.

We need to work together. Global warming cannot be averted unless *both* China and the United States make substantial reductions in their emissions of greenhouse gases. While Europe has taken this challenge seriously, the United States still lags, paralyzed by powerful interest groups supporting continued dependence on carbon-based fuels and by a public that resists the imposition of high taxes on gasoline that is a reality elsewhere in the world. We need courage and leadership to confront this issue back at home, but we must. The last twelve months have offered the first signs of hope that a bipartisan coalition may be developing to take global warming seriously.

China has certain advantages in pursuing environmental remediation. It will be planning large cities from scratch, opening a wide range of possibilities for innovations that would be much harder to retrofit in established cities. And, because it will soon be the world's largest producer and consumer of coal, it has a powerful incentive to develop new technologies for the conversion of coal and the sequestration of the carbon by-products of its combustion. China could easily become the worldwide leader in these technologies, which will have a huge market worldwide.

International collaboration will be essential in confronting the environmental challenge, and here, too, Yale is proud to be doing its part to work with China, along with a number of leading U.S. NGOs, including the Energy Foundation and the Natural Resources Defense Council. For the past three years, in partnership with Tsinghua University, our School of Forestry & Environmental Studies has been training Chinese mayors and vice-mayors responsible for urban planning and development. And, along with Tsinghua, Shanghai Jiaotong, and China's Center for Environmentally Sustainable Technology Transfer, we have developed executive training courses in industrial ecology, promoting a comprehensive approach to recognizing, measuring, and managing the environmental impacts of an enterprise's total activity.

Conclusion

The challenges confronting China's efforts to sustain economic growth are substantial, but they are surmountable. We need only hope for more of the farsighted leadership that China has displayed since 1978, for continued openness to international collaboration, and for recognition elsewhere that China's continued rise benefits the whole world.

Patents in Global Perspective

I AM neither a banker nor an expert on banking and financial matters, but, as a longtime student of the economic impact of intellectual property rights, I hope that I might contribute something useful to the discussion of a topic that is highly salient in India at this very moment.

As you know, ten years ago, India, along with the other members of the World Trade Organization designated as developing countries, obligated itself to bring its intellectual property laws and enforcement practices into conformity with the Agreement on Trade-Related Aspects of Intellectual Property Rights no later than January 1, 2005. The obligation to conform to the so-called TRIPS standards has engendered much debate here in India. Two weeks ago, Parliament adjourned without amending India's patent law as required by the treaty. Two days later, the President issued an ordinance, as permitted under Indian law, that temporarily satisfies India's treaty obligations by allowing, for the first time since 1970, the patenting of food products, agricultural chemicals, and, most controversially, pharmaceuticals. The 1970 law permitted the pat-

Sir Purshotamdas Thakurdas Memorial Lecture, Indian Institute of Banking and Finance, Mumbai, India, January 7, 2005.

enting of manufacturing processes used in producing these products, but not the patenting of the products themselves. The presidential ordinance does not end the debate, however, because Parliament must act to endorse or modify the decree in the first six weeks of its next session; otherwise, the ordinance lapses.

Opponents of the ordinance fear the destruction of a strong, indigenous industry that produces generic substitutes for drugs discovered elsewhere and supplies these generics both domestically and to other developing countries at a fraction of the cost of branded originals. Those seeking to protect the prosperous domestic industry are joined by public health advocates who fear that India's compliance with TRIPS will eliminate all hope of providing affordable treatment for the millions afflicted with HIV/AIDS throughout Africa and Asia, and raise the cost of health care generally within India.

I am going to take what I regard as the progressive, forward-looking side in this debate, but, before I do, I want to suggest, somewhat surprisingly, that the current discussion in India has a direct analogue in a quieter, but not insignificant debate on patent law reform that is under way in the United States. In both cases, progressives, or, shall we say, internationalists, are seeking to change domestic law by bringing it into greater conformity with prevailing global practice. And in both cases, parochial elements, for reasons both altruistic and self-interested, are resisting change. I will admit to being a partisan in the current U.S. debate. I am the co-chair of a committee of the National Academy of Sciences that recently reported on the state of U.S. patent law and proposed reforms that the U.S. Congress is likely to take up in the year ahead.[1]

---

1 Committee on Intellectual Property Rights in the Knowledge-Based Economy, *A Patent System for the 21st Century* (2004). Most of the principal recommendations of this report were adopted as law seven years after publication, in the America Invents Act of 2011.

In short, I will argue that, like the international trading system, the patent system encourages economic growth and creates wealth when viewed from a global perspective. And, like the arguments used to justify protectionism in international trade, the arguments used in the United States as well as India to justify exceptionalism are ultimately self-defeating. They may serve a narrow domestic interest for a period of time, but ultimately each nation gains from full participation in the global system.

To understand why India, among other developing countries, has resisted full entry into the international patent regime for more than thirty years, we need to understand the perfectly rational, but time-bound and ultimately parochial arguments that justified India's refusal to grant product patents on foods, agro-chemicals, and pharmaceuticals. And this takes us back to basics, to the classical argument for patent protection embedded in English common law and advanced in Article I, Section 8, of the U.S. Constitution, which was drafted in 1787.

A patent is a grant by the government of exclusive rights to the use of an invention for a specified period of time in exchange for a published disclosure sufficiently detailed to permit one skilled in the relevant arts to understand and "practice" the invention.

It has long been recognized that the grant of an exclusive right, whether the inventor herself practiced the invention or licensed it, potentially confers market power on the inventor. This would be especially true if a patented product were unique or had only highly imperfect substitutes (such as many new prescription drugs) or if a patented process enjoyed substantial cost advantages over other methods of producing the same product (such as the planar process for semiconductor manufacture, which was virtually indispensable in the 1960s and early 1970s).

Society gets two advantages in return for the temporary grant of exclusivity. First, the requirement of public disclosure ensures that others can have access to the knowledge that a patent creates, and they can use that knowledge to make further improvements, either after the original patent expires, or by taking a license during the period of exclusivity. Some of my early work describes how the existence of patents facilitates the development of efficient markets for cross-licensing in the semiconductor industry, where technological progress is cumulative, and continued advance is impossible without access to scores, if not hundreds, of previous patents.[2]

Second, when developing a patented product or process requires considerable investment and involves risk, inventors will not normally make the necessary investment without some likelihood of earning a return. Given the very costly and time-consuming burden of meeting the regulatory requirements in most developed countries, inventors would be most unlikely to develop new drugs or pesticides or food additives without the incentive that a patent's grant of exclusivity provides. The framers of the U.S. Constitution explicitly recognized the incentive effect of patent grants more than two centuries ago.

Of course, these classical arguments justifying patents do not specify how long or how broad the grant of exclusivity should be, but it is easy to show that the social loss from the monopoly power conferred even by a strong product patent is small relative to the potential gains from accelerating technological progress through both the disclosure and incentive effects that I just described. But, and here is the crux, the classical arguments are all framed in the context of a unitary, closed society containing both the inventors and the consumers who gain from innovation. Thus, the arguments for the desirability of a patent system hold in a nation that is closed to trade, foreign investment, and international technology transfer. And these arguments also hold for the world taken

---

2 Richard C. Levin, "The Semiconductor Industry," in Richard R. Nelson, ed., *Government Policy and Technical Progress* (1982).

as a whole. But they do not necessarily hold for a single nation that is open to trade, investment, and technology transfer.

In the 1950s and 1960s, there came a growing recognition that the classical arguments for the benefits of a patent system might not apply to the case of many developing countries, and a counterargument, made most forcefully in the work of Edith Penrose, was advanced to provide the ammunition for many developing countries – most prominently India – to abandon at least in part the patent regimes inherited from their colonial rulers.[3] The counterargument rests on the premise that a developing country lacks sufficient scientific and technical capability to produce economically significant patents on its own. If this is the case, the classical argument breaks down because granting exclusivity in the domestic market has little impact on domestic innovation. Moreover, if the developing country's market is but a small share of the world market, a grant of exclusivity has little impact on the incentives of foreign inventors. Under such conditions, patents granted to foreigners and practiced in the domestic market simply transfer wealth from domestic consumers to foreigners. This conclusion holds whether the patented goods (or goods produced with patented processes) are imported or licensed to domestic producers. Thus, in a country with little indigenous capacity to invent, the patent system yields increased rents to foreign inventors without producing significant domestic benefits.

It was such perfectly logical reasoning that led India, in 1970, to eliminate product patents on food, agro-chemicals, and drugs. India stopped short of completely eliminating the patent system, presumably because it recognized that domestic inventive capacity was not entirely absent. Thus, patents on other types of products and patents on manufacturing processes were retained.

This approach proved ideal for the development of an indigenous

3 Edith Penrose, *The Economics of the International Patent System* (1951).

capacity to copy drugs and chemicals invented and patented abroad, and to produce them with processes that could be patented domestically. Given that the cost structure of such products, especially pharmaceuticals, involves very large up-front investments for development and testing and very low costs of production, Indian firms had the advantage of "free riding" on the development of new drugs and producing them at a small fraction of the cost of their imported, brand-name equivalent. Before long, India developed a large and efficient domestic pharmaceutical industry, supplying the domestic market with generic drugs at low prices and, eventually, exporting them to other developing nations in Asia and Africa that, like India, did not offer patent protection to pharmaceutical products.

And then along came TRIPS, an agreement which many developing countries regard as having been forced upon them by the United States. This is not entirely a fair claim in the case of India, where the government and some of the successful generic drug companies recognized in the early 1990s that an eventual transition to a regime allowing pharmaceutical patents might be in the nation's long-term interest.

The TRIPS agreement, informed by both the classical argument for patents and the developing country counterargument, made a distinction among three classes of nations. Developed countries were required to bring their patent regimes into immediate compliance with the agreement. Developing countries, India and Brazil among them, were given ten years, and the least developed countries, mostly those in Africa and the Middle East, were given even more time. This differentiated timetable makes sense – for both developing and the least developed countries, and, specifically, for India.

Now let us ask: what has changed that made India's Patent Act of 1970 reasonable at the time but makes conforming to TRIPS standards reasonable now? I would suggest three factors: (1) India's growing size in relation to world markets; (2) its increased capacity to innovate; and

(3) the flexibility inherent in the TRIPS agreement that will allow India to avoid most of the adverse consequences envisioned by the opponents of reform. Let me discuss each of these factors in turn.

First, India's rapid growth rate and its large and rapidly expanding middle class will likely create a preference among some consumers for branded as opposed to generic drugs that simply wasn't present in 1970. Moreover, as the Indian market grows, the previously negligible effect of an Indian patent system on the incentives of foreign innovators becomes measurable. This incentive effect could be especially important in inducing foreign investment on drugs aimed at treating previously neglected diseases prevalent in India and similarly situated developing countries.

Second, even more significant than India's growing market is its increased capacity for indigenous innovation. India's largest pharmaceutical firms and some of its research institutes now have the scale, the trained personnel, and the technical capacity to develop new drugs, either alone or in partnership with foreign firms. The availability of domestic patents, combined with the low cost of performing research and development in India, could help to make India's largest pharmaceutical companies very successful globally. Moreover, a number of government institutes and private enterprises have developed the capacity to do large-scale, highly cost-effective clinical trials. With product patents in place, India is likely to become a major center for "outsourced" clinical trials undertaken by U.S. and European pharmaceutical giants. Without domestic patent protection, neither India's potential for indigenous discovery nor its potential to become a leading center for clinical trials will be fully realized.

Third, some of the adverse impacts feared by opponents of reform are likely to be less severe than imagined, and others can be mitigated by effective use of the flexibility permitted under the recent Doha declaration. The notion that drug prices and the overall cost of health care will skyrocket as a consequence of the government ordinance is exaggerated, because 90 percent of the drugs currently classified by India as essential medicines are either unpatented or the patent has expired. The prices of drugs patented before 1995 (including some of the most important antiretroviral treatments for HIV/AIDS) will not be affected, because these drugs will not be eligible for Indian patents, and generic substitutes produced domestically are likely to continue to dominate the market. It is true that those domestic producers that have been successful in copying foreign drugs without developing a capability for independent research are likely to be hurt, but, as I mentioned, the largest firms are likely to benefit from the opportunity that domestic patent protection will provide.

Finally, there is little substance to the concern that India's conformity with TRIPS will seriously hamper the battle against the HIV/AIDS pandemic in Africa and parts of Asia. Under the exception recently created during the Doha round, countries are free to impose compulsory licenses to deal with public health emergencies and to export such drugs to countries lacking manufacturing facilities. Thus, India will have the latitude to make sure that all significant AIDS treatments (including those patented abroad since 1995) continue to be produced domestically and exported to developing countries without indigenous production capability.

Moreover, we too often forget that most of the large global producers of AIDS treatments have dramatically lowered the prices of their drugs in developing countries. Yale is proud to have led the way in this development three years ago, by encouraging our licensee, Bristol-Myers Squibb, to lower its price in Africa for Zerit, an antiretroviral discovered at Yale, by 98.5 percent, from ten dollars per daily dose to fifteen cents. Other developed country manufacturers have followed suit, reducing the price of the standard AIDS cocktail in Africa to just over one dollar per day, a price close to that offered by Indian generic producers.

It is worth noting, however, that even at these much-reduced prices, it would require a significant fraction of the GDP of the poorest African nations to supply treatment to their infected populations. It is not the international patent regime that is preventing universal access to drug therapies; it is the crushing poverty of the nations most heavily infected with HIV/AIDS and the insufficiency of aid provided by developed countries.

All things considered, India's move toward conformity with the TRIPS standards would appear to promise significant national benefits, without incurring many of the costs feared by the critics. The government's ordinance has several features especially designed to mitigate potential hardship on various domestic interest groups, and, while this may be politically desirable or even necessary, care must be taken to ensure that these provisions do not undermine the efficiencies created by broadening eligibility for product patents. For example, a fair compromise without any adverse impact on efficiency is the provision that domestic generic producers will not be liable for past infringement; patents filed since 1999 in anticipation of the January 1, 2005, change in regime will be enforced from the date they are granted, not from the date they were filed or published. On the other hand, some government actions permitted by the ordinance – such as aggressive use of compulsory licensing (or the threat of compulsory licensing) to bring down the prices of patented drugs – could destroy the very incentives the patent system is designed to create. And such action might in fact prove illegal under the TRIPS agreement.

Now let me turn to the situation in the United States, where significant pressure is building for patent reform of a different kind. The issues under discussion may not seem germane to India at the current moment. But if India comes into compliance with TRIPS, and if, over time,

Indian firms succeed, as is likely, in building substantial international patent portfolios in pharmaceuticals and software, the issues currently under discussion in the U.S. will be of consequence to them.

At the risk of oversimplifying, our study found two major problems with the current patent regime in the United States. Let us call them the "cost" problem and the "quality" problem.

The cost problem arises from two sources. First, the process of securing global patent protection is unnecessarily costly and inefficient, and, second, the cost of litigation required to enforce one's exclusive rights is excessive.

Even though it is now possible to use a common application to secure patent protection in most countries, the patent offices in the U.S., the European Union, and Japan each independently determine whether an applicant's claims are novel, useful, and non-obvious to those skilled in the relevant arts. Although some progress has been made toward accepting in all jurisdictions the literature searches done in one of the jurisdictions, we urged the bolder step: that the U.S., Europe, and Japan move toward full mutual recognition of applications granted and denied. Thus, by gaining patent protection in one of the three jurisdictions, an inventor will have secured a patent in all three. This would reduce the fees paid by inventors and eliminate wasteful duplication of effort by national patent offices. Developing nations could choose to conserve resources by foregoing independent examination and recognizing patents granted in the U.S., Europe, or Japan.

Suing a potential infringer in U.S. courts — whether the lawsuit is intended to prevent use of the patented technology, to force the infringer to take a license, or to recover damages — is frightfully expensive. Parties to infringement litigation frequently run up bills in the neighborhood of $2 million to $5 million. And it takes several years to get a decision.

Our investigation found that the cost of enforcing a patent is much greater in the United States than in Europe or Japan. Part of the difference is due to features in U.S. law that introduce highly subjective elements into litigation, and thus require an extraordinarily costly and time-consuming process of discovery to establish facts and motivations. We found four specific legal doctrines — all unique to the United States — that in combination significantly raise the cost of litigation. In each case we recommended changes in U.S. practice.

The first area of concern is the way that priority is established if two or more inventors claim the right to the same invention. Outside the United States, priority is established by a simple objective fact: which inventor first filed a patent application. But in the U.S., priority is established by determining which inventor first conceived of the invention and reduced it to practice. This typically requires an extensive review of documentary evidence and witness testimony, involving hundreds or thousands of hours of legal work. We recommended that the U.S. abandon the cumbersome doctrine of first-to-invent and replace it with the globally dominant standard of first-to-file. The simpler doctrine may occasionally lead to an unjust outcome, but the cost of the more subjective doctrine is prohibitive.

A second discovery-intensive element in U.S. law is the requirement that an inventor must disclose the best mode of practicing a patent. If an infringer can prove that an inventor withheld information about the best way to implement her invention, the court will declare the patent invalid. This entails an investigation into the state of an inventor's knowledge at the time the patent was filed. We recommended the abolition of the best mode requirement, again to bring the U.S. into conformity with prevailing global practice.

A third subjective element in the law is the doctrine of inequitable conduct, whereby a patent can be declared invalid if an alleged infringer can prove that the inventor intentionally misled the patent examiner. Again, an inquiry into the inventor's subjective state of mind involves the costly and time-consuming review of documents and the deposition of witnesses. We recommended the elimination or substantial modification of this doctrine.

A fourth subjective element is the doctrine of willful infringement. If the court finds that a patent has been knowingly infringed, the infringer is liable for treble rather than actual damages. This also requires extensive discovery, raising the cost of litigation. But the process also has the perverse effect of discouraging inventors from doing a thorough search of previously published patents; one can't deliberately infringe a patent of which one is ignorant. In this case, too, we recommended elimination of the doctrine.

In all four of these cases, the idiosyncratic nature of U.S. law leads to unnecessary cost. By harmonizing legal doctrines, the cost of enforcing a patent can be significantly reduced, just as by introducing reciprocity, the cost of obtaining a patent can be reduced.

We turn now from the "cost" problem to the "quality" problem.

With the surge in global patenting that occurred during the boom of the 1990s came a growing perception that many patents were being granted that failed the common-sense test for novelty or that appeared to lack a perceptible inventive step. Examples abound: consider a patent on a computer algorithm for searching a table to determine the sine or cosine of an angle, or a patent on selecting a song from a server by clicking on a list of the available titles, or (and the economists among you will appreciate this) a patent on a computer program to aid pricing decisions, based on a formula implying that prices should be high when the elasticity of demand is low. Such inventions may be novel (in the sense of having no exact precedent), but common sense tells us that they would be obvious to a person possessing ordinary skill in the relevant arts.

Some have argued that the granting of low-quality patents is simply a consequence of the overwhelming increase in applications, which have grown much faster than the pool of trained examiners. But we found that the problem has another important dimension. Most of the patents failing a common-sense test for novelty or non-obviousness were issued in new areas of technology, such as genomics and Internet-enabled business methods. The case of Internet-enabled business methods is particularly interesting, because the published writings that might have invalidated many recently granted patents were not to be found in the *scientific* literature routinely searched by patent examiners, but in the literature of business and economics.

Our diagnosis was that the U.S. patent system is not well designed to cope quickly and effectively with emerging areas of technology. This failing is due in part to the lack of trained examiners in emerging fields and the lack of analytic resources within the patent office to anticipate the need for training as new technologies emerge. To remedy this defect, we recommended that the U.S. patent office develop an interdisciplinary analytic staff to study trends in technology and to work with outside experts and advisers to craft guidelines for examiners in emerging technologies.

The failure to cope effectively with emerging technologies is also attributable to the time and cost required to clarify standards of patentability through litigation. Currently, in the United States, there is no simple mechanism to challenge the validity of a patent. There is no pregrant opposition procedure, as there is in India, and the post-grant procedure is limited to challenges on very narrow grounds. Ultimately, it is the courts that decide whether patents are valid or invalid, and the decisions reached in particular cases serve as the definitive standards for the patentability of future inventions. As I noted earlier, litigation takes years; meanwhile players in the arena of emerging technologies face unnecessary uncertainty, not knowing whether inventions under development will be patentable.

To complicate matters further, it is impossible under U.S. law for a person to challenge the validity of a patent in court unless the patent holder has first sought to enforce the patent against that person, by suing for infringement or by threatening to sue. Thus, for example, a competitor seeking to overturn a patent must first infringe it in order to have the standing to mount a legal challenge. This requirement can distort investment decisions in both directions. Because of the time, cost, and risk involved in developing a new process or product using a patented technology that turns out to be invalid, some competitors will be deterred from entering the market, depriving the consumer of the benefit of competition. On the other hand, some rivals will wastefully sink costs to compete with the holders of patents that turn out to be valid after challenge.

The obvious solution for the U.S. is to conform to prevailing international practice and establish a system of post-grant administrative review that allows challenges based on the full range of statutory standards for patentability. Potentially, such a system would allow standards in emerging technology areas to be clarified quickly, thus resolving pervasive uncertainty and aligning the private and social incentives for investment. To be effective, the new system must be not only faster but also less expensive than litigation in the courts. We made a number of suggestions about procedures that would achieve these goals. The post-grant review systems in Europe are not models to emulate; they are inexpensive, but the time lags are comparable to those in the U.S. courts.

The politics of solving the cost and quality problems in the United States are perhaps not quite so contentious as the politics of TRIPS compliance in India, but those of us advocating reform in the U.S. do anticipate opposition from certain interest groups. The Patent and Trademark Office is ambivalent about our proposals; they like the appeal for increased staffing resources, and they favor the establishment of a post-grant review system. But the bureaucrats are likely to resist statutory requirements intended to ensure that a new system operates speedily and inexpensively from the perspective of the challenger and patent holder.

The major association of intellectual property lawyers has endorsed our proposals, but there is bound to be some infighting to preserve some of the subjective elements in litigation, because they produce revenue for patent lawyers. And America's unique "independent inventor" lobby, which is very well organized, will resist almost any move toward harmonizing U.S. practices with the rest of the world. On the whole, however, research-intensive corporations, the patent bar, and most academic experts in law, economics, and technology support the reform package that we have proposed.

The moral of this story of reform efforts in two nations is that in an interdependent, globalized economy, a careful consideration of national interest will often lead to the recognition that harmonization of national practices is desirable. The more interdependent we become, the more we find it compelling to adopt rules and standards that are efficient from a global perspective. Within each nation, parochial interests will remain, but the powerful arguments of internationalists are increasingly likely to prevail. Such is the case with U.S. abandonment of its idiosyncratic legal doctrines and institutions, and with India's compliance with the TRIPS regime. In an interdependent world, we have much to gain from moving toward global governance.

Lessons from the Crisis of 2008

I SPEAK to you today not as a university president, but as an economist eager to understand what caused the crisis of 2008 and why we did not effectively mitigate its severity and duration. I focus primarily on the origins and consequences of, and the insufficient response to, the Great Recession in the United States.

I will take up six questions in turn:

- What was the crisis?
- What caused it?
- What could have prevented the crisis?
- What could have been done after the crisis occurred to restore the flow of credit?
- What could have been done after the crisis occurred to stimulate the real economy?
- What lessons should we learn from the crisis of 2008?

Based on a lecture given on numerous occasions at Yale from 2009 through 2012, and at the Asia Society of Hong Kong, May 9, 2012.

What Was the Crisis?

The crisis was in essence a breakdown of credit markets that led to precipitous declines in business and consumer spending. It began with a decline in housing prices that started in 2006 and accelerated through 2007, reducing the value of the mortgages held by major financial institutions. By early 2008 there was widespread concern about the solvency of some of these institutions, and a substantial decline in the value of their stocks. In September, one of the leading investment banks, Lehman Brothers, declared bankruptcy. This led, in rough order, to the collapse of the stock market, the commercial paper market, the financing of consumer credit, business investment, and the commercial real estate market.

The failure of Lehman Brothers in September 2008 turned a financial market crisis into a full-scale recession. The first-year decline in gross domestic product was the sharpest in fifty years, and the combined size and duration of decline made this the most severe recession in the United States and Europe since the Great Depression eighty years earlier. Unemployment in the United States rose from 5 to 10 percent in just over a year, and it went much higher in certain subpopulations. Unemployment peaked at 20 percent in manufacturing and 27 percent in construction. Unemployment for those nineteen years old and younger, as well as for those without a college degree, exceeded 20 percent. Interestingly, the unemployment rate for those with a college education never exceeded 6 percent, and quickly declined to the 4–5 percent range.

What Caused the Crisis?

Fundamentally, the crisis resulted from a dramatic overexpansion of credit in virtually every sector of the economy. Continuous financial innovation had led to a steadily increasing ratio of debt to GDP through the 1980s and 1990s, so that the total public and private debt outstanding by 2001 was equal to the previous historical high of 250 percent of GDP. Then the Federal Reserve lowered interest rates in response to the bursting of the Internet bubble, and maintained low rates for several years. Lowering rates was appropriate in the short term; it helped the economy to recover from the impact of the stock market decline. But rates were held below historical averages for at least four years, and this fueled an enormous expansion of credit in the private sector. By early 2008, the ratio of debt to GDP stood at an astonishing 360 percent, of which 300 percent was in the private sector (government debt was then only 60 percent of GDP). As a share of GDP, every category of private debt — mortgages, consumer credit, financial sector debt, and non-financial business debt — was far in excess of levels ever attained before.

The expansion of credit was encouraged not only by low interest rates, but also by an unprecedented relaxation of collateral requirements. Of course, mortgages were collateralized by the homes being financed, but the amount of cash buffer was greatly reduced. Securing home mortgages no longer required a 20 percent down payment, or even a 10 percent down payment. The lower the down payment, the more likely that such subprime mortgages could go "under water" in the sense that the value of a house might decline below the amount of unpaid debt principal. These subprime mortgages were typically bundled into securities and sold to large commercial banks, investment banks, and hedge funds. Bundles were diversified regionally, to spread the risk of a decline in housing values in any particular region, but, with such low cash collateral, these securities — ironically called collateralized mortgage obligations (CMOs) — were extremely vulnerable to a widespread decline in housing values that cut across regions.

The explosion of debt was accelerated by the growing use of largely unregulated derivative financial instruments. Although many of these instruments were intended to permit the more efficient management of risk, collectively their expanded use added significantly to economy-wide leverage.

The low-interest, low-collateral environment prevailing from 2001 through 2005 spurred a boom in residential construction, concentrated in California, Nevada, Arizona, New Mexico, Texas, and Florida. When housing prices began to drop significantly in each of these areas, it became clear that recently issued mortgages would soon be under water. By late 2007 financial markets began to manifest concern about the balance sheets of the major commercial and investment banks that held substantial amounts of CMOs among their assets.

As housing prices continued to decline rapidly, Bear Stearns, the smallest and least well capitalized of the nation's five leading investment banks, came under severe stock market pressure early in 2008. Analysts and investors recognized that, at a realistic valuation of the CMOs on its books, Bear Stearns was insolvent. Knowing that Bear Stearns had many valuable assets, and could turn solvent if housing values recovered, a much larger bank, JPMorgan Chase, with encouragement and assistance from the Federal Reserve Bank, stepped in and bought control of Bear Stearns at a stock price more than 90 percent below the previous year's high.

Several months later, in late summer 2008, investor confidence in two other investment banks—Lehman Brothers and Merrill Lynch—collapsed. On a fateful weekend in September, the Federal Reserve and the Treasury tried to find private sector rescuers for each bank. The Bank of America stepped in to rescue Merrill Lynch, but an attempt to arrange a takeover of Lehman by Barclay's failed, and Lehman declared bankruptcy on Monday morning, September 15.

The entire stock market began to plunge as investors fled risky equity investments and moved their funds to cash and Treasury securities. Within six months, stock markets in the United States lost 50 percent of their value. Interbank lending and commercial paper markets froze up, causing the failure of many small banks and businesses over that same time period.

What Could Have Prevented the Crisis?

Appropriate countercyclical monetary policy would have made a big difference. The lowering of interest rates in 2001 was appropriate, but the Fed maintained low interest rates longer than economic conditions warranted. Despite relatively low inflation in the prices of consumption goods and services, housing prices increased 64 percent between 2001 and 2006, and stock market values rebounded from the 2001–3 slump to historic highs. Most worrisome, as I noted earlier, was the tremendous accumulation of private sector debt, but the Fed essentially ignored this phenomenon.

Traditionally, monetary policy had used multiple instruments to control the amount of debt created. In addition to raising interest rates to dampen the creation of credit, bank regulators can raise the amount of reserves banks must hold at the Fed, or increase the amount of overall capital banks must hold. Other regulators can control the amount of leverage allowed on home loans or in the purchase of stocks. None of these potential mechanisms for holding in check the unprecedented growth of leverage was used. Nor was there any attempt to regulate new forms of increasing leverage through the design of derivative financial instruments.

This not-so-benign neglect of the largest expansion of private sector debt in America's history was more likely a consequence of ideology than ineptitude. From the Reagan years forward, a laissez-faire approach to financial markets had become orthodoxy, and there was widespread consensus among policymakers that the less the extent of regulation the better. The interest rate was used by the Federal Reserve exclusively to control ordinary inflation – that is, increases in the price level of consumer goods and services. Little attention was paid to curbing the economy-wide explosion of debt, whether indirectly through interest rates or directly. Since inflation remained low in the years prior to the crisis, there was little impetus to raise interest rates. And there was no inclination to use the other available regulatory instruments to reduce directly the amount of leverage taken by banks and homeowners, or to moderate the rise of asset prices to reduce the likelihood of "bubbles." More attention to the growth of leverage could have prevented the crisis of 2008.

One other important tool was not available to regulators, however, or at least the Federal Reserve, the Federal Deposit Insurance Corporation, and the Treasury did not believe that it was. None of them had the statutory authority to seize failing financial institutions that were not chartered commercial banks. Thus, when investment banks such as Bear Stearns, Merrill Lynch, and Lehman Brothers came under pressure, the regulators believed that all they could do was help to arrange a private-sector bailout by finding banks willing to acquire those that were failing.

What Could Have Been Done after the Crisis to Restore the Flow of Credit?

The government was understandably operating under tremendous pressure in the fall of 2008, as one major financial institution after another experienced a rapid decline in the value of the mortgages, CMOs, and other derivatives they held (such as credit default swaps), and the attendant collapse of their stock prices. With many commercial and investment banks in danger of failing, the government decided in late September to seek congressional authority and funding to intervene, by means of a newly created Troubled Asset Relief Program (the TARP).

The initial conception of the TARP, however, contained a critical logical flaw. The idea was to buy the distressed assets (mortgage securities, credit default swaps, and other derivatives) from the banks. The flaw was this: if the banks were paid the current market value of these assets, they would be insolvent. They would have more cash, but the total value of their assets would be less than the total value of their liabilities. Banks, of course, were reluctant to accept offers for their distressed securities that would have made their insolvency visible. From their point of view, uncertainty about the value of these assets was better than the certainty of insolvency.

Within two weeks, the Fed and the Treasury realized that they were on the wrong track and began to recapitalize the banks directly by infusing cash in return for preferred stock. This approach stabilized balance sheets and succeeded in preventing further failures of large financial institutions, but it did not give the banks sufficient capital, given the remaining uncertainty about the value of their distressed assets, to resume lending on a large scale.

A better approach was potentially available, but it would have required new legislation, as the TARP did. The government might have seized the troubled banks, and taken the "bad" assets off bank balance sheets and held them in a government agency for later sale to the private sector after asset values begin to recover. This was done in response to the savings and loan crisis of the early 1990s, and it is the conventional method of dealing with smaller, less complex commercial banks. Had the government taken this approach in the fall of 2008, it might have very rapidly sold stock in the reorganized banks once they were liberated from their distressed assets. These healthier banks, once in the hands of new shareholders, would have been properly capitalized and more likely to resume lending. This approach, moreover, would have had the benefit of mitigating moral hazard in the future, since the equity shareowners in the original failing banks would have been completely wiped out—

disciplined by the market for excessive risk-taking rather than having their losses partially covered by the government.

What Could Have Been Done after the Crisis to Stimulate the Real Economy?

By early 2009, unemployment was 8 percent, headed to 10 percent later that year. The economy was in full recession by the time President Obama took office in January, and it was clear to both political parties that some kind of fiscal stimulus was needed to prevent even more rapid increases in unemployment.

Unfortunately, the stimulus package enacted in February 2009 was too small, and it employed the wrong mix of tools. The total package of approximately $800 billion represented about 6 percent of GDP. By contrast, the Chinese stimulus package, put in place at the same time, was 15 percent of GDP; it quickly reversed a 30 percent drop in exports and allowed the Chinese economy to grow at 9 percent in 2009.

The mix of tools also limited the efficacy of the U.S. stimulus. First, only one-third of the package went to government spending that created new jobs; the rest was divided between tax cuts and the extension of unemployment benefits and other entitlements. Empirical research tends to confirm the view that in normal times, the effect of one dollar of government spending on GDP (the "Keynesian multiplier") equals the effect of a one-dollar tax cut. But the U.S. economy was not in normal times in February 2009. The economy was massively overleveraged. Households receiving a modest 2 percent payroll tax cut were, a priori, much more likely to use the additional income to pay down their credit card debt, or their home equity loan, than to spend the money, which would have had a multiplier effect on GDP. By contrast, a worker who transitions from unemployment to employment under a government-spending program is moving to a significantly higher level of income, and will surely spend some fraction of that additional income. In other words, when consumers are deeply in debt, direct job creation through government spending is likely to have a larger effect on GDP and employment than a tax cut.

Moreover, the spending on job creation authorized by the February 2009 stimulus package was too slow to have substantial effect. Less than $100 billion was actually spent on job creation in the first year, since many funds were allocated to construction projects that had to work through approval and contracting processes before they began, even if they were, in the parlance of the day, "shovel ready" in terms of design. A much more effective approach would have started by asking contractors on government projects around the country – whether local, state, or federal – "how many more workers could you absorb?" By working multiple shifts, or working on longer stretches of highway overnight, many workers could have been engaged quickly.

Despite the insufficient size of the February 2009 fiscal package, the political environment since then has rendered significant further stimulus through government spending infeasible. Instead, we have been forced to rely on extremely accommodating monetary policy, including both near-zero policy interest rates and the purchase of government securities (a textbook technique for expanding the supply of money and credit, recently renamed "quantitative easing" as if it were something newly invented). Of course, low interest rates are to be preferred to higher ones in the current environment, but, as the Fed's Board of Governors knows, we are in a classical Keynesian "liquidity trap," a situation in which the expansion of the money supply will not significantly increase capital investment or GDP. The Chairman of the Fed has indicated several times since 2009 that we need more fiscal stimulus to speed the recovery.

What Lessons Should We Learn from the Crisis of 2008?

The effects of the crisis of 2008 are still with us. Growth remains sluggish, and the economy is still overleveraged. Since early 2008, consumers have been deleveraging at a rate of 5 percent of GDP per year. As of early 2013, it will still take three years at this rate to reach the high end of what might be regarded as a "normal" range of leverage. The financial sector is deleveraging at a rate of 8–10 percent of GDP per year; it, too, has about three years to get down to "normal" levels. Until then, without direct fiscal stimulus, which is unlikely in the current contentious political environment, the recovery is likely to remain sluggish, and growth is likely to remain below the long-term trend.

My views — that the crisis was a consequence of our failure to control economy-wide leverage prior to 2008 and that the 2009 fiscal stimulus was insufficient — were controversial when I first expressed them early in 2009. Some economists believe that the crisis was a manifestation of a serious problem in the labor market: a growing gap between the skills possessed by workers and those required by employers. I agree that the mismatch of skills and requirements is a long-term structural problem that must be addressed, but I do not believe that it caused the crisis of 2008, even if it may to some extent make a speedy recovery more difficult. There are also skeptics who believe that the government is simply incapable of legislating and implementing a successful jobs creation program. Nonetheless, the views I have been advancing since 2009 seem to be gaining ground among mainstream economists.[1]

---

1 In February 2009, I pointed out to a journalist that of the relatively few voices calling for a substantially larger fiscal stimulus, most were Yale students or faculty colleagues of the late James Tobin. I noted specifically John Geanakoplos, Paul Krugman, William Nordhaus, Robert Shiller, and Joseph Stiglitz. This led to an interesting *Bloomberg* article on the subject,

To recapitulate, these are the principal lessons of the crisis of 2008:

- The Fed, as well as the other bank and mortgage regulatory agencies, should monitor the accumulation of debt and act countercyclically.
- We should use the full range of policy tools to prevent excessive leverage, including reserve requirements, capital ratios, minimum down payment standards, and margin requirements. The recently proposed Basel III standards, which will regulate bank capital requirements internationally and mandate countercyclical adjustment, are a step forward.
- The government should have the authority to seize systemically important financial institutions. This power was conferred by the Dodd-Frank Act.
- If a fiscal stimulus is needed when consumers are overleveraged, the government should create jobs directly through spending programs, instead of cutting taxes.
- If a stimulus is needed, use mechanisms that create jobs quickly, such as "doubling down" on ongoing construction projects.

Keynes understood that the forces leading to cyclical crises are inescapable in an economy in which financial markets allocate capital, because investor psychology will play a significant, and sometimes dominant, role in determining asset values. We cannot make these forces disappear, but we can, through wise policy, mitigate them, and, even if the pressures prevail and a crisis ensues, we can choose better or worse paths to recovery. Let us hope that that the lessons of 2008 become better understood before another crisis looms.

February 27, 2009. Much more recently, economists involved in the first Obama administration – Christina Romer and Lawrence Summers – have acknowledged that the 2009 stimulus package was too small.